THE CORPORATION

AND THE ARTS

BOOKS BY *Richard Eells*

CORPORATION GIVING IN A FREE SOCIETY
THE MEANING OF MODERN BUSINESS
CONCEPTUAL FOUNDATIONS OF BUSINESS (*with Clarence Walton*)
THE GOVERNMENT OF CORPORATIONS
THE BUSINESS SYSTEM: Readings in Ideas and Concepts (3 Volumes)
                                    (*with Clarence Walton*)
THE CORPORATION AND THE ARTS

THE CORPORATION
AND THE ARTS

Richard Eells

The Macmillan Company   *An Arkville Press Book*

THE MACMILLAN COMPANY, *New York*

COLLIER-MACMILLAN LIMITED, *London*

To

Armand G. Erpf

pioneer to venturesome outposts
in finance, in education,
in the arts

STUDIES OF THE MODERN CORPORATION

Columbia University Graduate School of Business

The Program for Studies of the Modern Corporation is devoted to the advancement and dissemination of knowledge about the corporation. Its publications are designed to stimulate inquiry, research, criticism, and reflection. They fall into four categories: works by outstanding businessmen, scholars, and professional men from a variety of backgrounds and academic disciplines; prize-winning doctoral dissertations relating to the corporation; annotated and edited selections of business literature; and business classics that merit republication. The studies are supported by outside grants from private business, professional, and philanthropic institutions interested in the program's objectives.

Courtney C. Brown

Dean, GRADUATE SCHOOL OF BUSINESS, COLUMBIA UNIVERSITY

Preface

For many years I have been interested in the developing role of the modern corporation in contemporary society. My concern with this subject led to a study of corporation giving in a free society, then to a search for the meaning of modern business and an appraisal of the conceptual foundations of business, and later still to an investigation of the government of corporations. More recently—still in pursuit of a clearer understanding of the role of the corporation in society—I found myself seeking to explain the interrelationship between the arts and the corporation as decisive institutions in our society. This facet of the inquiry was given a new edge a few years ago by my participation in a comprehensive study of the performing arts in America conducted by the Rockefeller Brothers Fund.

Meanwhile, the activities of American corporations as donors have continued to show remarkable staying power and growth. During the past thirty years, the donative trend, if one can call it a trend, has been both upward (in terms of larger dollar totals) and outward (in terms of ever-widening areas of involvement). Corporation donative activities have expanded from the more restricted, unimaginative and ill-planned contribution lists of many companies, to the present beginnings of donative policies that are fairly well thought out, and geared to the long-range goals of a company. All this has taken place in little more than three decades. And in the same period one can even trace a promising development of sound managerial decision-making concerning corporate financial support of external institutions.

Many organizations have contributed immeasurably to this development by making quantitative studies of the trends and by recommending ways to improve corporate donative policies. At the same time, sanction for corporate support of health, welfare, educational and cultural institutions and activities in the corporate environment has come from a combination of factors: favorable public policy in the form of tax laws, permissive legislation governing corporate powers, and judicial decisions upholding these powers in the donative area of corporate governments.

All of these factors have contributed steadily to the evolution of a rationale of corporate support, and especially for the support of external institutions that are vital to the survival and growth of the corporate enterprise system. However, as new demands are made on corporations for support—especially for support of cultural institutions—it becomes increasingly clear that the present rationale is inadequate. This inadequacy has been particularly evident during recent drives to find support for cultural and performing arts centers at a time when America is at the threshold of a cultural renaissance. Also evident is the fact that most corporation counsel tends to move with hesitancy into new areas of support, preferring instead to hold to older, established fields.

What is needed now, I believe, is not a mere extrapolation of older donative theories so as to include the arts, but rather a fresh investigation of a much broader and deeper theme: corporate ecology in its entire institutional reach. The task is difficult because the place of the modern corporation as a major social institution among other institutions in our society has not yet been comprehensively defined. We cannot even be sure of the conditions necessary for corporate survival—I mean specifically the survival of large corporate enterprises as viable private-sector organizations fulfilling far more than economic functions.

Corporate support for the arts is but one chapter in this larger inquiry into corporate ecology. What I have tried to do in this book is to survey the outer boundaries of that chapter, presenting the gist of the argument that must be considered in approaching the subject of corporate support of the arts with serious intent. We cannot go

on putting together the pieces of a public relations puzzle in order
to build a self-justifying case for the support of corporate donations
to cultural centers. Nor can we haphazardly select artistic movements and institutions as the beneficiaries of corporate support.

That the artistic and general cultural environment is vital to the
corporation admits of no doubt, I believe. One is reminded here of
Leslie White's definition of culture: "By culture we mean an extra-
somatic, temporal continuum of things and events dependent upon
symboling. Specifically and concretely, culture consists of tools, implements, utensils, clothing, ornaments, customs, institutions, beliefs,
rituals, games, works of art, language, etc. All peoples in all times
and places have possessed culture; no other species has or has had
culture. In the course of the evolution of primates *man* appeared
when the ability to symbol had been developed and become capable
of expression. We thus define man in terms of the ability to symbol
and the consequent ability to produce culture."

The reasons for affirming the vital relevance of the cultural environment to corporate institutions are not at all obvious to many.
And when the thinking is canvassed, there may be more doubts than
convictions. For those who would pursue the argument further, I
offer some guideposts to the philosophy of this book:

1. Although addressed to both the corporate community and the
diverse communities of the arts, the message is directed mainly to
students of the world of business and to corporate executive managements.

2. Essentially, the message is this: try to widen your horizons and
deepen your insights into the corporation-arts nexus in preparation
for policy-making in this general field for the decades ahead. Avoid
the narrow view that corporate financial support of certain of the
arts is the main issue. Try to conceive of the arts broadly and to
consider the implications of their interplay with the corporate world
of business. Try to imagine what business corporations, on the one
hand, and the art world, on the other, can do apart and in collaboration with one another to achieve their common objectives.

3. On the side of the art world, the relevant people and institu-

tions are the creators of works of art, the custodians of this element of high culture, and the transmitters of it through education and avenues of communication.

4. "Art" does not mean painting and sculpture alone, nor even the fine arts to the exclusion of industrial and popular arts. A broad position is taken in this book because corporate policy concerning the corporate-arts nexus cannot be limited nor can it be abstract. This is true especially because corporate business aims at comprehensive service to the widest possible population aggregates, is democratic for economic reasons alone, and is, besides, confronted with the necessity and opportunity for living and flourishing in the midst of a democratic culture. Furthermore, the need for the artist's contribution to the world of business is protean and unpredictable, so that all sources of creativity must be encouraged. The relationship between artistic and other kinds of creativity—in science and technology, for example—is so close and intimate that no alert corporation executive will prefer to draw hard and fast lines between the several elements of high culture, all of which promise to contribute immeasurably to corporate survival and success. Enlightened corporate leaders, therefore, will keep an open mind about the scope of "the arts," their function in society, their meaning for man.

5. On the side of corporate business, the main concern of this book is with the great institutional corporations, but not exclusively with these. The big institutional companies can be expected to lead the way toward more thoughtful policy approaches to the corporate-arts nexus; but leadership sometimes comes from smaller companies.

On the whole subject of the corporation and the arts it is time to lay the arguments on the table and to make more than a superficial attack on the entire problem of corporate-arts involvement. This book may not have all the answers, but it does try to shed some light into all of the corners.

Richard Eells

ARKVILLE, NEW YORK
Summer, 1966

Contents

xi

THE CORPORATION

AND THE ARTS

CHAPTER I

Two Major Institutions

The modern corporation and the arts, two major American institutions, are experiencing startling changes in their nature, status, and interrelationship. The immediate focus of this book is on the convergent development that has brought these two major institutions into closer contact. This convergence has profound implications for both the corporation and the arts.

What the outcome of this meeting of artistic and corporate personalities will be is still uncertain. Nor can anyone be sure of definitive answers at this early stage of the development. Even the fact of convergence seems less than clear to many. Nevertheless, it can be shown that the convergence is inevitable, is occurring now, and might well be directed systematically and expeditiously.

It is by no means obvious that closer relations between corporate enterprises and the arts will always be mutually beneficial. Today many people seem to assume that any advantage would be one-sided, that only the artists, or the companies, as the case may be, have anything to gain by a closer relationship. The potential gain, moreover, is said to be conditional on corporate giving to art institutions on a completely "hands-off" basis. The suspicion that corporate patrons of the arts will become "meddlesome Matties" has deterred many from even a unilateral or arm's-length relationship. Corporate patronage, like governmental patronage, could indeed be stultifying to the artist. But is this the necessary and unavoidable consequence of financial aid from these sources—aid without which it is difficult to see how the arts will thrive and make their contribution to the vitality of our cultural life?

These topical and urgent questions will not be erased by fears of philistinism. They cannot be exorcised by elaborate diatribes. The combined problem of the role of the arts in society and of the appropriate means of the arts contributing to cultural maturation cannot be sidestepped—and will not be. The reason is that the arts, in all their grandeur and amazing range of versatility, are recognized more and more by leaders in both public and private sectors as indispensable. And because they are not always self-supporting, many of the arts have to be supported somehow. Aid to the arts is fundamental and the issue will persist until we get reasonable answers.

But aid to the arts, and more particularly financial aid from private and public sources, is not the entire issue. Indeed, to focus the problem on corporate giving is to mistake the branch for the tree. The major issue is one of interinstitutional relationships on a broad scale, viewed comprehensively, historically, and comparatively. In other words, what is needed is a perspective in time and depth on the development of both the corporation and the arts, and not only in our own society. The parochial and temporally superficial views of these interinstitutional relationships can hardly be scientifically satisfactory or useful to policy-makers.

The need for comprehensive analysis is already obvious in most contemporary approaches to the business-arts nexus; the blinders of the so-called philanthropic approach can be quite damaging. Policy-makers in government and business tend to follow side-paths rather than the main trail, with lengthy and detailed inquiries into means instead of ends. The financial-aid problem, important as it is,

2

can only touch this question of means and not basically that of the goals of art and business.

For this reason a main purpose here is to extend the inquiry beyond the immediate financial-aid question to the teleological issues. The corporation and the arts are both examples of social institutions in the process of growth. We must try to imagine what the outcomes of growth will be. And there ought to be more discussion of these ends, in the sense of ultimate purpose. The issues of material and formal cause can be subordinated profitably until we have some reliable conceptions of the corporation and the arts in terms of final cause—what these institutions can be and would be if we were to direct and permit their growth to the fullest maturity.

The discussion of corporate-arts relationships requires at the start at least a tentative definition of terms. What do we mean by "the corporation"? What do we mean by "the arts"? And what is the significance of both institutions for a free people?

In chapters that follow, an attempt is made to embrace a latitudinarian view of "the arts" because doctrinaire and academic definition would not be serviceable here. Our purpose is not a refined view of art that restricts the term to matters of fastidious taste. For reasons that appear later on, the corporate interest in the arts is deep and wide. One cannot safely confine this corporate concern to a few of the "fine arts" and still do justice to the goals and requirements of contemporary and future corporate enterprises.

On the other hand, it is incorrect to assume a corporate disinterest in the so-called fine arts and in esthetic considerations. There is a growing public interest in all the arts, and this interest is shared by many of the leading corporations today. It would be impossible for any major institution such as the modern corporation to be a mere bystander in the "cultural explosion" that we hear so much about nowadays. The attacks of the elitists on mass culture and on an alleged vulgarization of art cannot be ignored; nor can the demands for the democratization of culture. The makers of corporate policy find themselves—as they did in the financial-aid aspect of the corporate-arts relationship—confronted by such conflicts of opinion.

Shall a company back only esthetically pure and aristocratic art enterprises, or shall it go in for the spread of culture far and wide throughout the country?

Those questions go to the heart of corporate social responsibility, a much-debated issue in the business world, one that now moves into the new realm of the business-arts relationship. It is an issue that will undoubtedly strike sparks in many places; the debate may even become furious because business and the arts are so widely regarded as disparates. If it was difficult for many of the traditionalists on business policy to accept the idea of corporate support of education, how much more provocative will the corporate-arts nexus be?

At first glance, the question appears to defy objective analysis and any sound basis for a "business" judgment. Yet the opposite is true, and mainly because art, like the economic institutions of society, has a well-established place that can never be underrated. The fact is that, of all social institutions, art is one of the most venerable and ubiquitous. By comparison, the modern corporation is historically an upstart. The sociology of art—the science, that is, of art as a social phenomenon—is in its infancy; but not the phenomenon itself. We are tardy in discovering the way to talk scientifically about most of our social institutions. And we are especially tardy about art. The subject of art has been left too exclusively to writers with little or no interest in other social institutions.

However, a start has been made in the other direction—toward a realistic treatment of artistic work as it relates to other kinds of creativity, and toward a realization by others that artists have a vital function in a well-balanced society. Like innovators in the business world, artistic innovators share the common concern of free men with a future less encumbered by barriers to man's pursuit of the Good, the True, and the Beautiful. Since Socrates, at least, the best of the Western tradition has insisted upon intimate relationships among these ideals both in theory and in practice. And in the traditions of the East there is perhaps an even greater emphasis upon the social functions of art.

In an age when business enterprise is becoming increasingly trans-national in its operational scope, the modern corporation becomes a social institution that casts parochial prejudice aside and prepares to flourish in all kinds of cultural orientations, dealing with people from East and West, from the southern as well as the northern hemisphere. The path to understanding peoples globally, whether for business, political, scientific, or other purposes, lies in part through the arts.

This is an important reason why we in the United States, with ever-widening economic and social relationships, have taken new and renewed interest in cultural achievements from every corner of the globe. For transnational corporate enterprises the interest is immediate and practical. But for all American business leaders the social implications of art have become increasingly significant—and not only because businessmen are being asked to support burgeoning arts centers. A more comprehensive view of the situation reveals that what the free enterprise businessmen have been talking about so long (and too often in cliché-ridden terms) is a kind of freedom and enterprise that their fellow-citizens in other walks of life are just as much interested in as they are. To discover this fact requires, it is true, a redefinition of terms: "freedom" and "enterprise" are both words that reveal a changing content.

More broadly conceived, these words embrace the aspirations of scholars, scientists, and artists, as well as businessmen. The discovery of this common ground is an underlying cause of the tide of cultural interests that now sweeps into the corporate ramparts. It is a welcome tide that will launch the most enlightened leaders of business and art on the seas of venture. To state the matter boldly, we are on the verge of a new era in our country's continuing reach for prosperity —but prosperity with a new dimension in depth. Threats of disaster beset mankind in this particular epoch, this "time of troubles." Yet it is not a little remarkable that there should be such a rising tide of cultural activities throughout this country—a tide supported in-creasingly by corporate enterprise. The trend may perhaps be taken as a sign of the forward-looking habits of our best business leaders and a penchant for trying out new schemes of value to society, as well as profitable to themselves.

As we move from a period of building the economic foundations of a continental social structure to the further, and essential, task of filling in the spiritual dimensions of a better society, the alliance of Business and the Arts is certain to become more and more firmly established. Already it is obvious that there is to be an alliance of Government and the Arts. A free society, while never fearful of such an alliance, will want to be sure that the government-arts nexus does not exclude a wide diversity of artistic enterprise; and one way to assure this diversity is to facilitate, encourage, and even insist upon active relationships among business and artistic enterprisers.

Clearly there are many implications of the corporate-arts nexus. At this stage of the inquiry, the main effort must be to lay down certain directional paths and to propose a number of routes. Such proposals, as well as a recapitulation of the chief arguments of the book, are offered in the last two Chapters.

CHAPTER II

What Are "The Arts"?

In the corporate-arts nexus—the interplay between the modern corporation and the arts—what do we mean by "the arts"? Actually, we are talking about three rather complex elements: (1) Art, with a capital "A"; (2) the arts, in the plural, which comprise a wide spectrum running from the "fine" and "higher" arts to adaptive skills that make little or no claim to esthetic purpose; and (3) the artist, probably the most important element in the equation.

To begin with, no all-purpose definition of Art, the arts, or the artist is possible. As Thomas Munro[1] has well said, one must fit the definition of art to the purpose. This does not mean to say that no agreement is possible on what persons, activities, and things are being referred to when "the arts" are discussed. Rather, we must recognize that some people are interested only in works of art, as they define them in some particular way; others are mainly interested in the creative process—the way works of art are conceived and presented to us; still others focus their attention on the creators of art, or on the craftsmen, as the case may be if reference is

7

being made to the arts at the lower end of the spectrum. In other words, the definition of "the arts" depends more on the interests of the definer than on anything else. In fact, such qualifying words as "fine" and "lower" become relevant only in certain kinds of discussions about the arts.

Our concern here is less with definition and more with the impact and scope of the arts in the environment of the corporation.

Scope of "The Arts"

To examine the interplay of the corporation and the arts one must be prepared to examine closely many viewpoints. At the outset it is unwise to limit the scope of the arts to the fine arts[2]—painting, drawing, sculpture, and architecture—because other fields also require our attention. The graphic arts, ceramics, industrial design, landscape design, city planning, for example, increasingly pose issues that the corporate policymakers cannot resolve within the framework of traditional prejudices about the preciousness of art or self-limiting doctrines about the scope of the arts.

On the other hand, to extend the meaning of the arts too far, would also be unjustifiable. The arts, defined in terms of skill in adapting things to the uses of human life, or defined to embrace all human contrivance and ingenuity, could include practically everything that modern industry makes or does. Yet there is wisdom in keeping even these sweeping definitions of the arts in mind when one examines the common denominators of creativity.

The productivity of the modern corporation depends far more than is generally realized upon astonishingly rare human resources which, when tracked down, often prove to be a species of genius that is difficult to classify as either exclusively scientific or exclusively artistic. The terms "science" and "art" can be quite misleading when applied to the creative process in the human organism. Some scientific hypotheses may be considered works of art. And art is neither the antithesis of science nor independent of it.

8

The arts, as mentioned in the Constitution of the United States, are linked to the progress of science. Article I, Section 8, Clause 3 says, "The Congress shall have power . . . to promote the progress of science and useful arts, by securing for limited times to authors and inventors the exclusive right to their respective writings and discoveries." The federal patent and copyright laws rest on the foundation of this important clause. "Inventive genius" is a major test of patentability for the "discoveries" of inventors, and it is evident from cases decided under this clause that the mental processes involved in such discoveries must display "more ingenuity . . . than the work of a mechanic skilled in the art."[3]

But do the "useful arts" referred to include the so-called fine arts or "higher" arts? Photographs and circus posters may be copyrighted, according to decisions of the United States Supreme Court. When in one case it was argued that a certain lithograph did not fall within the protection of the clause because it had "no other use than that of a mere advertisement," Justice Holmes declared that it was not for the courts to attempt to judge the worth of pictorial illustrations outside the narrowest limits.

Artists and authors are not properly protected under legislation adopted by Congress under the copyright clause, according to August Heckscher, special consultant on the arts to President John F. Kennedy. In Heckscher's report on *The Arts and the National Government*[4] he made the point that creators of works of art are denied the rights available to holders of patents and other property under the capital-assets tax provision of federal law, thus subjecting writers and artists to higher capital gains taxes than inventors and others. Furthermore he urged that the copyright laws be revised to take into account technological and other relevant developments. "The equitable protection of fundamental rights as well as the recognition of the contribution of the creative writer, artist, composer, and playwright are at stake," he wrote. And he added that the outcome would be of "major significance in determining the degree of encouragement or discouragement this nation offers in the creative arts."

Some of the issues involved include the duration of copyright, proof and evidence of copyright protection, extension and character of rights, and existing limitations and exceptions from payment of royalties. The report expressed concern for performing artists, as well as composers and playwrights, and it raised the question of royalties on works in the public domain to be paid to the government and used to support and advance the arts—a method used in some European countries.

In the Copyright Act of 1909, works eligible for copyright registration included "works of art," "models or designs for works of art," and "reproductions of a work of art." Copyrightable works of art, according to the regulations of the Copyright Office, include works of artistic craftsmanship with reference to form but not the mechanical or utilitarian aspects of these works; mentioned are "artistic jewelry, enamels, glassware, and tapestries," together with "works belonging to the fine arts" such as "paintings, drawings, and sculpture." Copyrightable reproductions cover lithographs, etchings, drawings, photoengravings, and other similar kinds of copy.[5]

In contrast, for those who stress the "purity" of the esthetic experience, fenced off, so to speak, from all other kinds of human experience, it is anathema to talk about the arts in such prosaic terms. Art, for the esthetic isolationist,[6] is strictly isolated from any utilitarian purpose; otherwise the so-called work of art is in reality something else. Later we will discuss this point of view and the art-for-art's sake position. But let us first examine another approach—one that is more fruitful from the standpoint of corporate policymakers: art seen in its total context.

Are the Arts in Isolation?

Opposed to the isolationists are those writers who stress the continuities that exist between esthetic and nonesthetic values and experiences. John Dewey in his book, *Art as Experience,* falls into this category, as do those specialists in the sociology of art who take the contextualist position. From their point of view works of art deal with many subjects, serve many purposes for their creators, are points on continua in many kinds of history, and may be indicators of significant future developments within a culture (using that term in its anthropological sense). The contextualists see the creators of works of art as creative persons who might have channeled their energies into quite different human activities had they been given different circumstances in their lives.

In the contrast between isolationists and contextualists in esthetics a parallel can be drawn between similar intellectual camps in corporation theory. The isolationists view the traditional corporation as a "pure" enterprise run for the exclusive benefit of profit-seeking stockholders. This view of corporate purpose has recently given way to a contextualist view of the corporation as a major social institution with profound implications for corporate external relationships, which now include, and increasingly so, the corporate-arts interplay.

The attempt to isolate art from other aspects of a culture is not only unscientific. It is, as John Dewey observed, a pathological phenomenon. He regarded such isolation as one manifestation of the incoherence of our civilization. For Dewey it was an incoherence produced in part by new forces, so new that attitudes belonging to them and consequences issuing from them had not been incorporated and digested into integral elements of experience. Science had brought radically new concepts of physical nature, which were in contrast with concepts of the world that man inherited from the Christian and other traditions. Under the impact of science the things of the physical world and those of the moral realm fell apart, whereas, in contrast, the Greek tradition and that of the medieval age held them in intimate union. "From one point of view," wrote Dewey, "the problem of recovering an organic place for art in civilization is like the problem of reorganizing our heritage from the past and insights of present knowledge into a coherent and integrated imaginative union."[7]

11

The "inhuman" art of today may be a reflection of this incoherence. Artists try to probe the nature of man and the physical universe with the new tools of knowledge—physics and psychoanalysis, for example. They try to express what they see or feel in these new ways, casting aside naturalistic and representational techniques as archaic.

According to Dewey, science has entered into society diffusely, especially through industry where scientific applications have revolutionized business and contributed to the growth of the modern corporation. But science has also affected art in ways that are little understood. The Greeks divorced the useful from the fine arts in characteristic terms; their social theories erected universal propositions (which were false to Dewey) about the human slavery they took for granted. They relegated manual work, however artistic, to slaves. "Base mechanics," including even work such as architecture, sculpture, painting, and musical performance, were left to artisans. To the citizens of Athens was left the artistic use of *words*.

Dewey contrasts this view with the status of the arts in the age of science and modern technology. Mass production by mechanical means gives the old separation between the useful and "fine" arts a decidedly new turn, but not necessarily a more attractive one. The split is reinforced by the greater importance that attaches to industry and trade in the organization of society. The mechanical and the esthetic stand at opposite poles, with the production of goods now at the mechanical pole. The hand-craftsman's liberty of choice in fashioning his material has tended to vanish with the general use of the machine. He no longer directly observes and enjoys the use of the product of his work as he could before; his part in the productive process becomes so specialized and remote that the intimacy of art-and-use is denied him.

Dewey regarded this remoteness through specialization as possibly the most important factor in the status of art in our contemporary civilization.[8] But he rejected the view that industrial conditions made it impossible to integrate art into our culture. For Dewey there was now a new cleanness of line, a great gain in form and color in commercial products and in architecture. An esthetic revolution had been brought about by better adaptation of products to needs. Industrial surroundings were now working to create that larger experience into which particular products fit in such a way that they gained esthetic quality. The "habits of the eye as a medium of perception were being slowly altered in being accustomed to the shapes typical of industrial products and to the shapes that belong to urban as distinct from rural life."[9]

Art and the Antiesthetic

Dewey's observation about the pathological isolation of art in our time suggests that the significance of art in its larger context might be sought in its antinomy in the contemporary rejection of the esthetic. It is said that art was once the very center of life's text, but that in our scientific and technological age it tends to be shoved into the margin. It is not that science and technology are antiesthetic. The trouble is that art is too often regarded as a mere diversion or amusement, useful perhaps in a decorative way as a civilizer of manners but serving no vital function in society.

Against this is the view that art does have a vital function that must be taken seriously in our colleges and universities. The neglect of art in English and American education has often been the thesis of leading philosophers and educators such as Alfred North Whitehead, Sir Herbert Read, George Santayana, and Harold Taylor.

Taylor, for example, has emphatically denounced the "antiesthetic content of the curricula of the schools and universities where the arts are pushed out of the regular curriculum to make room for academic hack-work necessary for gaining admission to college and graduate school."[10] Unless some drastic reforms are made in the content of the educational system, Taylor warns, there can be no bringing of the arts to the center of national life. The "esthetic sterility" of the educational system now makes academic success practically impossible for students who are not gifted in the conventional academic sense, but who love to paint, to sculpt, to sing, to write, to dance, to compose, to act, to "celebrate their personal joy." Students whose talents lie in the creative and performing arts, he insists, are systematically eliminated from our educational system as it stands today. Instead of nourishing the growth of the sensibilities of our youth, thus maximizing their potentialities as creative persons as they mature, we teach them to value economic and social success as the outcome of the education they are offered—and, one might add, commanded to embrace on pain of social failure if they turn aside.

The social issue, which also is an element in donative policy in many companies, is a long-standing one. It is the issue that John Dewey raised when he said that "as long as art is the beauty parlor of civilization, neither art nor civilization is secure."[11] The same issue was raised in the Rockefeller Panel Report on the Performing Arts, which emphasized the arts as a community concern to be placed alongside our long-accepted responsibilities for libraries, museums, hospitals, and schools. John D. Rockefeller, 3d, observed in this report that meeting our basic physical needs falls short of attaining the end objectives of life—the emotional, intellectual, and esthetic satisfactions that constitute man's higher needs. Today, he said, the arts are more fully appreciated as one means by which man can achieve the satisfactions he seeks; the arts thus become essential to the human mind and spirit.

Do we have an *anti*esthetic culture in the United States, or is it only a culture indifferent to art? There are other alternatives; the esthetic elements in our civilization may be latently strong and still largely inchoate because we have been committed to other priorities. There is a decided tendency in some quarters to make a moral issue of this problem, identifying our alleged "materialism" with a relatively slow growth of the arts. Upton Sinclair in his earlier writings denounced "capitalistic art," which, though concededly produced by artists of sincerity and intelligence, was necessarily pessimistic because "materialistic capitalism" was dying. In contrast, he prized the optimism of "proletarian art," which was idealistic, permeated by a morality of brotherhood and service, produced by workers who could only act by hope and the dream of acting for a better future.

14

Aside from the fact that the intervening decades have brought new insights into the so-called proletarian regimes, introducing a special kind of pessimism of the Left, this species of moralistic case for an indigenous American and captalistic hostility to the esthetic quest has lost its force for other reasons. G. K. Chesterton declaimed in *A Defense of Nonsense* that "there must always be a rich *moral* soil for any great esthetic growth" and that "nothing sublimely artistic has ever arisen out of mere art, any more than anything essentially reasonable has ever arisen out of pure reason." As we shall see, the sociologist of art can make a strong case for the interrelationships of ethics and esthetics and the effect of social pathology on the state of the arts. But in our present inquiry we do not have to posit any identification of the Good and the Beautiful in order to get at the nuclear significance of art. That is to say, the nature and significance of art is not necessarily revealed by an inquiry into the state of our political and economic morals.

Art and Nonart

The heat now being generated by new developments in art may possibly yield some light on the nature of art and the function of the arts in society. The critics of, and the apologists for such developments as Op and Pop, the Theater of the Absurd, the Theater of Cruelty, and electronic music, to take some examples, help us to understand modern art if only by indirection. Denunciations are useful; they may point to the outer limits of art. From the din of the battle, and guided by seasoned observers of the social arena in its many aspects and phases, one may be able to draw useful conclusions about probable art trends and their implications for corporate policy as it relates to the arts.

Excluded from the category of art, according to some critics, is much of the contemporary "optical art" because the paintings are produced by a mechanical process. Op art was displayed at the Museum of Modern Art in New York City in 1965 at an

15

exhibition called "The Responsive Eye." At the Brooklyn Poly-
technic Institute an Op "painter" exhibited "paintings" he had
produced with a movie-patterns kit that anyone could buy for less
than ten dollars. The equipment in this kit could generate, by a
purely mechanical process, an infinite number of designs.

Anthony West complained that these designs, when transferred
to a prepared board or a canvas, should qualify for entry into the
Museum of Modern Art as a work of art; and he attacked the
"abysmal simplicities" in such shows as no creations of *artists*,
even though there is a school of painters who call themselves
"perceptual abstractionists" using color "to produce purely subjective impressions of the mind."[12] He contrasted the computer-
produced colored cover of the February, 1965, issue of the *Scientific
American*, which lacks an artist's signature. A research worker at
Bell Telephone Laboratories had programmed the computer for this
design, but not, said West, for esthetic or artistic ends; the research
aimed at the production of information about the capacities of the
eye as a receiving mechanism. The resulting design was beautiful—
but was it art?

Whether it is or is not art, of course, depends on one's definition
of art. We cannot adjudicate the conflicting claims here. All we
can do, and must do, is to note the fact that these productions are
sufficiently recognized as having a place among the arts of today
to merit their inclusion somewhere within the long spectrum of the
arts. Machine-processing is irrelevant, though it may be important
in esthetic evaluations and spectrum positioning. Let us concede
that in certain spectrums (there will be as many spectrums of the
arts as there are criteria of artistic excellence) these alleged
"works" of the "perceptual abstractionists" are indeed simple.
But simplicity and mechanical production are not universally
acceptable as the criteria of art critics and estheticians. Certainly
in the corporate world these would be strange criteria. The arts
serve the corporation independently of such qualities and the
corporation serves the arts on a more catholic basis.

Nonart, again, is sometimes distinguished from art on elitist

16

principles. The argument boils down to this: the arts are not for the masses, whose taste can only "degrade Art." John Sloan, a professed democrat in political matters, took it as an axiom that the majority is always wrong in cultural matters. He is reported to have said, "Whenever a cultural matter rolls up a majority, I know it is wrong."[13] Today the proponents and opponents of "mass culture" quarrel with each other and with still others who would write off any "cultural boom" as nonexistent. These others are not necessarily antiart, antiesthetic, or anticulture; they may simply be pointing to the central problems of human survival in an age of nuclear capabilities and logarithmic population growth rates. The arts do not deal with these problems, therefore the arts lie at the periphery, not at the center, of public affairs—so runs the argument. It is very much like the traditional argument for limiting corporate policy to issues of profitability for the stockholders. In both cases the claim of the arts for support is a diversionary action to be resisted.

The fallacy of the propositions that nonart is in the realm of "practical" affairs and that the arts are "nonessential" is not evident to everyone. But the issue here is not abstract and remote. It is a corporate issue as well as an issue of public policy. As one probes deeper one sees the line between art and nonart shading off and finally disappearing. The method of defining the arts by the process of exclusion does not work in practice. This may not be good news to the purists in esthetics or to the traditionalists in economic and political theory, but there is no escaping it.

A Hierarchy of Arts?

Similar difficulties arise in attempts to place certain arts higher or lower in a hierarchy of the arts. As Susanne K. Langer has well said: "There are no higher and lower, partial and supplementary arts, but, as [Thomas Mann] puts it: 'Art is entire and complete in each of its forms and manifestations; we do not need to add up the different species to make a whole'."[14] An empirical approach to the scope of the arts, and thence to the nature of art, seems indispensable. One aspect of such objective studies is the method of comparative cultural analysis.

As one moves out of the more or less parochial and doctrinaire atmosphere of art commentary it becomes obvious that our Western and contemporary definitions of the arts must be revised. The non-Western approaches, now increasingly demanded by all whose lines of communication (in trade, politics, and science, as well as in esthetic pursuits), reach beyond Western cultures, are always interesting and suggestive. A Chinese classification of the arts, for example, reminds one of the ancient Greek prejudice against art produced by manual labor, but with the special twist of an Oriental culture in which literary effort is the criterion. Literary art, in the classical Chinese classification, included poetry, calligraphy, and painting—and these were for the real artists. Nonliterary art—for artisans—included music, sculpture, and architecture. But, as with the Greeks, there was no necessary exclusion of the lesser arts from the general spectrum. And, to quote Kenneth Clark, perhaps the ancient Chinese philosophers would have understood the Greek view that "nothing related to the whole man can be isolated or evaded," thus avoiding "the two evils of sensuality and estheticism."[15] This is also a more humane view than that of Samuel Johnson, who suspected that art might "play too wantonly with our passions."

The vertical grading of the arts on an ethical scale raises many questions. Can esthetic values be properly applied to any other kind of value, including some conception of the Good? Is not the Beautiful an independent value? Can one not grade the arts on the scale of Beauty? To do this, of course, necessitates a theory of Beauty. One is confronted, too, with the question: Is art for art's sake not downright heresy?[16]

Luckily, there is a way out of the labyrinth. Just as no all-purpose definition of art is possible, so no all-purpose scaling of the arts is either possible or desirable. A hierarchy constructed for the isolationist in esthetics would serve no purpose for the contextualist. Yet, it seems probable that, for corporations generally, it is the path of wisdom not to reject out of hand any approach to the subject, however conservative, that might lead to the better understanding of Art, the arts, and artists.

The reason is not that an eclectic position is convenient and avoids hard choices. Rather, one does not know nor can one predict, where the corporate-arts interrelationship will lead in the future. It seems probable that during the next decade corporate executives will encounter many new points of contact with more and more of the arts. They will face many new kinds of situations where they must be ready to make decisions based on a high degree of sophistication concerning the nature of the art. The old Philistine contempt for art in business circles is already quite outmoded inasmuch as corporate support of the arts is being sought and given in the drive for a higher level of culture in the United States. And this is only the beginning. The corporate-arts nexus is not a one-way street and not exclusively a donative street. Big business can and, indeed, must aid the arts. Moreover, there are vast untapped resources in the world of the arts which business has never exploited for increasing the productivity of this country.

The Esthetic Quest

All of these arguments point to the need in the business world for broadened understanding of the nature of art, philosophically conceived, as well as of the principle involved in its application to industry.

During the millennia since the ancient Greeks discussed esthetics, the primary concepts of art that writers have employed are so numerous that one is inclined to doubt any possible common ground. These various approaches have been made through such diverse concepts as play, illusion, imitation, beauty, emotional expression, imagination, intuition, wish-fulfillment, pleasure, technique, sensuous surface, meaning, form, empathy, abstraction, esthetic distance, and isolation.[17] The disagreements among writers may be more nominal than real, thus indicating essentially the multiple approaches that are possible when a subject matter so rich in variety as art is discussed and when the purposes of the writers are so various. The *creation* of art may be the major interest at hand for some writers; for others it may be the *objects* created; and for still others, the *act of appreciation* by the beholder. Among the critics, there is even an *art of criticism* in which the "meaning" of art gets a thorough going-over, with results that the layman may not fathom.

If one accepts the position of Morris Weitz that comprehensive labels (e.g., that all art is "emotional expression") for art as a whole ought to be avoided because of its multifarious manifestations, and that the better way is to treat separately the various constituents of the creative process, of esthetic artifacts, and of the esthetic experience, then it becomes somewhat easier to talk about "the arts."[18] The classical definitions of art are undeniably enlightening; they aid us in understanding the role of art in the history of thought and provide clues for future development of a social theory of art. They serve also to call attention to certain aspects of art that might otherwise be neglected or underrated, to recommend for consideration certain criteria of esthetic excellence, and to connect the theory of art with other kinds of theory, such as epistemology and ethics.

In Carritt's review of over forty representative estheticians' definitions of art, ancient and modern, he reaches the conclusion that art, as a creative process, is the expression of mood, feeling, and spirit.[19] There may thus be a common denominator for "art" in the middle ground between "the arts" as skills and the narrowly defined "fine arts," although Carritt clearly leans toward the latter category. For our purposes the estheticians' refinements of definition based upon some particular theory of beauty are of secondary interest. This is so because the arts in their relation

20

to the modern corporation involve far more than the pursuit of beauty alone.

An anthologist, such as Melvin Rader, or a writer, such as Thomas Munro, who seeks the deeper interrelationships must face the more comprehensive task of seeing the arts as a whole. For Rader art is the great reconciler. Art reconciles opposite poles that ordinarily exclude each other in our daily lives. It combines creatively such opposites as variety and unity, familiarity and strangeness, repose and stimulation, order and spontaneity, the Apollonian and Dionysian moods. The extreme intensification of emotions in great tragedy do not exclude a sense of repose; on the contrary, it produces a dynamic calmness, the Aristotelian catharsis.

Art also involves the harmonious working of the conscious and the subconscious; the dream is inserted into the texture of waking life; the unreal and the real are fused. For Schiller art reconciled law and impulse; the form, the pattern, the lawfulness of the experience became the expression, not the repression, of impulse. Art, for Schiller, makes man whole, and man is only whole in artistic experience. According to Jacques Maritain, the universal essence—art—merges into the specific image, and the more seamless is the unity, the more perfect is the esthetic moment. John Dewey declared that "Art is the living and concrete proof that man is capable of restoring consciously, and thus on the plane of meaning, the union of sense, need, impulse, and action characteristic of the live creature."[20]

The definition of art as "the practice of creating perceptible forms expressive of human feeling," offered by Susanne K. Langer in one of her many enlightening commentaries, more nearly satisfies our requirement of a comprehensive view of the arts. A work of art, in her view, is a symbol of feeling, and like a symbol, "formulates our ideas of inward experience, as discourse formulates our ideas of facts in the outside world;"[21] it "presents something like a direct vision of vitality, emotion, subjective reality."[22]

21

Langer's concept of feeling, it should be noted, is an important key to her view of the scope and significance of art. It is a concept born of empirical inquiry into the psychology of art. We shall not pause here to elaborate it because the discussion belongs more properly in another chapter on art as a way of knowing. Here, we only warn that Langer's "feeling" is not simply a matter of emotion and that the perceptible forms that artists create to express human feeling run a very wide gamut. The forms so created may not be acceptable according to some canons of beauty, but they may express, as no other means could, "such elusive things as rhythms of attention and the strain of thought, bodily relaxation or tension that cannot be reduced to any particular sensation, attitudes of mind, confidence in the goodness of life, of fundamental annoyance, boredom, cynicism, or again the countless modes of humor."[23] Art begins where science ends in the expression of some of these feelings, and without the artists we might be at a loss to express them.

The absolute need for art as "an independent mode of apprehension and expression" and as "the sensuous correlative, equal and opposite, of intellectual abstraction"[24] is the theme of educational reformers who deplore the visual, tonal, and tactical[25] illiteracy of presumably educated young people. The plea is not so much for a developed sense of beauty (although this is a part of it) as it is for awareness of the forms art offers for the expression of feeling in Langer's meaning of the term. Why go through life with blinders on, with untrained ears and eyes and other sensors? How can a high culture permit atrophy of these avenues of apprehension? A usual reply mentions the puritanical restraints on modern Western cultures. But the story is far more complex.

Curt Sachs has suggested one cause of the atrophy in tracing the history of the dance. He tells us that the dance is the mother of the arts. Yet he is reluctant to speak of the dance in this historic sense as an art. How can "art," he asks, refer without question to the idea of "rhythmical patterns of movement, the plastic sense of space, the vivid representation of a world seen and imagined," the things which "man creates in his own body in the dance before he uses substance and stone and word to give expression to his inner experiences?"[26] The dance is not art in the usual sense, he insists, though he wants to include within the term *art* "all rhythmical motion not related to the work motif."

Art, says Sachs, in the narrower sense and in the higher cultures, becomes a spectacle designed to influence men rather than their spirits; it then disintegrates into guild art and social enjoyment. It is no longer "the means of re-creating things seen and heard, the giving of form and substance to the intangible and irrational perceptions of the half-conscious, and the experiencing in the creative process of the divine rapture of another world and self-forgetfulness." Dances had become works of art as early as the Stone Age, and on the threshold of the Metal Ages legend seized the dance and raised it into drama. But today the drama "denies its paternity," the new religions reject the old rounds and dances, and there is renunciation of rhythm by play and physical exercise. Yet, although modern religion has lost the capacity to "pray with the feet," like the beautiful gypsy Preciosa of Cervantes, every higher culture does retain the spiritual inheritance of a distant past, "the lofty conception that all supermundane and superhuman motion is dance."[27]

These observations on the dance in historical perspective indicate both some of the reasons for atrophy of modern feeling for "prayer with the feet," as well as the clearer notion we seem to have today that the dance *is* an art. Sachs quotes an old Mexican Zuñi who declared: "We dance for pleasure and for the good of the city." Who dances today for the good of the city? The dance becomes a separated "art form," whereas for the Zuñi it was somehow integrated into the life of his civilization. Similarly we often take other art forms *in vacuo*, and thereby lose the connection with their ethnic roots.

It is a dangerous exercise in the theory of art, John Dewey once observed, to contemplate the Parthenon *in vacuo*. Its esthetic, as well as its historic significance emerges only after one has turned from the edifice itself to "the bustling, arguing, acutely sensitive Athenian citizens, whose civic sense was identified with a civic religion, of whose experience the temple was an expression, and who built it not as a work of art but as a civic commemoration."[28] The very existence of works of art, such as the Parthenon, makes theorizing about art hazardous because we build a wall of prestige and convention around them and the wall prevents us from getting at the originating conditions of the works themselves. Those indigenes who created, observed, and lived with the dances and the temples might have formulated theories about them that would be strange to us.

On the other hand, as Dewey has said, "Esthetic experience is a manifestation, a record and celebration of the life of a civilization, a means of promoting its development, and is also the ultimate judgment upon the quality of a civilization."[29] Because esthetic experience has these dimensions, works of art provide many uses for the social scientist and for corporate policymakers. For the anthropologist and historian, extant works of art are indispensable clues—and sometimes almost the only ones—to problems to be solved in these disciplines concerning cultures, periods, trends. But this is only the passive use of art. Today and tomorrow we need to employ to advantage the creativity of the artist. And those who look at our time and place and culture in retrospect will assess the arts of our time in these terms.

Art for Art's Sake?

When we draw the boundaries of the arts so wide, is the way being paved for a purely utilitarian view, a conception of the arts as mere adjuncts of corporate enterprise? The answer is No. Art is autonomous in an important sense, and it can meet the corporation, as an institution, on even ground. The modern corporation, indeed, must give ground to the arts, and paradoxically enough, in the process of doing so corporate enterprise will be greatly enhanced. The case for this may not be readily seen. We must start from certain positions taken by those who emphasize the art-for-art's sake argument as though a corporate-arts nexus were thereby precluded.

To be rejected out of hand at the start, of course, is the notion that, as Sir Herbert Read has expressed it, art is only "some kind of decorative facade to be applied (literally 'stuck on') to any utilitarian object merely to hide its naked purpose."[30] But Sir Herbert goes on to say that a distinction must be drawn between the ideological and legitimately utilitarian functions of art. In its "ideological function," art expresses mental perceptions in a material form; but it can, and does, do more. Our practical needs can be satisfied by our making instruments that are merely minimally efficient; or they can be satisfied by our making instruments that meet the needs of the human being as a totality. That totality, he insists, includes an esthetic impulse as well as various practical impulses; "a concern for the form as well as the efficiency of production"; and "unless this instinct for form is satisfied at the same time as the functional need, a disturbance will be set up within the social totality: the pattern of the culture will not be integral."[31] He is arguing for the distinction between the fine arts and the applied arts—one that had been much abused but also much misunderstood. Sir Herbert's attention to industrial design is significant in this respect; he will not admit that art must be a mere servant of industry, but he urges that if art is not applied in industry there is danger of social pathology.

Sir Herbert emphatically rejects the servitude of art to the intellect, but he insists on art's role in a balanced life of the psyche. He deplores the Hegelian assumption that a *science* of art was more urgently needed than art itself—a well-directed blow at the pseudoscientists of esthetics who would have esthetic realities superseded by intellectual truths of a transcendental kind, leaving the arts below and behind. Art is not, he insists, a mere aid to thought, any more than it is a mere adjunct of industry in good industrial design; it is a *mode of thought* in its own right. A philosopher might well find it necessary to reach a comprehension of reality through the sensuous medium of art, but art is "the fundamental necessity," and its maintenance in full creative vitality requires an "open cultivation of the sensuous and instinctive elements of the personality" by educational techniques that Sir Herbert has elaborated in great detail. In his opinion no civilized society has yet realized the full creative vitality of art, and he asks whether ours can do it, now that we have the promise of relief from fear and oppression through the techniques of modern psychology and the growing determination to win for humanity the benefits of modern methods of production. Through these and other means the conditions of a great art might be created. This at least is "a possible faith to oppose to all who would leave us in despair and cynicism, without pleasure, without joy, without that highest and subtlest ecstasy of which the human mind is capable—the ecstasy of art, of poetry, the creation of a world of imaginative reality."[32]

Evidently this view of art, while it condemns the Philistinism that brushes art aside as "an expendable form of mental or physical gymnastics," as Sir Herbert puts it, leaves a good deal of room for those arts that are regularly excluded from the higher arts. He will not have art as "something that can be imposed on a culture, like a certificate of respectability," but at the same time he sees it as developing a favorable climate of social amenities and cultural aspirations. Art and the arts have their uses, even though art is autonomous and no mere instrument. The preferred outcomes—social action where art is a behavioral element—need not necessarily exclude nonartistic goals that are closely associated with the esthetic. This concept raises difficult questions concerning the esthetic goal.

In the art-for-art's sake school of thought, the esthetic goal is defended against all comers as a sufficient goal without regard to other goals. But one must distinguish the too-often caricatured view of this school from the varied views of its proponents. The supposed originators—Theophile Gautier and Baudelaire—were

26

perhaps the originators of a phrase but not of a philosophy. *"L'art pour l'art"* meant for Gautier an almost total indifference to contemporary social issues that others have insisted upon as being inseparably related to the work of the artist. In the recent books by Huntington Hartford[33] and William Snaith, for example, art is judged by moral and political standards, and Snaith, in particular, repeatedly denounces the "dehumanization" of art which, he says, stems largely from the *l'art-pour-l'art* heresy.[34] Yet George Saintsbury, the English critic, has observed of Gautier that he was neither immoral, irreligious, nor unduly subservient to despotism; but morals, religion, and politics (to which we may add science and material progress) were matters of no interest to him. A humanist and a humorist, Gautier was, in Saintsbury's opinion, of a singularly kindly and genial nature and his writings were full of extraordinary charm. His power was a literary power, pure and simple. Saintsbury brushes aside the accusation that Gautier lacked ideas as being a charge by "those who have not cleared their minds of cant," and as being characteristic of the criticism that favors "philosophical" treatment of the arts rather than attention to form.

This is a debate that one prefers not to enter into, but one has to take notice of it in any detailed discussion of the relationship of the arts to the modern corporation. Bound to arise, sooner or later, is the issue of art allegedly deflected to corporate purpose, and on the other side, of corporate objectives deflected to irrelevant esthetic goals. "Art for art's sake" is in part a defensive cry against those who would subordinate the esthetic quest to other values. Art that marches along *with,* but not subordinate to, other human effort may need a degree of autonomy that opens it to the charge of irrelevance and even the alleged "dehumanization" we hear so much of. The observation is relevant to discussions of functionalism in art.

The functionalism of contemporary architecture, for example, has been attacked by some estheticians for its sterile utilitarianism. But the case for functionalism in architecture was put by Gropius in clear, and clearly esthetic, terms. The guiding principle at the

Bauhaus, he said, was that artistic design was neither an intellectual nor a material affair, but simply an integral part of the stuff of life. The revolution in esthetics has given fresh insight into the meaning of design, just as the mechanization of industry had provided new tools for its realization. Their ambition was to rouse the creative artist from his other-worldliness and reintegrate him into the workaday world of realities. At the same time the aim was to broaden and humanize the rigid, almost exclusively material, mind of the business man. "Thus our informing conception of the basic unity of all design in relation to life was in diametrical opposition to that of 'art for art's sake,' and to the even more dangerous philosophy it sprang from: business as an end in itself."[35]

Sir Herbert Read, citing this passage observed that it implied "an opposition between intellectual (imaginative, creative) activity and practical, mechanical activity, and their integration in a unity which is precisely the art of architecture," but not "that this identical opposition is present in every work of art." Other arts, he said, have other ends, and though there may not be such a thing as "art for art's sake," the other element in art is not necessarily a practical one. There is a dialectic in all art, according to Read. The functional purposes set limits to the creative freedom of the artist. Function may be regarded as "an aspect of reason, reflection, utility, etc., whose dialectical opposites are unreason, impulse, imagination, etc.; and art like architecture, *in so far as it is an art*, is a synthetical resolution of just these contradictions." Modern architects like Gropius "fully recognize the necessity of allowing some play to impulsive and irrational elements."[36]

Functionalism carried too far leads to the subordination of art to other human activities without adequate justification of the implied scale of values. The reason for the lacunae in the argument is perhaps that a certain hierarchy of values, in which art falls at the lower end of the scale, is assumed to be acceptable to almost everybody. This assumption is usually vulnerable. It would

28

be very difficult, even in a tightly disciplined totalitarian regime, to identify a universe of opinion where the assumption holds. One is reminded of a wise observation of Ernst Kris in commenting on the confusion of art with religion and propaganda. The message of a work of art, he wrote, is "an invitation to common experience in the mind" and not a call to action or to a common spiritual experience, as propaganda and preaching would be. The close linkage of the arts to such distinguishable purposes sometimes misleads one to see the call to action rather than the art.[37]

Esthetics and Science

The trend today is strongly in the direction of a more scientific approach to esthetics, partly under the influence of the functionalists, who could link art and its application with complete respectability (against the onslaught of the isolationists), but perhaps more significantly because of the growth of the sociology of art. The development of this branch of the social sciences has been attacked by isolationists of the arts. However, it is a development that cannot be stopped and will contribute substantially to the understanding of the interplay of the corporation and the arts. Some attention must therefore be given to this significant literature.

Norbert Wiener, the mathematical genius and one of the fathers of the computer, in his article in *Encyclopedia Americana* speaks of esthetics as "the science of beauty and art" and seems to accept the Kantian view of it as the science of sense-perception. He points out that the subject can be treated under three headings. First, from the *scientific* standpoint—the empirical investigation of the actual qualities of the different varieties of beauty and art; second, from the *historical* standpoint—an exposition of the views held in the past on the nature of art and beauty; third, from the *systematic* standpoint—independent investigation of the philosophical question of the nature of beauty. If art is defined, he says, as that human activity which has as its end the production of the beautiful, then there arises the question: What is beauty? The three distinct approaches to this question and to the nature of art itself are often confused in so-called critical writing about the arts. Although criticism is an important branch of the literature on the arts, it is probable that few have examined the three different categories of writing on esthetics that Norbert Wiener has indicated.

Thomas Munro has written of the need for a more dynamic, operational approach to esthetics in view of the frequent overemphasis on the static, cognitive aspects of expression, symbolism, and meaning in the works of art. He points out the possibilities of studying works of art as "operative mechanisms" and from a functional point of view. As to the experiences of art, can we not ask relevant questions about the "purely" esthetic meaning, as well as the psychological, educational, and sociological functions of works of art? Munro declares that the esthetic function of art is but a part of its larger social functioning. This broader function includes the interaction of art with other social factors such as governments, churches, schools, and business enterprises. In this regard the arts are treatable as types of occupation. Artists and those associated with them in the production and administration of art are seen as subgroups in society. The varied and changing roles of artists can thus be described with reference to different periods and cultures. The role of artists in medieval Europe was significantly different from that of artists in modern times, and in a capitalistic democracy their roles differ from those in a community dictatorship. "The social functioning of the artist as a man, or of art as a métier, is not the same as that of works of art. To study the former leads to questions about who supports the artist and his family, what socioeconomic status he has, and who can direct or influence his work."[38]

To speak of a sociology of art is not to preclude the application to this problem of other disciplines. The significance of art in our time is hardly discoverable, in fact, short of a strongly in-

30

terdisciplinary approach. Nor is it to be expected that the
specialists in corporate matters will alienate themselves, or permit
themselves to be alienated, from this inquiry. Teamwork among
the students of society is proving to be of great value, not only
to the specialists of the various disciplines themselves, but also to
policymakers at the centers of influence and power throughout
the social structure. This is obvious to one who reads *Items,* a
publication of the Social Science Research Council, but it is a
truth that constantly impresses the higher echelons in governmental and business research.

Yet there is still a peculiar difficulty in linking up, for analytical
and policymaking purposes, such apparently disparate subjects
as art and the corporation. The disparateness is only apparent,
but it is a bar to the breadth and depth of studies that are now
urgently needed in this particular interrelationship of social institutions. The neglect of studies of art in its relationships with
economic institutions is not a unique or special case.

The interplay of art and politics, as H. D. Lasswell has pointed
out, is a good example of neglected research opportunities in
political science. He predicts that political scientists will concern
themselves more in the future with this interplay in order to il-
luminate the impact of the arts on politics and of politics on
architecture, literature, music, graphics, plastics, and the dance.
On the side of the arts, "the esthetic interest will find creative
expression in the criticism of power, rectitude, and in fact of all
values."[39] He sees evidence of this trend in the work of T. V.
Smith,[40] the witty philosopher-politician who followed in the tradition of George Santayana in speaking on behalf of the enjoyment
of the imperatives of conscience.

Lasswell offers some guidelines for this cross-disciplinary field
of politics and the arts. In suggesting the necessary developmental
constructs in these two related areas he proposes, as one might
expect, the kind of analysis he has long advocated as to the shaping
and sharing of values. In the "esthetic perspective"—a term that
has specific meaning in the Lasswellian approach[41]—the "shaping"

31

phase is seen in the skills of the craftsman, the "sharing" phase in the contemplative skill of the connoisseur. Political analysis requires one to examine any one value in relation to the others, and in the interplay of politics and the arts one does not begin and end with attention fixed solely upon the esthetic quest in terms of gratification. Craftsman and connoisseur cannot always be assumed to aim for the esthetic goal alone in an art-for-art's-sake quest, and when there are mixed criteria for preferred outcomes the intrinsic esthetic criterion must give way to others. Thus, Lasswell suggests that if we evaluate sculpture or music as instruments of power, wealth, or other nonesthetic values, the evaluation is in terms of events other than art.

This suggestion for further research into the interplay of politics and the arts applies with special force to the assessment of contemporary criticism in the arts. Writing about the arts would undergo basic changes were the Lasswellian approach to be adopted. The so-called dehumanized art of today, which is often bemoaned but seldom explained, might be seen, for example, as a case of more or less conscious effort by artists to "devalue power" in an age when "the imperatives of power are pressing heavily on the lives of men," and when the esthetic quest offers one way of turning away from, or reducing as far as possible, one's commitment to power.[42] Here is an example of analysis that avoids the sterile conclusion that certain developments in the contemporary arts are nothing but a senseless cut-off of art from life. The opposite may be true: the artist may have been overwhelmed by life, and what appears to be an isolated quest for *l'art pour l'art* may in fact be a strongly negative demand on other values—power not necessarily being the only one.

Art and Society

The sociology of art, using that term now to include not only the imprimatured sociologists but the specialists of many other disciplines as well, is really in its infancy. As Robert N. Wilson has observed in the preface to a recent symposium on the subject, "the art object is complex and the artist is complex; a single-factor or unidimensional analysis is almost certain to be inadequate."[43] In most of the literature on art, that is what we get.

The relation of works of art to the societies in which these works are produced is a very difficult problem, although it is not one that completely resists a translation into testable hypotheses, as Sanford M. Dornbusch has indicated in the same book. The talk was to be sure, mainly about the "higher arts," but it is probable that the observation applies quite as well along the whole spectrum of the arts. Methodological rigor, Dornbusch suggests, is not an inappropriate area for much current research in the higher arts, despite the resistance that one meets to any scientific inquiry whatever in this field of human activity. A search for methodological sophistication, he rightly insists, will not endanger the study of esthetics as a branch of philosophy or the appreciation of the creative impulse. Students in the humanities sometimes regard the behavioral scientists as pretentious interlopers of their own home territory, he says, adding that the sunrise is no less beautiful because one understands light rays and prisms.

For the imprimatured sociologist, the value of a sociology of art is that certain technical sociological problems, such as the nature of social interaction, the formulation and maintenance of collectivities, and the ways of cultural change, may thereby yield more ready solutions.[44] The symbolic forms found in art, for example, seem to be significantly related to more general categories of communicational signs that students of social institutions must examine in their effort to understand the cementing processes of social communication. All of the arts may have essential functions in social structure and social process, even though the artists themselves and the estheticians might wish to deny these functions, or perhaps read them erratically.

Sociologists have been attracted to art as significant to their discipline, partly because (1) artists are regarded as "sensitive perceivers who often see what is going on in the society or the psyche a good bit earlier than other men do,"[45] and (2) the artist is often "remarkably sensitive to tensions in the social order, and his work will, in all likelihood, reflect his awareness."[46] T. V. Smith spoke of artists as "messengers of discontent."[47] Arnold J. Toynbee says that "every civilization creates an artistic style of its own," and that if one wants to "ascertain the limits of any particular civilization in space or time . . . the esthetic test is the surest as well as the subtlest."[48] And Meyer Schapiro observed that the arts provide indispensable data for the understanding of the "life style" of a civilization.[49]

The sociological study of art from the scientific (as distinguished from the more usual humanistic) point of view had already begun in the nineteenth century.[50] Madame de Staël, Karl Marx, Ernest Gross, Herbert Spencer, Hippolyte Taine, and Jean-Marie Guyau made certain contributions. De Staël, for example, related the arts to her views of social progress, insisting that literature and the theater should portray the trends toward social justice and pay more attention to the lives of humbler citizens. Marx, characteristically, specifying the system of production and the nature of the class struggle at a given time as the determinant of artistic style and content, declared that the norms of art are relative, shifting from time to time with the preferences of the dominant class which usually contrasted with those of the underclasses.

In this way art becomes an integral part of the great debate about deterministic revolution in contemporary society. Ernest Gross and others, following to some extent the Marxian line, took the position that art reflects the stage of economic organization in a society and that the function of art has undergone basic changes in historic time. Spencer also took an evolutionary position (not Marxian) on art as on social institutions generally. With Spencer's emphasis on human ecology as the touchstone to an understanding of social institutions there was a relegation of art to those aspects of an advanced culture in which surplus human energy, after the basics of social adaptation, could be used in leisure-time activities.

In this attitude there is something of what Alfred North Whitehead later called the "stone-blind" attitude of nineteenth-century English philosophers toward art as a useful activity. Art, of course, has seldom been regarded by artists as a surplus activity. Indeed, it has always been drawn into the polemics of political and other social issues. Parrington speaks of the "war of *belles lettres*" in the long struggle between Federalists and Democrats: "Gentlemen forgot their manners and indulged fiercely in tall language,"[51] engaging in slashing attack and counterattack in fictional literature. In Taine's view, "a work of art is determined by an aggregate which is the general state of mind and surrounding circumstances"—a state of mind describable by his "race-environment-time" formula.[52] Taine thereby underlined the social basis of art and especially the way in which the public affects the creative output of the artist. For Guyau, art works were so intimately related to the social milieu that he dismissed the isolated artist's creative expressions of private pleasure as decadent.

At the close of the nineteenth century there developed in Germany the new discipline of *allgemeine Kunstwissenschaft*, or "Science of Art," that was carefully distinguished both from aesthetics and the conventional history of art. It began with the historical and sociological orientation of the art and architecture of the western Christian world, but, as Helmut Hungerland has pointed out, excluded any esthetic evaluation from its investigations. The major purpose was negatively this normative avoidance, and positively the discovery of general laws concerning the evolution of artistic forms. A pioneer in this scientific movement was Heinrich Wölfflin, whose major contribution to scientific esthetics was published in 1915 and appeared in English translation as *Principles of Art History* in 1932. Others in this general movement were Paul Frankl, Alois Riegel, Wilhelm Worringer,

Frederick Antal, Hugo Spitzer, Max Dessoir, Hippolyte Taine, E. Hennequin, E. Galabert, and Charles Lalo. Societies have been established in Europe and in the United States for the scientific study of art, historically, comparatively, and in relation to other disciplines.

The first general approach to a science of esthetics, including not only the science of art in Wölfflin's historical perspectives but also other kinds of interdisciplinary inquiries, is often attributed to Gustav Theodor Fechner. His work in the 1870s stressed the empirical, as well as deductive philosophical methods of investigating art. Later investigators, on both sides of the Atlantic, used experimental methods to explore the nature of esthetic sense-perception, as, for example, Lightner Witmer's and L. W. Lwgowski's further investigations of the Fechner hypotheses concerning the esthetic appeal of various geometric ratios; E. Bullough's and G. J. von Allesch's experiments with colors; and many kinds of empirical investigations in the field of music. Controlled experiments in listener response to music, for instance, cast doubt on long-held doctrine about the joy-sorrow antinomies of major-minor modes; and Farnsworth[53] presented experimental and statistical data that raised questions about the inherently "good" and "bad" in music. Traditional concepts of literary criticism and style were subjected to quantitative analysis.

In the twentieth century the sociology of art has included writers such as Max Weber, Charles Lalo, Ernst Kohn-Bramstedt, Levin Schücking, H. Sauermann, E. Souriau, Lucio Mendieta y Nuñez, V. Loos, Pitirim Sorokin, Robert N. Wilson, and Dennison J. Nash. Sorokin's conclusion that the several arts fluctuate in time between two polar conceptual types—the Ideational and Sensual—is among the more arresting ideas of modern sociologists of art. Ideational types of art have other-worldly and religious qualities; sensate types, by contrast, are characterized by secular and sensual qualities. With great time sweep, Sorokin sees (in 25 centuries of art history) swings of the pendulum from one pole to the other, both in aristic works and in the general cultural integration. Sorokin takes a general sociological approach. In addition, many monographs and specialized studies of particular arts or phases of the art-society nexus have appeared recently. Most of these have focused on literature and music, but there is a current tendency to extend the serious sociological inquiry of the arts to other facets, such as the performing arts, painting, and architecture. An example of the specialized approach is the current interest in alienation as an artistic theme and substratum of artistic motivation. There is also heightened interest in the interrelationships of the arts, as indicated in the studies of Thomas Munro.

Barnett has deplored the narrow focus of most studies. In his view, sociologists have directed their attention too exclusively to *works* of art in literature, music, the visual arts, and, less frequently, the drama and the dance. He has urged the broader scope of studies of "art as a process in which the artists, the work of art, and the art public are interacting elements."[54] The artist does more, he insists, than express his convictions in esthetic form; he expects to elicit some kind of response from some public—favorable, perhaps, but in any event usually some desired response however positive or negative. This broadening of the scope of the inquiry brings into the picture such elements as art galleries, publication houses, boards of directors of symphony orchestras, museums, arts centers, impresarios, private, corporate and governmental donors, critics, pollsters, educational and professional-training centers, and so on: "the initial recruitment of the individual artist, his training, his career as a creative artist, his artistic creations or performances, and the public response to them—all can be seen as aspects or elements in the *art process*."[55]

All of this calls for systematic inquiry into these elements in the art process, "perhaps concentrating on the social relations, social structures, norms, and roles which characterize the vocation of the artist."[56] A related approach, Barnett suggests, would involve a detailed study of the arts because "the various arts possess distinct technical 'cultures' " and there is "the possibility that the social situations of the creative artist in music, literature, and the visual arts may be markedly different in the same society at a particular time."[57] The art process in one art may not be paralleled at a given time with that of another. He mentions the Armory Show in 1913 which gained public attention for modern painting and the favor of a small but powerful art elite at a time when modern music had no such experience.

A further problem mentioned by Barnett is the identification of "serious" works of art that are worthy of the sociologist's attention and placement in the historical development of a particular art form. This task would require the close collaboration of art historians, critics, and other specialists so as "to discriminate between matters of style, imagery, subject matter, and the like that reflect important social and cultural influences and those that express merely the dominant esthetic conventions of an art at a specific time."[58]

Hungerland has observed that, in the scientific approach to esthetics, success depends on the formulation of hypotheses that are relevant to esthetic phenomena but not on a method that is peculiarly esthetic. This means that the interdisciplinary approach is indispensable. It also means that the serious discussion of art is no longer the exclusive domain of an elite of "criticism." On the contrary, art is too serious a subject to be left to either the artists or the critical elite. For corporate policymakers the more useful literature comes from other sources, and especially from the writings of those who have undertaken the development of a science of art. For the *works* of art, of course, one can turn only to the artist. But there are allied fields of creativity to which the policymakers must turn for guidance in the corporate-arts interrelationships. This implies not the slightest lack of respect for, or estimation of, the artist as artist. A great creative artist is not necessarily the illuminating verbal commentator on his own work, and especially on the interpretation of his work in terms

38

of its social implications—nor, for that matter, is any one of the specialists in the social and behavioral sciences.

As a tentative generalization, one might hazard the guess that the most illuminating commentary on the social implications of art are likely to come from those who are not too narrowly specialized in one of the disciplines at the expense of others. Here, again, the parallel with too-highly specialized commentary on the modern corporation is suggested. If one relies too heavily on one kind of specialist for an understanding of the social implications of the corporation, the results are almost certain to be a distorted picture. The jurist alone, or the economist alone, cannot supply a balanced analysis and a comprehensive synthesis. They are necessary, but not sufficient specialists in the total task. So it is with the social implications of art, and more particularly with those implications that directly concern corporate policymakers, who dare not rely on any one school of thought about the nature of art.

One of the most interesting aspects of the scientific approach to esthetics during the past century has been that of the psychologists. The psychoanalytic methods have been especially important. Ernst Kris, in *Psychoanalytic Explorations of Art* (1952), is perhaps the most useful guide in this respect. Many writers in the field have been noted by Hungerland. In addition to the great pioneers, Freud, Jung, Adler, there are R. Müller-Freienfels (methodology), Ernest Jones (analysis of *Hamlet*), Westerman-Holstijn and Karl Jaspers (van Gogh's art), Anton Ehrenzweig (perception process), Max Wertheimer (pattern structure), Kurt Koffka and Herta Kopfermann (depth perception), James J. Gibson (textile gradients), Edgar Rubin (analysis of figure-ground relations), Jerome Bruner and David Krech (interrelationships between perception and personality), Adalbert Ames, Jr. (perception), and Susanne K. Langer (process of feeling). The social psychologists' insights into such phenomena as the Theater of the Absurd, the New Wave in motion pictures, Pop Art, and other recent movements have been more useful than, say, the apologies and philippics of the debating arena.

39

The general effect of these and other scientific incursions into the field of esthetics is to widen and deepen our understanding of man's need for and uses of art and artists.

Classification of The Arts

One of the most difficult problems for the sociologist of art is a determination of the boundaries of the field of study. What are "the arts," and what kinds of creative activity are to be included? Barnett has advocated a provisional attitude on these key questions and the avoidance of a rigid system of classification at the start. He noted that the fine arts—music, literature, painting, sculpture, and architecture—are the traditional core of pure art in the western world but that the modern dance and the "serious" theater can also lay claim to being pure art. The applied arts, such as ceramics and textile design, on the other hand appeared to him to lack the intent to embody and communicate the significance of experience through esthetic forms which he saw in the "pure" arts. He thought that there was limited capacity of the applied arts "to symbolize more complex and abstract ideas and emotions through esthetic forms" as compared with the traditional fine arts. Yet he believed that the applied arts might provide a promising area of research as indicating "the functions of arts publics in the over-all art process."[59]

Still a further problem Barnett considered was the place of the mass media in the art process. The magazine story, radio play, the television play, the motion picture, sometimes sought to "reach beyond the function of entertainment and attempt to symbolize experience and the express ideas and emotions that are not mere documentary reflections of daily life."[60] Reaching thus beyond the goals of mere amusement and instruction "in terms of familiar events and conventional patterns of belief and behavior," the mass media occasionally "criticize, evaluate, and offer new interpretations of the 'human condition.' " And when they do so they take on the character of art.

40

The "marginal arts," then, become proper subjects of the sociologist of art not only because the mass media are such powerful agencies of social communication but also because they are on occasion genuinely creative forms. And he cites Thomas Munro's view that, because great changes in techniques and materials are occurring in many of the marginal arts, it would be unwise to restrict the label of art to only a few activities.

Barnett's tentative classification of the arts follows:

1. *Fine arts*
   music
   literature
   the visual arts
2. *The combined arts*, such as
   the dance
   the theater
   opera
3. *The applied arts*, which include such specialties as
   ceramics
   textile design
   miniature painting

He concedes that this is somewhat arbitrary and only tentative, and adds that there can be cross-classifications that are useful for the investigator: the popular arts (for entertainment) such as motion pictures, jazz music, the magazine story, and the radio and TV play. There is no question-begging here; the arts are not restricted to the "legitimate" arts. There have even been suggestions recently that TV commercials and documentaries may on occasion be classified as art works.[61] This is not necessarily an extreme view. Richard Buckminster Fuller's comments on design indicate that creative people are not to be intimidated by the conventional wisdom about art any more than they are by the establishment's views about science. Fuller speaks of "freedom-increasing design" and the "externalization of human function" as the basis for architecture, and his insistence that design capability is what makes man unique is applicable to the spectrum of the arts. Our spectrum is useless if it tries

to prescribe limits to this human capability and hold it within orthodox channels. Nor will the real innovators in business try to constrict
the conception of the arts.

Kinetic art is another novel category. It is art that involves motion
in the artist's product. It bears an organic relation to the "new" art
of "constructivism" as adapted by Group Zero, founded in Duessel-
dorf in 1957. It is said to emphasize the "spiritual significance of
light," and, perhaps by extension, the significance of sound—although the witticisms of these moving and sound-emitting constructions is sometimes more evident than any esthetic purpose. In the
English periodical *Signals*, the announcement is made that the new
gallery by that name in London aims "to provide a forum for all
those who believe passionately in the correlation of the arts and art's
imaginative integration with technology, science, architecture and
our entire environment."[62] The *Groupe de Récherche d'Art Visuel*,
centered in Paris, calls for a complete reconstruction of our habits
of seeing and requires that art integrate image, motion, and time.
The *Groupe* deplores variety of visual experience for its own sake,
insisting that the energy used in achieving variety ought to be used
in "contemplation of central problems of space-time."

The need for a more up-to-date classification of the arts, for purposes of corporate policy, is indicated not only in these avant-garde
perspectives. It is obvious in the trends of public policy concerning
the arts. In New York, for example, Governor Rockefeller has announced "State Awards for a More Beautiful New York" to be given
annually "for the enhancement of material and man-made beauty"
as determined by the State Council on the Arts. The Council was set
up in 1960 "to encourage appreciation of and participation in the
fine and performing arts." In announcing the awards, the Governor
said that these new awards were based on the philosophy that "there
is nothing in the laws of nature or the nature of man to require that
a state which is big and vital and productive must also be mundane
and dirty and ugly." In making the awards, the State Council was
to be guided by such broad considerations as urban renewal and
planning, architecture, landscaping, arts design, restoration and

preservation; and it was urged to look into progress in playgrounds, parks and recreation areas, community beautification, highways, and educational and religious institutions.

The very size, complexity, and vitality of the state, according to Governor Rockefeller "equip us more than most to meet the challenge of matching productivity with grace, of preserving diversity while achieving distinction." He suggested that the Council study transportation terminals and facilities, and industrial and commercial developments. Office buildings, hotels, and motels were to be included in considering the beautifying program. The bases for the awards were to be kept flexible; but the main objective was clear: "We are a people who care about and value beauty in all its aspects along with the more utilitarian necessities of life."[63]

Conclusions

One must conclude that for our purposes "the arts" deal with many kinds of media, serve diverse purposes for their creators, are points on continua in history that are not easy to discern, and are indicia of future developments that may have great significance for the general culture or an age or a nation. Narrowly drawn definitions will not serve the purpose, nor will they serve the cause of art. We must leave behind, for example, the idea of the "Seven Arts" as comprising painting, music, dance, poetry, theater, sculpture, and architecture, and no others. Nor can we accept the premise that there is some eternal law of legitimacy that determines whether this or that work is to be classified as "art" and whether this man is an artist but that one is a mere artisan. To assert, for example, either that there is not beauty outside of art or that the function of art is the creation of beauty, is to raise large anterior issues; yet we know that the arts are related to concepts of beauty, and doubtless to other values.

A watertight definition of Art and "the arts" is not a prerequisite for our exploration of the interplay between the corporation and the arts. We shall simply have to be satisfied with an eclectic and empirical approach. In other words, we take at face value many of the current views about the scope of the arts and try to relate these views to corporate policy on the interplay. Those who have searched as philosophers into the nuclear nature of Art may have thrown much light on the problem from the standpoints of metaphysical, epistemological, and ethical theory; esthetics is an important branch of philosophy, but it is one which cannot here be entered into profoundly—nor need we do so. On the contrary, our task is of a different order. Perhaps, for the esthetician, it is a part of the empirical task of surveying the field of the corporate-arts relationship in order to discover what, in fact, are today *regarded* as relevant vectors in this relationship. One learns a good deal about the nature of a subject by exploring its peripheral boundaries where other fields are touched. So it is with the arts: as one finds new and interesting tangential relationships where the arts affect corporate policy, one learns new things about the arts as well as about the nature and functions of the corporation in our society.

It seems clear that there are trends both in public and business policy toward a better understanding of the arts and their function in society. But this recognition is itself the result of a more comprehensive conception of art, by public and corporate officials on the one hand, and by those, on the other hand, whose careers are in the arts. There is, in other words, a convergence of trends. Paradoxically enough, at the very time when there is so much talk about the "dehumanization" of art and the "alienation" of art from society we are seeing the strong forging of a nexus between the arts and society which has never been so remarkable since the Renaissance. It is small wonder that the farsighted business leaders of today are seeking counsel on the corporate-arts nexus.

The nature of that nexus, however, can be variously interpreted. And those who accept interpretations without breadth and depth are likely to go astray in the formulation of corporate policy concerning the relationship. Corporate approaches to artists and the arts can be based on a broad conception of the past, present, and future dimensions of art; or they can be futilely sprung from sectarian notions that reduce art to a kind of dispensable sideshow of civilization. The approach adopted will determine the validity of the corporate policy, whether it be a donative policy concerning support of the arts or other kinds of policy that interlink the common purposes of artists and businessmen.

The arts are now broadly defined, as a matter of public policy stated in the National Foundation on the Arts and Humanities Act of 1965 (79 Stat. 845), as including, but not limited to "music (instrumental and vocal), dance, drama, folk art, creative writing, architecture and allied fields, painting, sculpture, photography, graphic and craft arts, industrial design, costume and fashion design, motion pictures, television, radio, tape and sound recording, and the arts related to the presentation, performance, execution, and exhibition of such major art forms." This Act also declares that both governmental and private agencies should collaborate in fostering and supporting a form of education in the arts and the humanities "designed to make men masters of their technology and not its unthinking servants," for "democracy demands wisdom and vision in its citizens." This Act, in providing for substantial federal support, at the same time declares that "the encouragement and support of national progress and scholarship in the humanities and the arts" is "primarily a matter for private and local initiative." The problem of central concern in this book is the role of the corporation in this initiative.

CHAPTER III

Freedom of Creativity and Innovation

Freedom to create and to innovate is one of the necessary conditions for the flourishing of the arts. There is no free society where this freedom has been suppressed or snuffed out.[1] In the interplay of enterprise and the arts this freedom is basic to both. Nor is it too much to say that the artist's freedom to create works of art, untrammeled by authoritarian and totalitarian commands, shrinks most disastrously in precisely those regimes where economic enterprise is most comprehensively and systematically subordinated or "coordinated" to something else.

Coordination, or as the Nazis termed it, *Gleichschaltung*, is both a totalitarian and an authoritarian method of bending all individual wills to the will of a leader or an elite. Whether of the Right or of the Left, national movements of our time which purport under the the guise of national interest to "coordinate" the lives of peoples emerge at length as monstrous despotisms that invade the cultural and economic spheres indiscriminately. Neither sphere escapes subjection if the other is successfully attacked.

The Lessons of Totalitarianism

Our contemporary experiences with such despotisms of the Right and the Left have taught us new lessons and reminded us of old ones concerning constitutional government. Constitutionalism is no longer taken for granted in democracies.[2] It has had to be defended against Right and Left. Its meaning and its mechanisms have become vitally important. We now know (better than we ever did before) that the vigilance that is the price of liberty has to be directed at quite specific points in our free societies if they are to guard freedom. In our own country, we give renewed attention to the structure of private rights, for example, and develop more systematic constructs for understanding the plural society that seems necessarily to underlie those rights. We seek additional security against arbitrary exercise of governmental power, not only over the private sectors but also within these sectors, where individual rights of free men depend on a species of private government harnessed to due process of law.

The plural society, about which so much has been said and written in recent years, is not, in constitutionalist terms, a society of disparate groups coexisting in some symbiotic way. That is what pluralism means in some countries, but that is not what it means here.[3] We have our racial and other group-interest problems; but they are not to be solved pluralistically in the sense that members of diverse ethnic, racial, religious, or social groups maintain an autonomous participation in and development of their traditional cultures and special interests within state or nation. Pluralism as a devaluation of sovereignty and a bold claim that one group can stand against the state is likewise ruled out of the idea of a plural society being requisite to constitutionalism.

The pluralism insisted upon here is rather a national unity of purpose based on diversity and not uniformity—diversity especially in organizational ways and means of achieving common goals.

Freedom of association is essential in this diversified approach to national purpose, and this freedom applies to many kinds of association. For the businessman it has meant, above all, the freedom to do business in corporate as well as unincorporated form. And out of the relative freedom to incorporate (the few limitations hardly match the pretentious concession theory of the law which would make incorporation a matter of Sovereign grace) has grown a vast corporate structure of the economy—to be contrasted with the coordinated structure of the so-called Corporate State of fascist doctrine. Our pluralism in the private sector of the economy is a remarkable example of the social value of constitutional freedom of association, and it applies to labor as well as to capital.

This pluralism applies across the board in a free society. The freedom to associate is a right of intellectuals and artists as well as of businessmen and workers in their respective private sectors. The universities, the professional societies, the artists' leagues, are all part of the same pattern: a highly diversified pattern that no one person in authority has laid down at the beginning and required all of us to conform to. It is a mosaic that is constantly changing, yet in general, it produces everything from works of art to the produce of the economy. It is, indeed, so highly productive a system that one wonders how it is possible to propound, and get accepted, social structures based on the contrary principle of subordination or coordination under authoritarian and totalitarian control.

The Authoritarian Posture Versus Constitutionalism

The authoritarian posture is that of a leader or an elite group who is not constitutionally responsible to the people, who, in turn, are expected to submit to authority without question. Totalitarian regimes are authoritarian, but they also reach into every nook and cranny of the lives of those who are subjected to the rule of a leader or an elite.[4] From the standpoint of the democratic constitutionalist, authoritarian government is bad enough, but totalitarianism is even worse because it obliterates the private sectors entirely—or at least claims the right to do so—leaving no room for initiative that has no public sanction.

One of the lessons of constitutionalism, bought dearly in two world wars, was that this authoritarian posture cannot be permitted to make a toehold in a plural society. Nor can the totalitarian pretense be allowed official sanction. There are many other aspects of constitutionalism that have received renewed emphasis in recent decades: an independent judiciary, an equipoise of powers, a free press, a party system with a healthy but loyal opposition, and a truly representative government based on a modernized electoral system, are typical. But it is doubtful that there is any more vital principle than that which goes to the heart of the matter: the right of a man to decide for himself the content and direction of his creative efforts.

All of the constitutional devices are "adjective law" compared with this imperative of human dignity. Yet enterprisers and artists need to remember that, although they all have a common purpose here, the requirements of this adjective law are not simple. For this reason it is of paramount importance, in speaking of the interplay between the corporation and the arts, to emphasize the procedural aspects of the question. We shall discuss later the more substantive aspects of the interplay: the common interest in access to knowledge through the arts, in the development of esthetic and ethical norms, and in lifting our own society to a higher level of culture in the comprehensive sense of that term. But first, we must pause to look at the prerequisites of creative freedom.

Rather than get into this subject through a textbook analysis of American constitutionalism, let us look instead at the contrasting political systems in which art and enterprise have been coordinated, creativity suppressed. The exercise of both the innovative talents of the enterpriser and the creative talents of the artist has been subjected to drastic controls under communism, national socialism, and fascism. A twice-told tale to the specialists in these contemporary social and political movements, the matter is nonetheless of continued importance to laymen—especially in the democracies, where a certain complacency tends to undermine efforts to sustain the *procedural* and *structural* foundations of creative and innovative liberties. The indispensability of these foundations is clear when one examines the practices of contemporary authoritarians and totalitarians.

Freedom and liberty have a changing content when one moves from discipline to discipline, from country to country, from politics to the nonpolitical. An ideology devoted, as communism is, to ends that are hardly less than anarchistic freedom—liberty, that is to say, defined as absence of any coercive power over free men—seems easily to justify completely authoritarian control by the state over both art and economic enterprise in the transitional period between now and a distant future of idealized freedom. Fascist doctrine, which never made a pretense of eventual human freedom, could—and still does here and there in the world—proceed on totalitarian and authoritarian premises to careful and comprehensive disciplining of both the arts and economic activity. In both communism and fascism the purpose is to bend the arts and enterprise to the authoritarian directives of the political elite. The political elite in these systems is also the cultural and economic elite and not, as in liberal and constitutional regimes, an elected officialdom committed to the rule of law, which in turn is a code for representative government.

It does not impress the authoritarian that law based on consent of the governed is the embodiment of Justice, nor that the defense of human freedom is the touchstone of legitimacy in a government. For one who pins his faith on more mystic outcomes, freedom of enterprise and freedom for the artist are ridiculous "bourgeois" prejudices and liberal shibboleths. And it ought not to escape the attention of artists and enterprisers in this country that the authoritarian attitude sometimes prevails here at home, as well as abroad, in quarters that make no claim to communist or fascist doctrine and would reject the appellations. Yet, innovation and creativity are no less threatened when intentions are purified by anticommunist and antifascist postures. In the case of the arts and economic enterprise the

50

question is whether one is for or against the conditions of creativity and innovation.

These conditions are necessarily nonauthoritarian both as to the *structure* and the *processes* of power. The necessary conditions for freedom to create and to innovate are parallel to those which are vital to a democratic society. In such a society power, respect, and knowledge are widely shared and are not limited by law and custom to political, cultural, religious, economic, or other elites. In authoritarian regimes the opposite is true: the most highly valued activities and outcomes are limited to defined groups, classes, institutions and persons, whereas the structural and procedural devices for securing privileged status are not open to question. The contrasting method of constitutionalism in democratic regimes is often advocated as a formula for liberty without specifying content. But a close inspection of the constitutional law of these regimes reveals their content quite clearly. In our constitutional system, for example, limitations are placed on governmental power—that is, on political elites—to protect the rights of persons.

Totalitarian "Coordination"

Under the Nazis, the Reich Chamber of Culture embraced in theory all the agencies of "culture," as that term was then understood: authorship, the press, radio, the motion picture, music, the arts, authors, musicians, and artists. At first the control of these was in the hands of Goebbels, but authority over some of them was later delegated to others. Press, radio, and other media were completely subordinated and "cooordinated" (*gleichgeschaltet*), and the nonconformists were liquidated. These media became the outright propaganda instruments of the Reich, or more specifically of the Nazi party. Authors, musicians, and artists were carefully censored, and the official or controlled Nazi newspapers and journals directed their withering critical fire at all who did not reflect the new *Weltanschauung*. The *Gleichschaltung* of art was a political-moral neces-

51

sity, in Hitler's view. The State had to "prevent a people from being driven into the arms of spiritual lunacy" by decadent artists. For Hitler, there was but one art—German-Nordic art. He had all examples of expressionism, for example, removed from the Weimar Museum, because they were the expression of a mankind subnormal from a racial point of view—"excrescences by which our culture is bound to perish sooner or later."[5] Such art was among the "symptoms of decay of a slowly rotting world," Hitler warned, and "Woe to the nations which are no longer able to master this disease!" To him "a single German march" was "worth more than all the junk of these new musicians—these people belong in a sanitorium."

In retrospect we see this ranting as pathological in itself. Among the art collections, seized after the war and now stored in the warehouse of the U. S. Defense General Supply Center in Richmond, Va., there are paintings that Hitler considered beautiful, especially the massive portraits of himself, crowded with Nazi swastikas and banners, and the canvases glorifying German soldiers and degrading Allied troops. The Nazi view of the place of art in society was closely specific and systematized. Art glorified the State and above all the *Volksstaat*, the presumed executive organ of a nation with racial homogeneity. The particular race—Germanic, Aryan— was held to be superior to all others, and the *Volksstaat* was more important than the individual. Here, there was no place for any individual freedom in the liberal, constitutionalist, sense, to say nothing of freedom for the artist.

The Nazis were thoroughgoing statists, and like the Fascists in Italy, they were firm believers in the doctrine that the state should dominate every phase of the citizen's activities and thought. The "bourgeois" and "liberal" truncation of the "political" aspects of life were denounced as decadent and positively harmful. In democracies, the "license" that prevailed for literature, the drama, and the arts generally, was regarded as immoral. Under National Socialism it became "the business of the State to combat injurious influences and encourage those that are valuable, actuated by a sense of responsibility for the well-being of the National community—so ran

52

the statute instituting the Reich Chamber of Culture, which also prescribed that "all creative forces in all spheres must be assembled under Reich leadership with a view to the uniform molding of the will."[6] Membership in one of the Chambers of Culture—all of which together made up the Reich Chamber—was compulsory for every intellectual or artist. Expulsion for "cultural misbehavior" could mean starvation. Purge of the undesirables was more important than the creation of a new art and a new literature.

In making the present inquiry into the place of the arts in a free society, and more especially in a society where freedom means freedom for corporate survival and growth, one must keep in mind the vast difference between the "corporate state" of fascism and the "coordination" of national socialism, on the one hand, and on the other, the corporate freedom of a free and democratic society, where freedom of association means, if anything, freedom for artists as well as enterprisers.

In national socialist totalitarianism there could be (1) no rational division of functions among the several branches of government, (2) no organization of the governing agencies with legally defined powers assigned to each so that one could be sure that these agencies would act within the rule of law, and (3) no constitutional limitations that could effectively curb (even in theory) the powers of governmental officials in the interest of private rights. There simply were no private rights in this sense. As far as the arts were concerned, in Nazi Germany it was authoritatively declared that the totalitarian state recognized no separate existence of art and rejected entirely the idea of art for art's sake. "It demands that artists take a positive position towards the state, towards the German nation, towards the German cultural heritage."[7] The old "vicious" freedom of teaching without limitation, as Alfred Rosenberg, the semi-official philosopher of the Nazi party, called it, disappeared from the German universities. It was replaced by "true freedom," the freedom "to be an organ of the nation's living strength."[8]

The freedom that the national socialists denounced and eliminated so effectively from the universities was the kind of academic freedom of professors to teach, of students to learn, that is taken for granted in liberal and constitutional regimes. It is a freedom, moreover, that is protected by specific limitations on the powers of academic governments as well as the powers of state and federal governments. Under Nazism in Germany, however, such restraints were incompatible with doctrines of statism and "purity of blood." The purpose of teaching in any field of knowledge became essentially propagandistic. Particularly in the social sciences and history, the permissible aim was to elaborate and spread the racial myth. As Sabine has said, the apex of absurdity was probably reached in a Nazi treatise on physics which declared that "science, like every other human product, is racial and conditioned by blood."[9] The possibility of doing creative work in science and the arts under such conditions was seriously reduced. It is of course true that the military strength of the nation in war was enormous. But might not victory have been within grasp had the national socialist *Gleichschaltung* of the intellectuals not taken place? The answer to this can never be known. Yet the postwar era in German literature and art shows how slow the recovery has been and how barren the Nazi period was.

The Arts Under Communism

The picture is essentially no different under communist rule.[10] "All genuine Soviet artists are dedicated to strengthening Socialism and building Communism. . . . The literature of every society is guided by forces more fundamental than itself; in Soviet society, it is guided by public opinion and its vanguard, the Communist party— guided toward solving the tasks of building Communism." These are the words of a contemporary Soviet cultural arbiter, Aleksandr Borisovich Chakovsky, editor of *Literaturnaya Gazeta* (Literary News) in Moscow.[11] Art cannot flourish independently of politics, he insists, and in this respect Socialist society is immeasurably superior to capitalist.

Asked whether any book that casts aspersions on the October

Revolution of 1917 could be published in the U. S. S. R. today, Chakovsky replied that he did not think so: "By definition, every great
work of art must be moral—it must be imbued with the concepts of
fairness, justice, human progress." And he demanded to know
whether there had ever been a great work of art concerning any
period of history which spoke out against these concepts. "To reject
the October Revolution in any literary creation is to deprive it of its
moral substance as a work of art," he concluded. On moral grounds
he likewise condemned abstract art as corrupting and confusing people, "leading them away from the true and the beautiful and from
our tasks as a society." Abstract art "tears art away from real life";
it is "a commercial device, a fraud, a mockery of true art." "Our
art," he said, "is based squarely on the principles of Socialist realism. . . . We will not stand by and let these things harm us. We have
a definite line in art—not laissez-faire, laisser-passer." Socialist
realism was "the truthful, veracious reflection of real life, taking into
consideration the tendencies of life's development." Communism does
not mean freedom for the artists in the traditional sense, he warned.
The Marxist-Leninist line must be followed.

The parallel with Nazi insistence on "moral" grounds for the "coordination" of artists is clear. In both cases the totalitarians reject
freedom for the artist, who has prescribed civic obligations that govern his creative work. But the shoddy national socialist and fascist
theory in support of this coordination did not compare well with
communist theory. The German and Italian doctrine was a waste-
land compared with the work, for example, of Georg Lukács, the
leading Marxist philosopher of esthetics today.[12] The dialogue between Lukács and his followers, on one side, and Western defenders
of artistic freedom, on the other, is of a different order than the
critique of Nazi and fascist doctrines. Lukács has been accused of
"rightist deviation" and conservatism by his communist colleagues
because he has criticized Stalinism as an unscientific simplificaton
and distortion of Marxism. He regards Marxist method as a necessary tool in analyzing reality in the arts. His emphasis is on the
continuity and evolution of human thought and artistic expression,

and he rejects the too-dark "*Angst*" literature of Kafka and others for the "critical realism" of some Western as well as Soviet writers.[13] He has said that the iron discipline over the arts, so characteristic of the Stalin era, has been considerably relaxed, and that Communists today are not rigidly bound to take a single view of the arts.

Other, especially Western, observers of the artistic and literary scene in communist countries have different interpretations. In January, 1965, after the removal of Khrushchev and the installation of Brezhnev and Kosygin, *Pravda* editorialized that the "so-called progressive" trends in art were dangerous "formalism" and "digressions from realism." Art was an ideological matter, and in that area there could be no "peaceful coexistence" with the enemies in the West. The Central Committee of the party declared in June, 1963, that art had to continue as a "sharp weapon in the struggle against alien bourgeois ideology." The party would not allow "even the tiniest cracks to open through which the enemies could rush." In the new regime there was pointed editorial reference to this view, together with the warning that ideological errors, concessions and compromises, by artists could not be accepted, even though the works of "talented people" would not be condemned in entirety for an ideological mistake that might appear in one poem or one painting.[14]

In a *Pravda* article some weeks later, Aleksi M. Rumyantsev, the new editor, declared that progress in science, literature, and the arts required "the existence of different schools and trends, different styles and genres competing with one another." But "socialist realism" would still be the guiding principle. Socialist realism means, among other things, that the Theater of the Absurd is not seen in Moscow, although it is in Poland. This official care for the morals of theater-goers is matched in some of the communist countries by regard for the character-formation of music-lovers. In Peking, for example, there has been an offensive against "Western bourgeois music"—and this includes almost anything from Bach to the Beatles. More revolutionary homegrown works are preferred, especially operas, plays, and films that satirize and attack "reactionary" types such as American and Japanese capitalists, militarists, and "imperialists." Faithful comrades beat their breasts in abject public re-cantation over errors and failures to follow the party line on art.

The Maoist party line on "ghosts, spirits, wizards, and fairies," for example, sets out guidelines for playwrights that preclude any-thing but pejorative reference to these, except perhaps for "progres-sive spirits." "Bourgeois music" is condemned. And in Cuba, the Committee of Revolutionary Orientation has censored as subversive certain kinds of "Western" music. Jam sessions are not permitted on radio, for example; however, the new "Mozambique" rhythm, in-troduced by Pello el Afrikan, a Cuban Negro bandleader, is highly favored as honoring rebels against Portuguese rule in East Africa.

The Arts and Constitutionalism

In the *Esquire* case, U. S. Supreme Court Justice William O. Douglas said that "a requirement that literature or art conform to some norm prescribed by an official smacks of an ideology foreign to our system." Yet, we do have the remnants of official censorship, and it is not likely that these remnants will soon be removed. In the United Kingdom, stage censorship prevails under the terms of the Theaters Act of 1834, although the Lord Chamberlain's refusal to license plays does not stop presentations by "private clubs" in theaters such as the Royal Court in London. The Lord Chamberlain will almost certainly bar disrespectful references to the royal family and lam-poons of public figures or "persons" held to be "divine."[15] His authority, however, is broad, and it is doubtful that any clear stand-ards can guide playwrights and producers.

It is anomalous that the country in which the famous blast against the licensing of printing was let loose by Milton should still have theater licensing. Yet in our own country the licensing of film-pre-sentations to the public still prevails in the form of state police power, albeit with restraints on this power now made somewhat tighter by the Supreme Court of the United States. The point is that, arguably, there is only a difference of degree, and not of kind, in our official control of the arts, as compared with that of the totalitarian regime. The case is further supported by the existence of customs barriers against the importation of some works of art under widely discretionary authority delegated to officials, some of whom have no credentials for art censorship—if, indeed, there can legitimately be such a thing in a free country.

It is true that the grounds for official control of the arts in totalitarian countries are of a different order. In the United States, the assumption is made that public governments must not encroach on private sectors except for well-established reasons of public interest and public policy duly adopted through constitutional procedures. In totalitarian and authoritarian regimes the contrary is true: there are no truly private reserves where anterior rights are a bar to governmental encroachment as a matter of procedural regularity that is enforced by courts. In legal theory, at least, we place all the devices of constitutionalism at the command of the citizen to debar arbitrary and officious "coordination" of the arts. The basically pluralistic character of our society, not only as a matter of constitutional law but also derived from an older Western political heritage, makes it very difficult for a would-be Commissar of the Arts to work his will even in limited areas. Added to this is the singularly indifferent attitude of most politicians toward the arts, in general, and the remoteness of any idea of national "purification" of culture on Nazi lines.

To these caveats there is certain to be bitter rejoinder on the part of many. The surging interest in moving America to a higher level of culture, together with new public policies as well as private efforts to make the move possible, has aroused widespread suspicion of a meddlesome agency lurking just around the corner to tell us what good art is. Fear of official encroachment on the sovereign realm of the arts has been voiced as we edge nearer full-scale federal and state support of cultural projects—such as the John F. Kennedy Memorial Center for the Performing Arts in Washington, and Lincoln Center in New York. The issue was raised during the debates on the establishment of a national foundation for the arts. No one believes there is any real danger of nazification or communization of culture.

Nevertheless, the essential problem of creative freedom remains. And this problem, for corporate executives, is closely enough related to the issue of innovative freedom in enterprise to require attention.

Corporate Support of Creative Freedom

One of the more usual arguments for corporate support of the arts is that the imperative of creative freedom for the artist demands such support. The syllogism runs somewhat as follows: creativity in the arts depends on the preservation of private sectors for the artist; if the corporation does not throw its weight on the side of this artistic autonomy, then there is danger of governmental control resulting from governmental support of the arts. On the positive side, there is also the argument that corporate support of the arts is closely related, as we have argued here, to corporate interest in innovative freedom for scientists, technologists, and enterprisers, and that balanced educational preparation for work and living in a society where both these attributes of creativity and innovative capacity are prized and indeed indispensable requires equal attention to both. It is often urged, and properly, that American society as a rule has not been characterized by balanced attention to these issues. The arts have suffered from preponderant attention to science and technology, to the material requirements of our culture, and to the busy world of affairs where men compete for these material fruits.

For all of these reasons, interested business and political leaders have repeatedly urged that our collective efforts toward the transformation of American society into a higher culture must not be entirely, or even mainly, governmental. The other private sectors must help the artistic private sectors to survive and flourish. Corporations should be among the biggest helpers financially because they have the most money and the most at stake. This puts the matter bluntly, but honestly. It remains to be seen whether it puts the matter fully and in proper perspective. But the case for keeping a brake on public governmental cultural projects by stimulating private-sector aid is motivated in part by the fear of an official art, a "so-cialized" cultural program.

On this point the words of President Kennedy's special consultant on the arts are pertinent. August Heckscher, in proposing a national arts foundation, sketched in what was to become a permanent policy giving form to the relationship between government and the arts. He advocated a limited policy, with a distinctly marginal role for government. He did not want a policy copied after European models. Ours, he said, should be keyed to the particular conditions of diversity and decentralization that prevail in the United States. Although there would always remain those who would feel that art and government must exist in different spheres, having nothing to do with each other, the fact remains that the federal government constantly comes up against choices and decisions where esthetic considerations are involved. More than this, the nation has an interest in artistic talent and creativity, Heckscher pointed out, as resources that are vitally important to the nation. "The well-being of the people is related to progress in the arts as surely as to progress in fields such as recreation and education where government's responsibility is fully recognized."[16] There were things that government could properly do, both confidently and expertly, in the field of the arts, he said, even though the role of government must always remain peripheral. Individual creativity and private support will be central.

Washington and the Arts

Heckscher undoubtedly expresses the preponderant view in the United States, although there will be great differences of opinion concerning emphasis. There is the federal question, for example, and the issue of distribution of authority and responsibility concerning the promotion of the arts as between state and national governments. Within the states, there is the question of local responsibilities versus state action. Some critics would exclude all governments, state and national, from the field of the arts. But, as Heckscher has shown in numerous cases, government is already inextricably involved, whether one likes it or not. And the involvement is not likely to diminish in view of demands that are made for governmental action. There are also the questions of what arts are to be promoted, the means of promoting them, and for what ends. Current trends run strongly in favor of the performing arts, but this is not the whole story.

When President Kennedy set up the President's Advisory Council on the Arts by executive order in June, 1963, he hoped that Congress would grant statutory authorization for this body.[17] He had in mind the arts on a fairly broad spectrum. The executive order defined the arts as inclusive of "music, drama, opera, dance, painting, sculpture, literature, architecture, and such allied fields as urban and landscape design, photography, graphic arts, crafts, motion pictures, radio and television." It should also be noted, under point five in the following paragraph, that there is a reference to "cultural institutions" generally.

In carrying out its functions under the order, the Council was directed to undertake five general categories of functions and responsibilities:

1. Surveys and assessments of the needs and prospects of the various arts, the means used to encourage creative activity and to afford opportunity for participation in and appreciation and enjoyment of the arts, and the relative roles of governmental and nongovernmental institutions in relation to the arts.

2. Evaluation of existing federal legislation, policies and programs that directly or indirectly affect the arts as to current and potential effects on the development of cultural opportunities and institutions and on the character and quality of federal activities in the field of the arts.

3. Reports and recommendations to the president.

4. Encouragement and facilitation of the most effective use of resources available for support and development of the arts through advisory and consultative work with governmental agencies, educational institutions, foundations, and other interested institutions.

5. The promotion and stimulation of public understanding and

61

recognition of the importance of the arts and cultural institutions to our national welfare and our international interests.

The Council was further directed to provide opportunities for "interested government and non-governmental agencies and organizations and private citizens, including practicing artists and others professionally engaged in the arts" to present their views and recommendations to the Council for its consideration.

A careful reading of these provisions of the executive order, together with the comments of the President himself and those of his special consultant on the arts, make it quite evident that this was a cautious and measured approach to the government-arts nexus. It bore no resemblance to the authoritarian and totalitarian approach. As members of the Advisory Council on the Arts, President Kennedy was to designate twelve heads of federal agencies, the special consultant of the arts, and "no more than thirty members[18] appointed by the President from among persons in private life who are widely recognized for their role in the arts, including practicing artists, civic and cultural leaders, and others professionally engaged in the arts." The President stated that these private members would be drawn from such categories as museum directors, producers, managers, and union leaders, as well as artists. With the Council so formed, he said, the arts, for the first time, would have some formal government body that would be specifically concerned with all aspects of the arts and to which the artist and arts institutions could turn to present their views and their problems. He thought that there was urgent need for such a body.

President Kennedy's reasons for urging the establishment of the Council are especially interesting in retrospect. The new memorial center in Washington will attach his name permanently to the advancement of the arts. If it was his wife, and not he, who was notably active in the White House as a promoter of federal encouragement of the arts, it is nevertheless true that his administration marked a turning point. It had never been widely supposed that the nation's capital was the focus of attention in such matters. The art capitals of the country were elsewhere. The federal government, in the minds

62

of artists generally, was a realm of the prosaic. Artists seldom had much interest in it as a source of esthetic inspiration or artistic aid. But the Kennedys changed that. The President's statement supporting his executive order underlined the need for opportunities for the young to develop their artistic gifts and to participate in an active cultural life. He wanted public recognition of excellence in the arts. He was concerned about employment opportunities for the decade ahead and the danger that the development of creative talent would thereby be seriously discouraged. Art was in need of an adequate financial and institutional base. The "concept of public welfare should reflect cultural as well as physical values, esthetic as well as economic considerations." In all of this, President Kennedy also recognized the plural, decentralized structure of culture in the United States and the need for preserving it.

Read in conjunction with the comments of his special consultant on the arts, these observations make it abundantly clear that anything like totalitarian "coordination" must be avoided at all costs. Instead, the line of action for the federal government should lead in quite the opposite direction—toward vitalization of the arts throughout the United States and under local and private auspices so far as possible. The purpose of federal action was to be advisory, informative, stimulative, encouraging, and approbatory. Any suggestion of shift of authority over the arts to the federal center was completely absent and would have been sharply at odds with the tenor of the President's directive. Kennedy would have preferred statutory creation of the Council; however, he had little hope of Congressional action at the current session, nor had he yet made public the names of his appointees to the Council at the time of his death on November 22, 1963.

An advisory group[19] recommended to President Lyndon B. Johnson early in 1964 that the White House continue the strong interest in the creative arts started in the Kennedy Administration. President Johnson chose Roger L. Stevens, New York theatrical producer, for the post of special consultant on the arts—a post previously held by August Heckscher. Stevens had been selected by Kennedy as chairman of the board of trustees for the projected Center for the Performing Arts, so he now held two closely related posts. It had been Kennedy's intention to use the Center as a stimulus for artistic endeavor in the nation.

President Johnson urged the passage of a bill to create a National Council on the Arts, and the bill was signed into law on September 3, 1964. The new Council—now on a statutory basis—has twenty-six members and is headed by a full-time chairman. Its duties include: (1) recommending ways to maintain and increase the cultural resources of the nation; (2) proposing methods to increase private initiative in the arts; (3) advising and consulting with other state, local, and federal agencies on methods of coordinating existing resources and facilities for fostering artistic and cultural endeavors and on the use of the arts, both nationally and internationally, in the best interests of the country. There is specific prohibition of any federal direction, supervision, or control in the administration of the Act over the policy or program determination of any group, state, or state agency involved in the arts. There will be no *Gleichschaltung* or the laying down of a party line on the arts and culture generally —but then no one had ever considered this as a real possibility. The words of the act simply underline the plural character of the arts in our society.

Although it was the Kennedy Administration that gave the greatest initial push for this kind of legislation, Senator Claiborne Pell of Rhode Island pointed out the protracted development of the idea. He called the legislation precedent-setting, but he also called attention to the fact that such concepts had been pending before Congress since 1877. Representative Frank Thompson, Jr., of New Jersey, the author of the bill, said that its passage ended a long, hard effort that had begun 87 years earlier. He had worked on it himself for ten years, and now, for the first time in the history of the republic, the federal government had at last given recognition to the arts. Pell and Thompson were Democrats, but there were two Republican sponsors as well: Senator Jacob K. Javits and Representative John V. Lindsay of New York.

64

President Johnson's moves on behalf of the arts were somewhat delayed, but they indicated more than casual interest. The President did not make his appointments to the new Arts Council until the end of February, 1964. The names included many well-known leaders in the arts, the press, education, and theatrical production. There was no doubt about the independent-mindedness of the people in this group; and in the press the "strictly advisory" role of the new body was stressed. But the President's plan did not stop here, nor were the proponents of federal encouragement of the arts satisfied with this start, however meritorious. Many bills were before Congress for further action and looking toward substantial federal financial aid for the arts.

The Council still had no money to underwrite the arts. To provide the necessary aid, the President asked Congress on March 11, 1965, to establish a National Foundation on the Arts and Humanities. The Pell-Thompson bill for this purpose—with many co-sponsors which included Senators Javits of New York and Ernest Gruening of Alaska, together with Representatives Hugh L. Cary and James H. Scheuer of New York—was designed to parallel the legislation that had set up a National Science Foundation fifteen years earlier. Its declaration of purposes stated that a "high civilization" must not limit its efforts to science and technology alone, but must give value and support in "the realm of ideas and of the spirit."

Two national endowments were provided for in the Pell-Thompson bill, one for the arts and another for the humanities. Financial aid in the humanities would emphasize the academic and scholarly humanistic studies: teaching, learning, and research. The arts were to include not only the traditional fields, such as drama and creative writing, but also photography, costume fashion design, motion pictures, television, and radio. In practice, the Council on the Arts has named program directors for the fields of architecture and design, the visual arts, theater and allied arts, and music. The language of the bill stated that the term "humanities" would include, but not be limited to, "language, literature, history, and philosophy; archeology; the history, criticism and theory of the arts . . . and those

65

aspects of the social sciences which have humanistic content and employ humanistic methods."

President Johnson, in the message accompanying the bill, said that "no government could call artistic excellence into existence, but that it could seek to create the conditions under which the artist and scholar can flourish." He added, "pursuit of artistic achievement, and making the fruits of that achievement available to all its people, is also among the hallmarks of a great society." Mr. Pell noted that this was the first time in our history that a President of the United States had given his administrative support to such a comprehensive measure "which combines the two areas most significant to our nation's cultural advancement and to the full growth of a truly great society."

The emphasis on freedom in the arts was clear in the President's message. No government, he said, should "seek to restrict the freedom of the artist to pursue his calling in his own way. Freedom is essential for the artist, and in proportion as freedom is diminished so is the prospect of artistic achievement." The bill specifically prohibited any department or employee of the United States from exercising the slightest control over any nonfederal group dealing with the foundation. On the other hand, the President observed the value of federal recognition of achievement in the arts, of aid to "those who seek to enlarge creative understandings," of increasing "the access of our people to the works of our artists," and of establishing the arts in the public mind "as part of the pursuit of American greatness."

The National Foundation on the Arts and Humanities Act was passed by Congress in 1965 and signed by the President on September 29. At the signing ceremony at the White House Rose Garden, President Johnson said that with the help of state and local governments and private groups the new Foundation would create a National Repertory Theater to bring ancient and modern classics to audiences all over America; support a National Opera Company and a National Ballet Company; create an American Film Institute, bringing together leading artists of the film industry, outstanding educators, and young men and women "who wish to pursue this twentieth-century art form as their life's work"; commission new works of music by American composers and support our symphony orchestras; and bring more great artists to our schools and universities by creating grants for their time in residence. The new Foundation, he said, would have "an unprecedented effect on the arts and humanities of our great Nation." Congress had created the instrument for channeling money to areas that had been "in the basement" so far as federal financial aid is concerned. The President thus gave unprecedented Administration blessing to a conception of governmental support of the arts that is a commonplace in Europe but has always been a source of controversy here.

The new national programs for the arts and the humanities have been modestly financed. The councils for the two endowments, consisting of distinguished people in their diverse fields of specialization, had about $20 million authorized (less was actually appropriated) for their first year's work. There were provisions, however, for grants-in-aid to the states and for matching grants that would invite further support from private donors. The legislation thus may have a multiplier effect for the support of the arts and the humanities far beyond the actual federal appropriations. The first gift from a corporate donor came in 1966 with an unrestricted grant of $300,000 from the Bristol-Myers company to the National Council on the Arts. The Council, using this gift together with a matched amount from the National Endowment for the Arts and $25,000 from individual donations, then made an award of $625,000 to the Educational Broadcasting Corporation for educational television. It should be noted, also, that federal appropriations for other purposes, as in the Education Act of 1965, will at times parallel and enhance the effect of the work of the two Councils.

The United States had indeed taken a momentous step with the creation of a National Foundation on the Arts and the Humanities. During the preceding generation science, with justified government support and encouragement, had become a dominant strain in our national personality. But now, eminent spokesmen of the academic community, humanists, artists, and scientists alike, had come forward to ask the Federal government to help right the balance. The government had responded. And not only with the Foundation. Federal concern for the esthetic element in national life was spreading into many quarters of governmental activity. August Heckscher has shown this in his survey of the government's established role in the arts—from stamp designs to USIA's creative films—but there were also new departures. A federal War on Ugliness has been declared, and it is a war ecologically associated with the war on disease and poverty. The first White House Conference on Natural Beauty was no exercise in abstract esthetics. A ban on roadside billboards and junkyards; beautification as a by-product of the Interior Department's study, in the Office of Saline Research, of the use of trash and garbage as fuels for operating desalting plants; the same department's study of a process for filtering sewage through coal, here again with the prospect of cleaning up the nation's dirty rivers; the Agriculture Department's study of new plants, grasses, and shrubs especially adaptable to the urban environment; soil surveys to help in the selection of the best sites for area-wide suburban development; studies of ways to speed junked cars through the scrap cycle and back to steel mills; and master planning for river valley development —all of these and more, at both federal and state levels, have come in for serious debate. Some have led to legislation.

Yoking—or Advancement—of the Arts?

The public reception of these major legislative steps toward federal stimulation of the arts has not been uniformly favorable. Disregarding for the moment those criticisms that have nothing to do with the subject in hand—that is, the conditions for free creativity in the arts—is there danger in the present trend? Or is it true that these moves at the federal level on behalf of the arts really do help to provide at least some of the necessary conditions for cultural development based on freedom of artistic and intellectual work? Given the lessons of contemporary totalitarian and authoritarian regimes, are we to be on our guard against even the modest steps now being taken here toward governmental support of the arts?

To some critics the first Council on the Arts, with no money to spend and with mere advisory functions, seemed little more than a graceful gesture from Washington. Yet they saw that a forward step had been taken with official commitment by the federal government to the principle that the arts are important and that there is a federal duty in the premise. And, as one writer put it, there had been a hard fight even to get this far. "Were it not that the arts have become fashionable in recent years," he wrote, "the persistent opposition, which looks upon culture as something abstruse, highbrow, sissy and downright un-American, would not have been overcome. You may be sure that those who suspect the arts have not been silenced. If you read recently in these columns of John Houseman's recollections of the troubles of the Federal Theater Project, you know how the self-appointed guardians of conformity pursued those who expressed bold ideas in novel forms. If you recall the clamor over the choice of artists and art to be sent abroad, you are aware that evidences of difference or dissidence were hunted down and excoriated."[20] These are the words of drama critic Howard Taubman.

Taubman went on to say that it would do the arts little good if, in the process of receiving official benediction, they are obliged to behave as ingratiatingly as house-broken puppies. Artists worth their salt would not take government money on such terms; a proud national culture could not arise from "safe" dramatists, poets, novelists, composers, and painters. He suggested that the new National Council on the Arts make it a first order of business to draw up and publish a bill of rights for the artist in relation to governmental authority. The declaration would affirm that "the artist owes no duty other than to explore himself, his fellowman, his natural environment, his social setting and his spiritual quest, and to express his perceptions with all the truth and imagination within his gifts." It would also "assert uncompromisingly that even unpopular ideas must be heard," and it would "establish the principle that interference by politicians of any party is anathema in a free land."

Government patronage of the arts would probably be no more than "ornamental" under these conditions, Taubman continued, and he spoke of the struggling regional theatrical companies with professional aims as potential recipients of federal aid. "Certainly such institutions are as valuable to Americans as carriers, bombers and national parks"; yet they were now walking a thin line between success and collapse. But it would be hard for Congress to invest national funds in so controversial a field as the drama. The day must come, he concluded, when words of approval would have to be backed by financial support unafraid of controversy. Had this nation the maturity to work out a plan as effective as the British to bring the government's resources into the arts without impinging on freedom of expression? An answer to this question would be enough to justify the existence of the new Arts Council.

The strong preference for private, as against public, patronage of the arts, as a condition of free creativity, has been reasserted repeatedly now that the federal government is at last taking a broad interest in culture. The case was put by James J. Kilpatrick, then editor of the *Richmond (Va.) New Leader*, in his usual straightforward and acerb style.[21] He had just visited Huntington Hartford's Gallery of Modern Art. The patron's taste may be "square," says Kilpatrick, but that's the way he likes it and it's his money. "So long as patronage of the arts is free and voluntary, Guggenheim and Hartford, and Wright and Stone, can compete fairly in the marketplace. You pays your money and you takes your choice. But once the really big money in the arts begins to come from the federal government, you still will pay your money, all right, but the dominant choice will be Big Daddy's." He sounded the warning against "regal taste-making," against "a despotism of taste," and the wide discretionary powers he saw in the "two cultural czars" who would head the endowments for the arts and the humanities. He looked in vain for adequate safeguards against the arbitrary use of power in

70

these two chairmen, as, for example, assurance that there would be a reasonable turnover in membership on the governing board. But it is doubtful that mere amendment of proposed legislation in this category would satisfy Kilpatrick, who takes the position that Congress has no more power to pass such laws than it has to make Harry Truman a duke. The basic issue, then, is really whether any federal aid to or promotion of the arts is admissible, on constitutional or other grounds.

On this issue, the summary view of the Rockefeller Panel Report on the Performing Arts was that "while private support should remain dominant, the federal government—together with state and local governments—should give strong support to the arts, including the performing arts, by appropriate recognition of their importance, by direct and indirect encouragement, and by financial cooperation."[22] The panel did regard the danger of federal interference as real, but it thought that safeguards were possible. Financial help from the federal government has been administered in other fields with adequate protection against abuses, the panel pointed out, referring to the work of the National Science Foundation and the National Institutes of Health. In these cases there has been massive federal support far beyond anything currently contemplated for the arts, and there has been no compromising of intellectual and scientific freedom and quality. Ways and means can be, and are, devised to prevent unwanted encroachments on the freedoms of the intellectual community, and machinery can be developed to provide similar protection for artistic freedom, given time and study to the problem. Nor, in the opinion of the panel, was there any evidence, from extensive studies the Rockefeller Brothers Fund had made of public support for the professional performing arts in Europe, that public funds had impaired artistic freedom. The Federal Theater Project in the thirties had indeed fallen victim to politics, the panel conceded, but that was a quarter of a century ago. Since then "our country has grown in artistic sophistication."[23]

On the other hand, the panel makes it quite plain that "no form of government aid to the arts should vitiate private initiative, reduce private responsibility for direction, or hamper complete artistic freedom," and that "these must remain the prerogative of the citizens who direct the performing arts institutions and of the artists."[24] This injunction would of course apply to all of the arts, and a repetition of the doctrine with frequency and force will be salutary. The panel recommends putting governmental support as close as possible to the local level, and asserts the duty of local governments actively to enter the field, as many of them already are doing. The responsibility of the state governments is stressed when the local communities cannot afford to take the initiative on a large enough scale.

Governmental aid is usually thought of in terms of financial grants to artists and institutions. But one of the great contributions of the Rockefeller Panel Report was its comment on other possibilities, and these apply to all of the arts. In addition to the question of direct and indirect financial support,[25] the federal government is involved with the arts in important ways that escape the attention of most people because the involvement is incidental to other governmental functions that appear to have little or nothing to do with the arts. Special tax burdens fall on the professional theater—and thus on the performing arts. Reference was being made to the 10 per cent excise tax on admissions, and on professional musicians because of the 10 per cent tax on the sale of musical instruments. "No other worker pays such a tax on his tools," the panel observes.

By omission rather than commission, too, the federal government imposes special burdens on artists. The copyright law allows the jukebox industry to get off without royalty payments for its use of copyrighted music; the loss to creative artists from this source alone is quite substantial when it is remembered that jukeboxes take in about a half a billion dollars a year in gross. Also, by comparison with that in England, for example, the copyright protection is skimpy in that when the 56-year period runs out many aged artists cannot continue getting their royalties. The indiscriminate copying of plays and other literary products also deprives many creative artists of their royalties. These and other methods of pirating original material are not adequately policed by the federal government. The uses of federal taxing and copyright power to protect artistic enterprise as well as other kinds of enterprise should be of special interest to corporate managers who want to get to the roots of the corporate-arts nexus.

Another aspect of federal involvement in the arts concerns the government's informational programs and its urban renewal projects. The Rockefeller Panel discussed these programs and projects primarily with respect to the performing arts, but the issue has implications for all of the arts. The United States Information Agency and the Defense Department are both involved in projection of American cultural achievements overseas. These are not transient governmental efforts; they are here to stay, and as the Panel observes, they should go on even if cold war pressures decline. But the Panel also warns that these programs need to be maintained at the highest standards and insulated against interference on narrow political grounds.

The Panel points to the futility of arguing, as has often been done, that the federal government must get out of these programs entirely. The troops have to be entertained. The projection of the United States image abroad is an established policy and an indispensable one; in the prewar days when we had no overseas information or cultural *programs* we always had plenty of "projecting" by many kinds of people, some official and some private.

Private persons—businessmen, film producers, expatriates, writers, students, travelers, and so on—all carry out their own conceptions of American values and American achievements, including those in the arts. The difference is that, today, the method is more systematized, and in the systematization it is unavoidable that the arts play a large role. It is notorious that some projects and programs carry the stamp of mediocrity, partly because of political pressures, partly because of limited funds. We seldom send abroad the best theater groups and symphony orchestras, for example. Nor is it at all certain that in the armed forces information and educational programs the available resources make it possible for military personnel to take advantage of the best that the world of the arts has to offer them.

In the above-mentioned federal activities, as well as in others, such as the urban renewal program, in the work of fact-collecting agencies (e.g., the Department of Commerce production of statistics on occupations and business trends), and in public recognition of excellence through awards, the Panel sees only tardy recognition of the role of the arts and artists. The Medal of Freedom now at last goes to artistic and cultural leaders as well as to those distinguished in other fields. Our public monuments may some day begin to reflect cultural achievements as well as national service astride cavalry mounts. Few poets, musicians, dancers, architects, and other cultural contributors are seen on granite pedestals.

The Conditions of Creative Freedom

The arts will flourish in the United States, given the appropriate conditions. Among these conditions is undoubtedly freedom for the creative artist. And this freedom, we have suggested, is not different in kind from the freedom required for innovation generally, including the innovative activities of enterprisers in the economic sphere. It is partly because of this common requirement of the conditions for freedom that those who are responsible for corporate policy need to give attention to the conditions for the growth of the arts. For the same reason, those whose field is artistic creativity do well to make common cause with corporate leaders in pursuing the goals of freedom in the broadest sense.

The nature of freedom is, however, an elusive subject. We seem to appreciate it most when we are deprived of it. In contemporary despotisms of the totalitarian and authoritarian brands there has been abundant experience with unfreedom; its consequences for art and industry are there for anyone to see if he studies the record. It is a dismal record for the liberal-minded. A directed economy and a "coordinated" culture are contrary to the goals of liberalism. And yet, it is obvious that these illiberal regimes work in some respects, and they work pragmatically in ways that cannot be denied: near success in war for the totalitarian regime in Germany, and the rapid rise of a new and deadly threatening empire of communism in the East. The negativism of dated liberalism has not been enough; the absence of governmental restraint on private individuals and groups is no sure road to freedom for the creative mind.

The minimization of restraint exercised against the individual, and especially the creative individual in the arts and in industry is of course still a basic requirement of constitutionalism in the best Western tradition. Systematic and effectively applied restraints upon power, public and private, are a necessity if the creators and the innovators are to rise from the mass of men and enrich our society. But something more is required. On the positive side we have seen the necessity for creative uses of governmental power, too, and this applies both in the arts and in industry.

The Constitution of the United States was itself an eighteenth-century response to that need—a response that met admirably the needs of the time with special reference to the development of a continental market on this side of the Atlantic. Such key powers of the federal government as the commerce power, the taxing power, the judicial power strengthened by the supremacy clause, and later, after the Civil War, the important equal-protection and due-process clauses of the Fourteenth Amendment[26]—these and other wisely endowed attributes of national governmental power opened the way to our own brand of common market and thus paved the way to an unparalleled national strength.

It is not too much to say that the growth of our great modern business corporations is due in no small measure to the legislative, judicial, and executive uses of national power to open up, and keep open, the entire market from coast to coast to a burgeoning industrial development extending over almost two centuries. The exercise of national power has at times been restrictive and illiberal. But on the whole it has been a necessary condition of material growth and prosperity. This is an aspect of constitutionalism that is sometimes forgotten or conveniently passed over in silence.

The point is significant with respect to the arts and creative freedom. Tardily, the national government has at last moved into first gear in the advancement of the arts and in positively promoting the necessary conditions for a fecund culture, especially for the nourishment of creative persons in the entire spectrum of the arts. We do not have to amend the Constitution to provide Congress with the power to foster other arts than the "useful arts" mentioned in the patent and copyright clause; an adequate scope of powers is there, but it has not been much used.

It is now time that these powers be used, not only to complement other vectors of national strength, but more emphatically to give our existing strength the most humane direction. In the arts there are such potentialities, even though our mores have tended to close our eyes to this. The first hesitant and small steps have been taken; others of larger purpose and dimensions will ensue, given the necessary push of the business world and more of the political temperament that we have seen in getting through the recent legislation and executive orders on the arts.

There are further necessary conditions for the advancement of the arts through creativity and innovation. In addition to those restraints that keep the holder of power off the backs of the creative people, and to that wise exercise of governmental power that opens up new opportunities for the creative talent to emerge and make itself-effective, there are two other conditions: (1) the actual existence of potential innovators and creators of works of art; and (2) an *awareness*—as Karl Deutsch has pointed out[27]—on the part of talented people of the reality of their own capabilities and of the "unrestrainedness" and opportunity in the environment of a truly free society. It may be useful to expand these two points a little.

The operative meaning of freedom as an effective range of choice brings up the question, when we talk of freedom for artists, whether we need it in view of the dubious capacities displayed by contemporary op-pop-sop types. Why become exercised about creative freedom when there are no creative people around? Conceding for the moment that much contemporary "art" deserves other names, how can we be sure that we have not encouraged the untalented and let the potential geniuses sink without a trace in an educational system that fails to discover the educable?

The system often succeeds; but does it succeed in bringing to the surface the boldest potential innovators, the unnoticed creative personalities—those in unlikely places like the slums, the racially discriminated against, those in the deviant groups? Do we know how to recognize the promising ones and to provide them in time with the skills they need for developing and eventually exercising their talents to the utmost? This is an aspect of the conditions for artistic and innovative freedom that makes great demands on those who can use their powers, in public office and in the private sectors, to open up opportunities. The problem has something to do with the negative aspect of "unrestrainedness," but more to do with positive action.

The other matter is that of awareness, or recognition, by potentially creative people of their own talents and capacities and of the doors that are open to them. One's range of choices may be wider than he realizes; and it is part of the strategy of a free society to increase the possibility that he will realize the full width of the range. This, again, goes to the educational system in the full-life meaning of that word. The full-life reference is not only to time—to the conception of education that reaches into mature years—but also to depth.

"Know Thyself," the Socratic injunction, entails the pursuit of knowledge into regions of the soul and of the universe that the ancient Greeks had no inkling of. We can now release energies of mind through techniques that were unknown to them, but it still is very difficult for the common run of men to take advantage of most of these techniques. One reason is faulty allocation of resources owing to the devaluation of education in this broad and deep sense, for fear that penetrating self-knowledge (of the self in relation to the universe) will destroy the conventional wisdom. But perhaps the main reason is simple inertia: hanging thoughtlessly onto received dogma and habitual ways of running our social institutions. A country that has traditionally not paid much attention to the value of art in education has to be strongly stimulated to introduce new departures. In a later chapter we shall return to this theme.

A practical and immediate question, of great interest to corporate managers, is whether we can achieve high standards in the arts in the United States without extensive governmental financial support and systematic policies in federal, state and local governments which make advancement of the arts a deliberate goal. The best evidence is that we cannot. Private support and private initiative will continue mainly to sustain the effort. But we cannot do what we know we must do for the arts without governmental participation. The problem, then, so far as freedom of creativity and innovation is concerned is the old constitutionalist issue in new garb—new, that is to say, for us on this side of the Atlantic, for it has been faced in Europe—the issue of freedom and restraint, of adequate but controlled powers.

There are still those who think that private patronage can still carry the burden. This is often the tenor of arguments for corporate support of the arts. But how far can corporate support reach? If all the foundations, corporate, and individual donors are added together, the total resources will certainly not cover the rapidly growing requirements for plant, equipment, personnel, expertise, and sheer deficit financing of cultural developments in the years ahead. The fact must be faced that these private resources are not an inexhaustible artesian well. And if this fact is indeed faced—together with the other ineluctable fact about the future of the arts: that the demand will not shrink conveniently to the point where governmental intervention can be written off—then we must accept the mixed public-private character of art sponsorship in this country for the long pull. It will do no good to assume that all one has to do is to hurdle the next few years of deficit financing, after which the arts will be self-sustaining. They will not and cannot be, any more than education can be.

Will creativity and innovation be gradually suppressed under these conditions? The answer must be that freedom to create and innovate depends not so much on the public-private mix of financial support of the arts and of the economic productive system as it does on two factors: (1) the firmness of the intention of citizens to keep creativity and innovation as high-priority goals in our society, and (2) the effectiveness of the ways and means chosen for reaching these goals. The latter question is not the prior one, as often appears to be the case. One hears too frequently the unsupported plea for corporate support of the arts or of education, for example, without due attention to the prior question of objectives. In the chapters following, an attempt is made to spell out those objectives—more broadly, the common goals of corporation and artist, and not merely the corporate goal of financial aid—with particular reference to the pursuit of knowledge and the reach for ethical value.

In the present chapter, however, we have had to focus on the second question, which is adjectival, procedural, an issue of means rather than ends. It has been necessary first to discuss the conditions of free creativity and free innovation—conditions that are hampered as little as possible by governmental and other restraints, but that require some degree of governmental intervention. We have seen that the necessary conditions also include corporate intervention, for without corporate support, along with continued support and initiative from other private sources—it seems highly unlikely that the arts will flourish.

The arts cannot be regarded as an alien field of activity for corporate managements, and not merely because they add a certain elegance to an otherwise drab, materialistic, and business-oriented culture. The arts are closely akin to the more obviously business-centered activities of corporate enterprises, mainly because they depend upon a quality of the human mind and personality that also produced the innovations without which business stagnates. The reasons for this relationship will become even clearer as we proceed.

CHAPTER IV

The Knowing Artist

"Art is only a more direct vision of reality." This dictum of Henri Bergson may make too much of the claim for art as one of the indispensable paths to knowledge. But it is a claim that demands the attention of every corporate executive who is alert to the potentialities of those fields and activities now commonly regarded as peripheral to business, but which are beckoning to the far-sighted policymaker. That the arts could potentially contribute to expanding business horizons has occurred to more than a few business executives, especially those who have hoped to cash in on the so-called cultural explosion in the United States in recent years. But this is only the superficial aspect of the matter. The truth is, not even the surface has as yet been scratched in a serious effort to develop statements of the common purpose of art and corporate enterprise in the search for knowledge and the communication of ideas.

The Common Purpose of Art and Enterprise

Of all the common purposes pursued by art and corporate enterprise, none is more important than the search for knowledge. This is perhaps more obvious to corporate executives than to artists. It has become commonplace to identify corporate purpose with the development of science. "R&D" (research and development) naturally go hand in hand in modern enterprise, and not only in those companies which rely on the computer. It is questionable, however, whether the average executive as yet appreciates the value of art as a path to knowledge. The search for new knowledge in all fields is the hallmark of progressive businesses; burgeoning technology, and especially electronic and other technology dependent upon modern physics, has dramatized the economic significance of science. The expansion of new frontiers of knowledge in *all* disciplines is characteristic of great corporations. The linking of science, technology and business development should not, therefore, be stressed at the cost of another significant new linkage: that of art with the knowledge now being pursued in many hitherto unexplored terrains of experience.

This linkage of art and knowledge is not necessarily a direct linkage with the kinds of knowledge that fall customarily under the rubric of scientific knowledge, although epistemological advances may at length show that there is such a direct linkage in all cases. One thinks of the classical theories of Beauty, for example, dating from ancient Greek philosophical literature, which saw a more direct linkage between the Good, the True, and the Beautiful than many modern epistemologists would concede. On the other hand, the neoclassicism of today attempts to refute these Ideas or universals. In much contemporary thought it is assumed that "science" means a nonevaluative, nonnormative account of the nature of the universe, while art and morals decidedly involve evaluation and the assertion of norms about the beautiful and the ugly, the good and the bad.

It is generally assumed, moreover, that esthetics and ethics stand apart as disciplines that do not yield the same kind of knowledge as the modern descendants of metaphysics—the natural and behavioral sciences. The latter disciplines are often thought of as the appropriate proving ground of both empirical and deductive methods that are not inherent in ethical and esthetic discourse. All of these propositions can, of course, be refuted and are not universally held; yet they are sufficiently widespread to require some attention when one begins to discuss art as a means of knowing.

Art as a Path to Knowledge

As a path to knowledge, art assumes considerable significance for policymakers in the modern corporation. Although other reasons for the corporate-arts nexus exist, this one is probably the most important. The reason is that the survival and growth of the great corporations depends upon a constant instream of knowledge from every available source, and one of the still unrecognized sources of valuable knowledge is the domain of art.

The lack of recognition of this fact is not due solely to the prejudices of a scientific age against ways of thinking that seem to counter the scientific method. Among artists, too, there is often antipathy to the view that art is a way of knowing and is therefore allied with science; they would keep art and science at swords' points. Thus we find that among some estheticians and in some artistic quarters great suspicion is aroused when the suggestion is made that art, science, and industry are somehow allied and pursue a common purpose.

The aim of this chapter is to show that there is potentially such an alliance, and that this potential alliance, more than anything else, accounts for the present tendency for art and the corporation, as two major social institutions, to merge efforts in the common purpose of augmenting man's understanding of the way things are. It is a purpose in common, too, with science, which seeks accurate statements about the way things are rather than the way we want them to be in our dreams.

If it be objected that this dream-world of hope and desire—which allegedly has nothing to do with the way things really are—is precisely the realm of art, then a counter-objection must be made. The artist who makes statements in esthetic form about his dreams is also likely, if the dream is part of a protest against the way things are, to make some interesting statements about the realities as he sees them. If we are wise we do not dismiss these artistic statements about the nature of reality merely on the ground that the artist's *scientific* credentials are not in order, or that his radical reformism disturbs us.

As to the demand for credentials, there is today a strong tendency to retrogress into a neoguildism that would require everybody to show his union card or risk the danger of being condemned as an outlaw when he practices an unsanctioned profession. In the supposed dichotomy between science and art, the world relegates the artist to poesy and the depiction of a dreamworld of unreality, and it opens the door wide to anyone who calls himself a scientist when "exact" knowledge is wanted. Some reshuffling of the union cards and some basic revision of the rules of admission to the guilds is in order now that we recognize the inexactitude of the allegedly exact sciences at their very core of nuclear physics, and the useful revelations, on the other hand, of artists with metaphoric insight.[1] And as to the radicalism and reformism of artists, it is well to remember that Nature does not always elect the eminently respectable and orthodox as vehicles for the revelation of religious, scientific, and esthetic Truth.

Facing the Human Condition

Dramatic and literary artists are often far more realistic than the so-called scientific writers on social structures and processes. The artist may achieve realism precisely because he declines (or is unable) to use the language of social science in describing and commenting on the social scene. In this respect the dramatist, the novelist, and the poet are indispensable to a free society that aims toward a truer understanding of the nature of man before it prescribes a rule of law for him. The human condition is variously described by contemporary playwrights and dramatists as good, bad, or hopeless. The intent may be merely to display human nature as they see it or to argue a point. Tennessee Williams' plays are probably less an indictment of the weaknesses and failures of men and women than sympathetic accounts. In many contemporary plays, a moral is drawn and the dramatist's approach to ethical problems is not to be ignored. Plays in this category, if they are widely seen and therefore appeal to a substantial public, are for that very reason significant in the social scene; the chord they strike has resonance because many people agree with the dramatist that a problem exists.

The freedom to state problems of an ethical nature is one of the most important freedoms. Solutions are not possible until the problems are stated, and stated forcibly enough to work up demands for solutions. The dramatist and his interpreters on the stage lend force to the statement that cold logic alone does not provide. This is the use of emotion in the cause of social justice, as evidenced in Ibsen's plays, for example. Essays on social criticism and dry reports of a clinical character may never achieve the results that a Zola could produce.

In this way the arts have a compelling ethical purpose. Yet something must be said for the social value of using the dramatic arts, not to state social problems or indicate solutions, but simply to comment on the human condition with a question mark. A playwright may say: "This is the way it is as I can see, but I propose no solution, nor do I even attempt to state solutions; I merely hold the mirror up to nature." Such works may in the end serve the purpose of a free society more effectively even than the "problem" plays. The reason is that they stimulate the imagination more than purely scientific statements of the human condition could possibly do, and therefore lead to more balanced views of social relationships.

84

It has long been obvious to serious students of society that this is so, and it becomes even more obvious today as the language of social science becomes more technical, its concepts more abstract and more recondite. We need the novelist, the poet, the dramatist, the painter, the sculptor, the musician, to help us to see human nature as a whole and to penetrate truths about man's feelings and aspirations— truths that may elude us as social scientists, "objective" reporters, and case-hardened administrators.

An "Instrument of Understanding"

In President Kennedy's plea for a national cultural center he said, "after the dust of centuries has passed over our cities, we will be remembered not for our victories or defeats in battle, or in politics, but for our contributions to the human spirit." And he added that art is "political in the most profound sense, not as a weapon in the struggle, but as an instrument of understanding."

One may take the key word to be *understanding*, in its broadest and deepest sense. And we may add that art is not only political in this sense but a civic necessity in the Greek meaning of *paideia*. In this broad civic-educational sense the arts are a necessity both for knowledge of the Good and for the knowledge of the True.

We will have an opportunity later to return to the paideutic concept of the role of art, particularly with regard to character formation in a society of free men. But now we are looking primarily at the pursuit of Truth in the scientific sense, and at the role of the arts in this pursuit. It is a subject in which one encounters difficulties and resistances. Difficulties arise from the common tendency of many to erect a wall between science and art. Those who resist the idea of art as a path to knowledge and an indispensable adjunct of communication include not only artists but men in the world of affairs.

Yet the virtue, and indeed the necessity, of art as a gateway to the understanding of scientific truths has been emphatically and irrefutably stated by our mentors. Art, as Alfred North Whitehead has observed, is an integral part of the adventures of knowledge. Art, others remind us, lends its intuitive judgment where logical analysis fails us. Art is a powerful dialectical activity of a special kind. It broadens the view of nature, gives a more realistic coverage of the life spectrum, the totality of experience. Art is apprehension of meaning that would otherwise escape us. It is a great simplifier, and yet it keys us into complexities of feeling that cannot so easily be stated in the language of today's science.

In these and other respects one can enlarge upon President Kennedy's designation of art as an instrument of understanding. And although such enlargement may be elementary to some readers, it may stimulate others who seek a more weighty corporate-arts nexus than is ordinarily encountered. The interplay of corporate enterprise and the arts, one must repeat emphatically, is not exhausted—nor even significantly touched—in simple proposals for corporate support of the arts. The essence of the relationship is more nearly approached in probing the common purpose of the artist and the enterpriser in stating "the way things are"—the metaphysical truth reduced to concrete situations and understandable terms. This is the justification for drawing together at this point some philosophical commentary on art as an instrument of understanding. Needless to say, this designation of art in no way reduces it to a subordinate role.

The Adventure of Esthetic Experience

The arts contribute to understanding by providing what Alfred North Whitehead called "adventures of esthetic experience." The merit of such experience was of major concern to this distinguished philosopher when he discussed the place of science in the modern world. An age of science and technology demands great rigor of intellectual analysis. And the training that leads to a scientific career is so demanding that one is apt to overlook, according to Whitehead, the "necessity of wandering." Why this necessity of wandering? Unwary observers of scientific progress have been misled by rigid doctrines of causality, failing to see that science, with its progressive thought and progressive technology, has made "the transition through time, from generation to generation, a true migration into uncharted seas of adventure."

This has meant adventures of thought, not rigidity of doctrine. These adventures of thought in science were, for Whitehead, integral with adventures of ideas, feelings, and esthetic experience generally. A major factor in the upward trend of animal life on earth, in Whitehead's view, has been the wandering faculty. Although he wrote before astronautical adventures, his comment is timely. He suggested that antediluvian armor-plated monsters had fared badly because they had no power to wander. "Animals wander into new conditions. They have to adapt themselves or die. Mankind has wandered from the trees to the plains, from the plains to the seacoast, from climate to climate, and from habit of life to habit of life. When man ceases to wander, he will cease to ascend in the scale of being. Physical wandering is still important, but greater still is the power of man's spiritual adventures—adventures of thought, adventures of passionate feeling, adventures of esthetic experience."[2]

Whitehead warned of the grooving of professional minds, trained too exclusively by intellectual analysis, into paths of abstractions that are absolutely essential for one's professional work but usually sterile for "the comprehension of human life" in all its myriad colorations and meanings. In the modern world, he said, there is a certain "celibacy of the intellect" that has succeeded the celibacy of the medieval learned class, divorced from "the concrete contemplation of the complete fact." In our age of extreme specialization with concurrent demands of these "grooved abstractions" of such indispensable professional value, we are in danger of giving no serious thought at all to experience beyond the world of these abstractions. The remainder of life gets superficial treatment within the confines of the imperfect categories of thought derived from one's profession. The esthetic experience was for Whitehead an indispensable way out of this difficulty.

For him, the "habits of esthetic apprehension" were to be inculcated not for more gracious and elegant living but for the purpose of "increasing the depth of individuality." The habit of art was the habit of enjoying vivid values. The arts provide more than entertainment. They provide paths to reality that cannot be provided by intellectual approaches alone. Through the arts, one achieves at length an immediate and intuitive apprehension of the "total environment . . . with a minimum of eviscerating analysis." Esthetic growth thus meant for Whitehead at once the liberation of a man from the too narrowly limiting abstractions of his grooved professional life and, more positively, opening up to him "the infinite variety of vivid values achieved by an organism in its proper environment." Science, scholarship, and technical proficiency are not enough. "When you know all about the sun and all about the atmosphere and all about the rotation of the earth, you still miss the radiance of the sunset."

But art, he insisted, was concerned with more than sunsets. Foreshadowing the more comprehensive approaches to the study of the modern corporation and its role in society, Whitehead observed that "a factory, with its machinery, its community of operatives, its social service to the general population, its dependence upon organizing and designing genius, its potentialities as a source of wealth to the holders of stock is an organism exhibiting a variety of vivid values." What we want to train, he said, is "the habit of apprehending such an organism in its completeness."

Whitehead declared that a century earlier the esthetic experience was regarded as important even by the best men with a stone-blind eye, whereas in the most advanced industrial countries today art is regarded as a frivolity. Probably that is no longer true. But we are still getting warnings from various quarters that something must be done to overcome the one-sidedness of our technological and intellectualistic civilization. It is not simply that there ought to be more "art appreciation." To reach full development, the creative person must be awake to the sensuous part of life as the artist sees it. Among the creative scientists, especially, the role of the arts in education and training is of great importance. An esthetic quality in the learner is said, for example, to aid in the understanding of "structure," which in turn is properly stressed in the intellectual schooling of students.

Art and Intuitive Knowledge

Aristotle declared that the aim of art is to represent not the outward appearance of things, but rather their inward significance. To him, this inward significance, rather than the external mannerism and detail, is true reality. Perhaps for some perceptions there is an artistic expression that cannot otherwise be communicated, an embodiment of truths in artistic form that men cannot otherwise know or understand.

Sir Kenneth Clark refers to Aristotle's observation that art completes what nature cannot bring to a finish, and that the artist gives us knowledge of nature's unrealized ends; a chief assumption here, Clark says, is that "everything has an ideal form of which the phenomena of experience are more or less corrupted replicas."[3] The artist, the poet, the mathematician, offer us the best statements of the ideal form.

Sir D'Arcy Wentworth Thompson, the scholar-naturalist, thus defends the rigor of mathematical definitions as a key to all but endless freedom: "the precise definition of an ellipse introduces us to all the ellipses in the world; the definition of a 'conic section' enlarges our concept, and a 'curve of higher order' all the more extends our range of freedom."[4]

The search for form in this artistic and mathematical sense is a process that eludes exact description. There is a "creative night" of poetic intuition, Maritain tells us, and he seems to mean by this that the creative process is hidden in an impenetrable darkness. Yet the poet, the artist, reveal by their work, as Maritain shows, something of the nature of that mysterious process. It is a creative process that adds immeasurably to human knowledge and demands of us every effort to protect and encourage it. The demand is the more urgent

89

in an age that respects empirical inductive and theoretical deductive methods of inquiry above all others and is apt to shunt aside the nonlogical and intuitive-artistic processes of discovery.[5]

The creative intuition that Maritain explores is not, in his view, an esoteric thing of exclusive concern to the artist; it is a powerful source of action, an elemental force of intellect.[6] And in this conception of action and power resident in the hidden recesses of artistry we reach some of the common ground on which artists and other men of action meet, notably the men of action in business. In discussing the "critical reason" and the obscure nonlogical processes so essential to creative intuition, Maritain comes closest to the common ground of poet and executive—strange as this ground may seem.

The worlds of the artist and of the modern corporation can meet in at least a number of points. One suspects that the common ground lies in that penumbra of the critical reason which Maritain refers to as the nonlogical, even though some in the business world might wish to abjure the nonlogical processes. They may appear to do so, but in fact they are like the poet who sings best when he reflects least. One is reminded of Maritain's comment about Charles du Bos: as a critic he was distinguished but his poetic activity had been "paralyzed by a prodigious development of the reflective faculties." The frequently well-grounded suspicion that businessmen are anti-intellectual may be because, like poets, they succeed best if they avoid the contemplative life and go in strenuously for the manipulative arts.

Action, indeed, is so much the essence of art that it is somewhat paradoxical that science—not art—has enjoyed priority in corporate philanthropy. The search for truth in the basic and applied sciences is supported by corporations both intramurally and extramurally (in universities, for example) because scientific truths and the training of people who can understand and use them have become so indispensable to modern industry. Yet the contemplative life of the scholar, without which scientific knowledge and the teaching of science would be impossible, is remote from the world of affairs. Risk-taking and decision-making of the entrepreneurial

90

type is so different from the ratiocination of the scientist and educator that it has been difficult for men from these disparate camps
to understand each other's ways of life. For the artist, however, there
is an active way of production that businessmen can understand
quite well.

The wiser men have always known that there are elements of truth
available only through what Bertrand Russell has called the "mystical way of feeling."[7] And, as Sir Herbert Read once remarked in a
critique of bourgeois academic art and its limited focus in reality,
there seems to be no reason why the artist should not take the whole
range of internal perception as his legitimate province—and, we
might add, no reason why practical men of affairs should hesitate
to consult the poetic insights that cover this range as perhaps no
other human faculty could. One dare not stretch the case too far.
There is prudence in Graña's observation that art is just what
Dewey said philosophy ought to be: an endeavor dedicated to the
apprehension of meaning rather than the discovery of truth.[8]

What Truths Does the Artist Discover?

When one speaks of the knowing artist, and of art as a path to
knowledge, it is essential that distinctions be made. For, the artist
may indeed discover and reveal to us some truths that the scientist
does not grasp, but can we depend on the "objectivity" of the artist's
report?

In Clive Bell's objective theory of esthetics, objects that provoke
the experience of a peculiar emotion are the starting point of all
esthetic experience. But it is not the objects themselves that the
artist sees, but rather a reality behind them that is latent in them.
Art, as C. E. M. Joad says in expounding Bell's theory, enables us
to glimpse a reality which lies outside the realm of normal awareness,
and the emotion we feel is unique; we do not have the feeling that
the object or the reality behind it is useful or instrumental for other
purposes; it is an end in itself.[9]

The concept of art as a window to reality differs from that of science as a path to truth. Originating with Plato, this view of the reality of the artist's observed object is one that presupposes a Form of Beauty or the Idea of Beauty. When we say that a picture or a symphony is beautiful we see or hear the manifestation of Beauty, that universal truth that lies beyond sensual description or scientific explanation. The artist does not see or hear all the details of an event or an experience and then relay it to us in the same exhaustive detail. Art is a kind of abstraction itself, a search for and an expression of beauty that is latent in things and events. There are, to use Whitehead's terminology, "eternal objects" that enter into the flux of events,[10] and these the artist comes nearer to apprehending than the scientist acting only within the limits of scientific investigation.

In contemporary comment on art one encounters so frequently an extreme view of the artist's special kind of access to reality that his objectivity often becomes suspect. This specialized access is at times so alienated that the truths these artists purportedly perceive will never be known to anyone else. They are incommunicable. This extremism bears no relation to the neo-Platonic conceptions of esthetic Form, nor to the position that art provides us with the means to penetrate to deeper strata of reality. Sociological and psychoanalytic theory have undoubtedly influenced this position far more than the revival of Platonic doctrine in esthetics.

Evidence of this influence is apparent in many contemporary works on art. Sir Herbert Read declares that the primary function of the artist, and the only one that gives him unique faculties, is the capacity "to materialize the instinctual life of the deepest levels of the mind."[11] At that level he supposed the mind to be "collective in its representations,"[12] and it is because the artist can give visible shape to these invisible fantasms that he has power to move us deeply. But the artist must exercise a certain skill in the process of giving these fantasms material shape lest the bare truth repel us, Read observes.

For Sir Herbert, it is absurd Philistinism to regard art as an expendable form of mental or physical gymnastics. Art must rather be recognized as the most certain mode of all expression that mankind has achieved, and one that has been propagated from the very dawn of civilization. All the time that man has developed the practical and scientific side of life, he has felt this to be inadequate. The mind he had developed from his "deliberate cunning" could only cope with objective facts. Beyond these objective facts was a whole aspect of the world which was accessible only to instinct and intuition. "The development of these obscurer modes of apprehension has been the purpose of art; and we are nowhere near an understanding of mankind and of the history of mankind until we admit the superiority of the knowledge embodied in art." But Read goes further to claim superiority for such knowledge because "whilst nothing has proved so impermanent and provisional as that which we are pleased to call scientific fact and the philosophy built on it, art, on the contrary, is everywhere, in its manifestations, universal and eternal."

With such a conception of art, Sir Herbert could not regard the function of the artist as merely "the production of objects within the economic field—not, that is to say, as the making of buildings, furniture, utensils and the more or less utilitarian things." Art tries to tell us something about the universe, something about man, or about the artist himself. As a mode of knowledge, the world of art is a system of knowledge as valuable to man as the world of philosophy and the world of science. Indeed, it is only when we have clearly recognized art as a mode of knowledge parallel to, but distinct from, other modes by which man arrives at an understanding of his environment that we can begin to appreciate its significance in the history of mankind.

Psychoanalytic Explorations in Art

The influence of Freudian and other psychoanalytic thought on the contemporary reassessment of the nature and function of art in society has been profound. This approach to art has been examined in depth by Ernst Kris, who deplored the fact that our education does not, in general, train us so that we have ready access to the specialized sorts of knowledge that come easily to the artist. Freud had spoken of the artist's "flexibility of repression." Artists have the capacity to gain "easy access to id material," writes Kris, "without being overwhelmed by it, of retaining control over the primary process, and, perhaps specifically, the capability of making rapid or at least appropriately rapid shifts in levels of psychic function."[13] We can gain a certain indirect access to this specialized knowledge, he says, through the works of art, but we are not *trained* to do so. Our education in this respect is neglected or sketchy. Art provides us with a vast unexplored field of *prepared* knowledge in this respect —a storehouse of invaluable information about human nature.

Freud had spoken of philosophers, writers, poets, as "the few to whom it is vouchsafed . . . with hardly any effort to salvage from the whirlpool of their emotions the deepest truth to which we others have to force our way, ceaselessly groping among the torturing uncertainties." Kris observes that the history of intuitive insight has yet to be written, to demonstrate, if for no other purpose, how the great are less than others subject to the limitations that cultural and historical conditions impose. The inference is that there is something of the artist in the great. But we may draw a further inference, with direct application to the subject at hand—the interplay of art and business enterprise: something of the artist, with his flexibility of repression and his intuitive insight, is a necessity in the creative person now so much in demand in modern business.

In a recent study by a group of sixteen experts on creativity,[14] one of the conclusions drawn was that the highly creative individual can generate a large number of ideas rapidly, can shift gears by discarding one approach for another, and can give original and unusual answers to questions, original responses to situations, and unusual interpretations of events. They respond more favorably to complex and novel art than to academic art. And they are more inclined to be absent-minded, versatile, daring, impulsive, excitable, sensitive, reflective, preoccupied, and moody, than people of low creativity. It is not clear from the findings that highly creative persons

94

have the "flexibility of repression" that Freud spoke of, or that they are potential artists. Yet they probably have access to that "art of thought" that Graham Wallas had in mind.

Kris has referred to John Dewey's view that esthetic creation and re-creation is a kind of problem-solving behavior. The artists' problems are not conditioned by the same "stringencies" as those of the mathematician or the inductive scientist, however. And therein lies an interesting key to the kinds of creativity that are required in corporate enterprise and decision-making in all large organizations. Kris observes that the stringencies of the artist's problems are so minimal that esthetic solutions—and even statements of the problems —bear quite personal stamps of the artist. Material and conventional limitations bind the artist as they do all creative people, but only in rigid academicism is he so bound that there is no room for what Kris calls "esthetic ambiguity"—a quality of mind that plays, in his view, a central role in esthetic creation and re-creation.

Without the flexibility provided by this esthetic ambiguity there would be no possibility of expression of an artist's unique style within the broad limits of his material and the conventions of his time and place, Kris believes. The art of a work appears not in the skills shown in the mastery of techniques with materials and within the conventional limitations, but rather in the expressiveness and inspiration of the statement. The importance of esthetic ambiguity is precisely that there is a "disregard of external stringencies," a relaxation of the ego functions in esthetic creation and re-creation. There is a controlling intellectual component in the vicinity, but it is at a distance. The acts and symbols of the artist are emotionally charged with a variety of meaning. The audience does not so much *react* as *re-create* as a result of the stimuli triggered by the work of art. Kris here draws attention to a special kind of communication between artist and observer that needs further exploration, especially at a time when there is perhaps undue emphasis on communicational precision at the expense of nonlogical processes of thought.

The variations in the kinds and levels of "stringencies" which limit artistic and generally creative production are of great interest to the sociologist of art. These stringencies vary from culture to culture, from age to age, and probably from social group to social group. They probably also vary significantly from company to company, thereby affecting the creativity of corporate personnel. In this regard, an interesting and little-penetrated question arises—namely, whether company profitability, productivity, and growth are not more directly affected by such variation in creativity than any other factor. The Hawthorne experiments point, of course, in this direction. On the other hand, they have not been followed by further explorations that develop hypotheses concerning esthetic ambiguity as a causal factor in productivity at higher levels of management.

Kris suggests that the scope for the interpretability of works of art probably varies with certain contemporary conditions. Sometimes there is full exploitation of ambiguity and correspondingly heavy demand upon the audience as re-creator and interpreter of a work of art. At other times and places there are minimal demands on the audience because of tight stringencies in the conditions of esthetic expression. These observations are useful for more direct application of his hypotheses to industrial productivity, and particularly to the decision process in its more creative and nonlogical aspects. He suggests that "art is likely to be characterized by low stringency (i.e., high ambiguity and interpretability) where systems of conduct ideals are in doubt or social values are in process of transition." We are in such a period now, he adds. The attention given to the art of children, primitives, psychotics, and apes is indicative of this, and artists themselves deal with high-ambiguity techniques, as in aleatory music.

The works of art produced in such a transitional period would seem to reflect a general ambiguousness with uncertainties and equivocations evident in many departments of life. Highly ambiguous art evokes a favorable response in such a period. But when stringencies rise again, as they might do, we can expect a return to the academic and ritualistic limitations on esthetic creation and re-creation. There may be a return to traditional problems in most artistic genres and to traditional ways of solving them. Alternatively, artists in such a period or such a culture might emerge as revolutionaries working on the basis of new stringencies, producing works that are at first obscure, but later recognized in terms of the new stringencies. What was at first obscure then becomes ambiguous with new and possibly rich significance. The ambiguities become stylized; the revolutionary becomes conventional; academicism flourishes once more.

This cycle, Kris observes, is repeated in the history of art; he draws our attention to the re-creators of works of art and especially to the audience as well as to the artist in this process. Rigidity of conventions inhibit the process of re-creation, while "high ambiguity allows for a wide range of interpretation, so that [a] work may be prized throughout various changes in cultural interests and values by being interpretable in a corresponding variety of ways."

Indicated here are several aspects of corporate policy in relation to the arts. Design, for example, whether in industrial architecture or otherwise, is peculiarly liable to obsolescence in certain periods of the cycle Kris speaks of, and under certain social and cultural stringencies" that affect the artist and his audience. Of less direct significance, perhaps, is the role of corporations as supporters, stimulators, and sponsors of artists and artistic activities. It is worth pondering whether the persons and activities supported have survival value, and whether too low or too high levels of stringency are related to survival of works of art.

Kris's pioneer work covers many other important aspects of the subject we are here considering: art as a way of knowing, as a path to understanding of man and his environment. The literature on this subject, with particular reference to psychoanalytic insights, is growing.[15] No attempt is made here to review comprehensively such a highly specialized field. But perhaps enough has been said to suggest its relevance to the interplay of art and corporate enterprise.

Cognition of Feeling

Some of the most arresting work on the psychology of art in its social aspects has been done by Susanne K. Langer, and it especially illuminates the function of art as the objective presentation of feel-

97

ing. The term *feeling* must be given special attention because in Mrs. Langer's analysis it cannot be equated loosely with emotion. Feeling is a much more inclusive term, but at the same time it is tied in with a quite rigorous psychological analysis. In a recent statement of her position she declares that the import of art is not the occurrence of emotional upheavals but "conceptions of feeling," artistic expression being an expression of *ideas*.[16] "The artist's idea of what feelings are like, how they rise and take shape, grow, culminate like breaking waves, and spend themselves" is the artist's *knowledge* of subjective reality, which he projects—in visual terms in the plastic arts, in tonal and verbal terms in music and literature.

By "feeling" Mrs. Langer means "everything that can be felt, comprising sensibility as well as emotion." Thus she goes beyond the usually accepted meanings of tactile perception, euphoria and dysphoria, moods, and so on. She signifies by "feeling" all these, and much more. There is a vast "private world of subjective immediacy" —those internal events that result from impingement of the external world on our peripheral sense organs: "inwardly, we feel the rise and pulse and cadence of emotions, the strains of concerted thinking, and the more or less voluntary evocation of images from some unknown deep sources of memory and fantasy."

Although "feeling" is thus broadly defined, and the artist's task is regarded as one of projecting feeling objectively, Mrs. Langer goes on to say that feeling, intellect, imagination, and perception are not separable functions. In the history of art one observes the interrelationships in various forms and degrees. The ways of the artist in expressing his conception of feeling have changed remarkably over time and as a consequence of new principles of representation. She points to the way, for example, in which the great originators of Renaissance art revolutionized the modes of representation of human figures and nature. In this respect, their theories of these modes of artistic representation were not always abreast of their actual practices as artists.

Renaissance artists thought that they were copying Nature exactly, writes Langer, but in fact they were developing inchoate laws

98

of representation that were not at all the same as the laws of vision through which they perceived Nature. She comments that the development of the camera and of photography as an art corroborates Britsch's thesis distinguishing the laws of vision and the laws of artistic representation, and that the human eye is a part of the mind, perceiving whatever is given to it as the mind conceives it. Even the eye does not see Nature as it presumably "is"; and her conclusion that the principles of representation follow the "intellectualized, conceptual, interpreting perception" of the human eye leads her to some significant further conclusions about the social influence of design.

This intellectualized, conceptual, interpreting perception of the human eye by the artists of the Renaissance led to works of plastic art that were radically different from those of earlier and later periods. What these artists "saw" and represented in their works was not the same world as that seen by others that preceded and followed them; nor are the differences due entirely to a change of scene. They stressed and abstracted their own imaginative concept of the world. And, what is even more important, as Mrs. Langer points out, they *created new perceptions that engendered new ways of feeling* about the world in those who looked on their painting, sculpture, and architecture. The creations of the Renaissance artist were followed by re-creations in the observer, with far-reaching effects on the observer's comprehension of the world and of man. The Renaissance artists made the average man see in nature what they had fashioned in their paintings and sculptures for his eyes, with resulting transformation of the observer's sense of reality. It was a transformation, also, of "the scope and organization of his feeling for the objective world." It was the revelation of a new world toward which human emotions were turned.

In Mrs. Langer's analysis of art as a kind of knowing—indeed one of the most important kinds historically because of the tremendous influence of artists, especially in the field of architecture—two lines of inquiry are indicated for those who seek answers to the interplay of art and corporate enterprise.

First, there is the question of the effect of the external world on the internal world of the artist: how does the external world—and especially that part of the external world over which the corporation has some degree of influence—shape the "intellectualized, conceptual, interpreting eye" of the artist? What are the social institutions and social processes involved in this conditioning of the artist's interpreting eye, and ear? What can and should corporate enterprises do to effect changes in this conditioning, regarded as an essential aspect of the total educational process? Given the vast influence of art and artists, what is there to be said and done in this broad field of developing a new conception of the world of man and nature—a modern conception moving with the times and consistent with contemporary (other) types of knowledge—for the specific use of educating artists?

Secondly, there is the question of the effect of the artist on the external world through his representations of feeling: how can the corporation contribute to the maximum beneficial effects of the arts as media for new perceptions that engender new ways of feeling? Warnings are in order against the narrow view of art simply as the handmaiden of corporate public relations; the policymaker who stops there sees only a little way ahead. The modern corporation has become a major supporter of education, but in general, education is still suffering from a failure to overcome tonal, visual, tactile, and kinetic illiteracy in a population largely unaware of the potentialities of art as objective presentation of feeling. These are dangerously neglected dimensions of a man's preparation for life. For corporate executives, the question arises: What is to be done to assure the flow of the artist's knowledge of feeling into the educational process for citizens, specifically those who will be responsible for key decision posts in the corporations of tomorrow?

Even though there is currently a new awareness among corporate leaders of the importance of the world of art for the world of business, one wonders about the depth of understanding of the problem. There is a general tendency to regard it essentially as a problem of applied arts, of using certain of the arts as means to specific and immediate corporate ends—public relations, for example. The purpose must be probed more deeply than that, still conceding that we are a long way from making the best uses of our artists and their special creativity for the everyday business objectives of a firm. Both corporate ecosis—the adaptation of the corporation as a social institution to its human and other environment—as well as corporate leadership through which the environment is itself adapted to human needs, require more extensive inquiry into the social functions of art.

Mrs. Langer's comment on these functions is suggestive. It is relevant, moreover, to the contemporary problem of rapid, almost breathtaking, social change which leaves man's emotional development far behind the changes rushing in from advances in technics. She speaks of the loss, in our time, of familiar expressive forms with the onrush of new modes of life, new machines, new industries, new ways of organized living, new buildings, new landscapes, and the rapid obsolescence and discard of traditional techniques, tools, materials, and furnishings. The resultant "subjective strain . . . affects such vast numbers of individuals that it emerges as a widespread moral uncertainty, confusion or loss of human values, a great increase of mental imbalance, and a nightmarish sense of more or less constant and pervasive insecurity."[17]

The psychological effects of this strain seem to Mrs. Langer to include two different kinds that lead in opposite directions. One of these is an indifferent, reckless, and superficial frivolity that really masks moral defeat and surrender. The opposite kind is undirected emotional tension, an increase in seriousness, and a search full of anxiety for a way out. The syndromes are both neurotic, but they have quite distinct artistic expressions. She calls the first a "cavalier reaction," often of irresponsible behavior; the second, an "intellectual reaction." The latter appears as "a nostalgic desire for medieval disciplines and institutions, return to religious traditions, a sentimental search for old customs and 'grass roots,' and preoccupation with the meaning of existence and the reality of human attachments." Art, at such times, is in a state of ferment. The traditionalist cast of mind makes one abhorrent of "modern art" and the advance guard, but with the gnawing fear that the old forms of expression will not do today. Painting and sculpture in the contemporary mode

101

may be rejected, but not necessarily the new architecture, the new design of things we use every day, the new departures of the more creative artisans. These arts of the immediate and the usual pursuits may be more easily accessible and more readily absorbed. They help us on the way to a new culture, to the eventual correspondence of emotional development and technics.

At this point in her analysis Mrs. Langer enters a caveat. For growth and stabilization, the cultures of the past have depended heavily on these artisans and their design of the tools of a civilization. They were craftsmen through whom "predominant feelings—*not only emotions, but the pulse of work and surrounding nature*— recorded themselves in the design of weapons and implements as a general style." (Emphasis added.) Yet today this responsibility of the artisan persists while the craftsmanship disappears. Instead of the artisan-craftsman we have the industrial designer; and next to the architect of today it is the industrial designer, she declares, who is shaping the visual scene. "It is in our things—our countless things, multiplied fantastically *praeter necessitatem*, so they always surround us—that we need to find some significance, some look of simple honesty in ordinary utensils and of dignity in silverware and technological elegance in our machines." Not only the industrial designers and the architects, but the planners must be relied upon to "shape the new vision of reality which will embody a new world-feeling, enigmatic and articulate as yet." But this is not going to happen overnight; we have to be prepared to take the turmoil, the confusion and even lack of style, until this readjustment occurs. We can do more than wait, however; we can encourage the creation and appreciation of beautiful forms and make an effort to stop that "corruption of consciousness" (R. G. Collingwood's phrase) produced today by the vicious influence of pernicious design.[18]

Mrs. Langer's highly sophisticated approach to the problem of the knowing artist and of the function of art in the articulation of feeling at this crucial stage in the development of American culture will not, perhaps, be widely shared on its philosophical and psychological grounds. But it is evident that there is increasing concern about the social implications of design—from the design of simple artifacts to the design of cities, highways, and regions—and for much the same reason, although in less elaborate justification, as she offers. Nevertheless, we have apparently reached a time in our national history when the urgency of good design in this broad sense is a matter of public policy.

Mrs. Langer's criterion for good art is: the objective presentation of feeling to a beholder's direct perception. It is not the expression of feeling, the emotional outburst of the artist. Bad art lacks the requisite element: "a logical projection in which feeling appears as a quality of the created object." And the images produced by the true artist, she insists, will have a great influence on all of us. For "our feelings are guided and shaped by the forms in which various artists have projected them."

Using this approach, but not necessarily the special language of psychology, we can readily see the importance of design all along the scale just indicated—from simple and small things we use every day to the shape of our cities, the contours of our national landscape in the automotive age, and the style of living. It has been said that the great architectural challenge of the present century in the United States is the control of explosive urban expansion through design, through planning the man-made environment for beauty, efficiency, and order: we are well ahead on the design of individual buildings but woefully behind on the architectural setting.[19]

The total ecological problem, in terms of principles of esthetics and ethics as applied to community planning on a large scale, has long been the theme of Lewis Mumford's writing. The evidence of growing concern is everywhere; it has stimulated governmental action and in turn more awareness in the business sectors of the dangers of ugliness and decay.[20] Nor is the problem one that resolves itself naturally into the traditional norms of health and welfare alone. Polluted streams and air are indeed bad for us and they weaken the national fiber.[21] But that is not all. We need good design throughout, in an environment of protected natural beauty, for the reasons that Mrs. Langer specifies—for the guiding and shaping of our feelings as citizens and as self-respecting members of the human race.

The White House Conference on Natural Beauty in May, 1965,

under the chairmanship of Laurance S. Rockefeller, was President Johnson's idea to promote natural beauty as a matter of national policy. But it covered much more: conservation, outdoor recreation, natural resources, urban renewal, and environmental health.[22] And despite the criticism that followed the Conference (the critics were not against the goals but questioned the means proposed to reach them),[23] the program could be a turning point in the way we use our land and build our cities. No one felt it necessary to argue for beauty in the abstract, although a good deal of attention was paid to the implications of sustained ugliness. It has become clearer that design, including design in its negative sense of noninterference with natural beauty, has a profound effect on the style of life and the tone of the nation.

The status of art as well as natural beauty has progressed in this country from that of limited and specialized appreciation by the elite connoisseur to a necessary commodity for a wide public that shares this "contemplative" skill in the arts. Few can be master craftsmen in the shaping of things of beauty, but there can be no arbitrary limits to the audience, to the observing eye of the common man. He needs an environment of beauty and will demand it.

The Esthetic Model of Anthropology

The artist as a special kind of knower of truths and teller of aspirations of civilizations has been the subject, in recent decades, of much study by historians and sociologists. Some indication of this have already been offered. Artists have at times complained that the sociologists, with few exceptions, fail to note that art is an "autonomous activity," a mode of knowledge in its own right, a unique way of reacting to our human destiny, a contribution without parallel in the process of civilization.[24] Is this a fair assessment?

In his discussion of the "models" that have hovered about and determined the theoretic course of modern anthropology, Robert Redfield gave considerable attention to what he called the "esthetic"

104

and "symbolic" models.[25] The reason for the several "models" used by anthropologists as theoretic constructs to explain their scientific subject matter is, as Redfield pointed out, the "holistic" and comprehensive nature of humanity, on the one hand, and the effort of the scientific mind to reduce the organic reality of man's nature and man's culture to elements amenable to analysis, on the other. The conflicting claims of analysis and synthesis in anthropology have made the use of various theoretic constructs exceedingly useful, even though no anthropologist would align himself exclusively with any one model. The alternative models are used, rather, for the purpose of achieving knowledge, or for organizing knowledge so as to communicate understanding and to provide foresight. From the natural sciences the anthropologist may derive some of these models, especially those that emphasize causal relations and functions. Some students of the subject warn against too great a reliance on such models and methods.

The esthetic model of anthropology, as one of the alternatives[26] to the causal and functional models, sees in a culture "a constructed work of art." This point of view is discernible in the works of Margaret Mead and Ruth Benedict. A culture is there conceived "in terms also appropriate to works of art: theme, plot, phrasing, style, classic, or romantic."[27] In Benedict's *Patterns of Culture*, for example, the emphasis on rites and ceremonies makes it possible for us to see these activities as a dramatic interpretation of the cultures she is comparing. Each culture is "a play written by the past for the present, each individual an actor of a role." Benedict had mentioned the influence upon her of Santayana's study of three great Western poets as "contrasting studies of the genius of three great civilizations." Thus, Redfield suggested, one might attempt to distinguish national or tribal character by concepts more familiar to the history of humanistic learning than to those of the behavioral sciences.

The relationship between the humanities, especially the arts, and the science of anthropology was further alluded to by Redfield in another theoretic construct—the "symbolic model." In such a model a culture is conceived as represented in its characteristic properties as a whole by certain symbolic representations such as epic, dance form, and allegory. "The symbols may be transformations of the reality represented and of the impulses projected of perhaps quite fantastic nature: assumed is the capacity of symbol-creating and imaginative beings to frame meanings for themselves." Cassirer referred to the relations of symbolic representations to culture. Warner's concept of symbol system is a further case in point. Here the reality conceived to be represented was emphatically the social structure. Other symbolic models, emphasizing religious conceptions or ideal behavior as that which is symbolized, can also be seen in studies of the mythology of primitive and other peoples.

Redfield placed the esthetic and symbolic models of anthropology at a distance from the natural sciences and nearer to the humanities, identifiable, indeed, with the arts. In the rigorous scientific mode of the most careful social scientists, he commented that "the validity of a characterization of a culture by any of the models employed, but especially those which approximate the esthetic, logical, or symbolic models, is not today established (whatever may develop in the future) by experimental or any other precise proof such as is demanded in many fields of the natural sciences." But he compared insight into the "truth" about a culture or a personality by use of esthetic or other models with the understanding of a work of art: "A part is played by an act of apprehension of the totality on the part of him who accepts the presentation as true."

Art and Augury

Can the study of trends in artistic expression be useful to policy-makers who must observe long-term possibilities in environmental analysis? Both positive and negative answers to this question can be found. But the denials can be countered by statements of respected authorities on art and society.

Factual science may collect statistics and make charts, but its predictions are but past history reversed, John Dewey wrote in *Art*

106

as Experience. "Change in the climate of the imagination is the precursor of the changes that affect more than the details of life . . . the first stirrings of dissatisfaction and the first intimations of a better future are always found in works of art."[28] Surveyors of contemporary art would possibly add that the works of art also portend a worse future.

In Toynbee's *Study of History* it is said that every civilization creates an artistic style of its own, and that "if we are attempting to ascertain the limits of any particular civilization *in space or time* we find that the esthetic test is the surest as well as the subtlest."[29] There is the further statement that "the upshot of our investigation seems to be that the abandonment of a traditional artistic style is an indication that the civilization associated with that style has long since broken down and is now disintegrating. Like the disuse of an established technique, it is the consequence of breakdown, not the cause." Toynbee expends many pages on the question of style in the art of civilizations. The results may not satisfy sociologists who demand more rigorous scientific analysis. Yet the question of style is itself a serious issue in contemporary sociology.

Meyer Schapiro has said that a theory of style adequate to the psychological and historical problems has yet to be created, but it is clear from the literature that many scholars have turned their minds to the subject during the past century. The serious concern of writers—such as Semper, Riegl, Löwy, Worringer, Wölfflin, Nohl, Fry, Dilthey, Coellen, Adama van Scheltema, Boas, Dvořák, Focillon, and Hauser—with the subject of style in the history of art as it relates to social institutions cannot be so easily dismissed, as some would do who deny altogether the predictive value of art style.

As befits a careful scholar, Schapiro's own conclusions, though tentative, are arresting.[30] Reviewing the many studies that have related particular styles and contents of art to institutions and historical situations, he concedes that the general principles applied in explanation and connection of types of art with types of social structure have not been investigated systematically. The nearest approach seems to have been the Marxian one, which is an undeveloped view that the higher forms of cultural life correspond to

the economic structure of a society, the latter being defined in terms
of the relations of classes in the process of production and the technological level. But Marxist writing on art suffered from schematic
and premature formulations and from crude judgments imposed by
loyalty to a political line. There was obvious need for further work,
Schapiro said, not only to develop scientifically Marx's indicated
hypotheses, but also to work out other hypotheses.

In the work of Paul Frankl,[31] Schapiro found the most serious
attempt in recent years to create a systematic foundation for the
study of art forms, though Frankl's was a work that had been
almost ignored in the scientific literature on the subject, possibly
because it appeared just before the outbreak of World War II.
Frankl's most original construct had to do with a model of stylistic
development in history based on the analysis of elementary forms
and a limited number of possible combinations. The model itself was
not intended to be representative of actual historical development,
but rather an ideal plan of inherent or normal tendencies of development against which one might better understand the factors—social
and psychological—that divert the innate tendencies and determine
other courses. The diversions would be otherwise unintelligible.

By style Schapiro means "the constant form—and sometimes the
constant elements, qualities, and expression—in the art of an individual or a group." He also applies the term "to the whole activity
of an individual or society, as in speaking of a 'life-style' or the
'style of a civilization.' " For the archeologist, he reminds us, style
is a "symptomatic trait," like the nonesthetic features of an artifact
that is studied "more often as a diagnostic means than for its own
sake as an important constituent of culture." And he adds that the
archeologist has relatively few esthetic and physiognomic terms for
dealing with style.[32]

Art as an Indicator

The historian, as Toynbee's work illustrates, must associate style
and esthetic terminology. Toynbee is not worried too much about

the rigor of the sociologist's method, which is not to say that Toynbee's observations on style and augury in art are to be taken less seriously. The needed hypotheses, to which Schapiro refers, are likely to grow out of the ruminations of men who have a vast sweep of historical—and thus empirical—knowledge at their command. Toynbee's extensive travels in time and space qualify him for this preparatory work, for which all must be grateful. Therefore, his comments on the predictive value of art trends are worthy of careful note. We can only present some examples here.

One of the most interesting examples occurs when Toynbee speaks of schisms.[33] The "schism in the body social" he regards as a collective experience and, therefore, as superficial. Its significance lies in its being the outward and visible sign of "an inward and spiritual rift." "A schism in the souls of human beings will be found to underlie any schism that reveals itself on the face of the society which is the common ground of these human actors' respective fields of activity." Then Toynbee goes on to say that in a disintegrating society this schism appears variously in the characteristic behavior, the feeling, and the life of people who play a part in the genesis and growth of civilizations. When a society is disintegrating these characteristic responses to a challenge are not creative; they are polarized into "passive" and "active" responses—options that are the only freedom left "to a soul which has lost the opportunity (though, of course, not the capacity) for creative action through being cast for a part in the tragedy of social disintegration." The movement is toward more and more rigidly limited alternatives.

In decadent civilizations Toynbee sees a loss of command over the environment, the decline of techniques.[34] This decline is evident in engineering, but also in the artistic techniques of architecture, sculpture, painting, calligraphy and literature. This tendency to abandon artistic traditions is not necessarily the result of technical incompetence. It may be, rather, the deliberate attempt to abandon a style identified too closely with tradition, which is more or less openly repudiated. People lose faith in their own civilization, so they discard the artistic media through which it is transmitted. The old style becomes distasteful, perhaps because it is associated with a past that people would rather forget. The abandonment of a traditional artistic style indicates that the associated civilization has long since broken down and is disintegrating. "Like the disuse of an established technique, it is the consequence of breakdown, not the cause."

Distinctiveness of style is "the sign-manual of fine quality," and in a disintegrating civilization Toynbee observes vulgarity and barbarism in its art. He speaks of "our archaistic flight from vulgarity into pre-Raphaelite Byzantinism" as well as the contemporary alternative flight into the barbarism of "the flight to Benin"—to West African sculpture, music, and dancing—and the "chocolate-box" style of our Victorian commercial art.[35]

These observations are not offered here as proof of their validity. The point is that the knowing artist in any age is regarded by the many historians and sociologists as a possible indicator of general social trends. No one seriously proposes that artists are prophets or that social prognosis is a peculiar trait of theirs. There is perhaps a sense in which the esthetic techniques of an age reflect the spirit of the age; those whose task it is to take the long view will not neglect trends in art. The indices of change are too valuable to the policy-maker to neglect any one of them, especially at a time of rapid movement in the whole social structure, in science, in cosmology. The artist does not stand outside of, and aloof from, these epochal trends.

Sorokin on Art and "Sensate Culture"

Pitirim Sorokin regards the "fine arts" as among the most "sensitive mirrors" of the society and culture of which they are an important part. If the culture is predominantly "sensate, sensate will also be the dominant fine arts." If the culture is "unintegrated, chaotic and eclectic also will be its fine arts." He regards Western culture as predominantly sensate, a culture in crisis. The crisis consists in "the disintegration of its dominant supersystem." The contemporary crisis in the fine arts will therefore exhibit "a disintegration of the sensate form of our painting and sculpture, music, literature, drama, and architecture."[36]

110

In the "fine arts" Sorokin distinguishes three cultural types. Ideational art's topic is the supersensory kingdom of God; its style is, and must be, symbolic without concern for *paysage* or *genre*, whereas its emotional tone is pious, ethereal, and ascetic. Sensate art, in contrast, is naturalistic, visual, and even illusionistic in style, and free from supersensory symbolism, its emotional tone is violent and changeful, whereas its style is marked by superficial beauty with "lavish use of pomp and circumstance, colossality, stunning technique, and other means of external adornment." Idealist art stands between these polar types of sensate and ideational art. "Its world is partly supersensory and partly sensory, but only in the sublimest and noblest aspects of sensory reality." It is art with saving graces, "intentionally blind to everything debasing, vulgar, ugly, and negative in the empirical world of the senses," and its style is "partly symbolic and allegoric, partly naturalistic," while its emotional tone is "serene, calm, and imperturbable." Idealistic art is regarded by Sorokin as "a marvelous synthesis of the ideational and the noblest forms of sensate art," and the artist becomes merely the *primus inter pares* of the community in which he is a respected member.[37]

The dominant form in the fine arts during the last five centuries in the West has been the sensate form, in Sorokin's view, although the idealistic form has occurred many times in certain places. The idealistic period closed at the end of the fifteenth century, however, and since then there has been a decline in the ideational form together with the progressive rise of the sensate form in most of the fine arts. We see this, he says, in the overwhelmingly secular character of the arts; in the formula "art for art's sake," as against the ideational relation of art to religion, moral, and civic values; in its emotional, *pathetique*, and sensational and even voluptuous tone; in its realistic, naturalistic, or visual style reflecting merely the surface of empirical phenomena; and in illusionistic devices tending "to produce a show, reflecting surface appearances rather than the substance itself."[38]

"Modernism" in all of the arts—impressionism, cubism, futurism, pointillism, expressionism, Dadaism, constructivism, and so on—indicates a revolt against the debased forms of sensate art. Sorokin does not regard this modernism as a new organic form of Western art that is destined to dominate the decades and centuries to come. When he spoke of this effect over twenty years ago Schoenberg and Hindemith were regarded as musical modernists; and of course now they have been displaced by others who are even more "modern." Nevertheless, Sorokin's point is still relevant: "modern art is one of transition from a disintegrating sensate to an ideational or idealistic form, . . . is revolutionary *vis-à-vis* the dominant sensate form . . . but has not yet arrived at any definite goal."[39] Its positive aim is not as clear as its negative program of revolution. It is "hypersensate" in that it is not yet devoted to supersensory or idealistic purposes.[40]

With this somewhat inadequate review of Sorokin's thesis before us we may well ask how it is that art adumbrates the fate of a culture? The clue, so far as the "sensate" culture is concerned, lies in the analysis of the roots of its disintegration. The modern sensate culture, in Sorokin's view, emerged with a major belief that true reality and true value were mainly, or exclusively, sensory.

Art, in this respect, is not so much a harbinger of a new day as it is a delicately poised indicator of the storm just ahead. But art, like other fields of human activity, is not merely a barometer. It is capable of reflecting and realizing the great values of a culture at its best, and particularly of that succeeding culture that hopefully lies ahead, whether it is to be ideational, idealistic, or integral. When, as Sorokin hopes, we shall have re-examined the main premises and values of the sensate culture, rejected its superannuated pseudo-values, and re-enthroned its discarded real values, then we shall have recognized that "sensory reality and value are but one of the aspects of the infinitely richer true reality and value; that these have a supersensory aspect of which we get a glimpse through our reason and through charismatic grace or intuition in its sublime forms; that this supersensory side is the supreme aspect of the value-reality, and as such it is absolute; and that the same is true in regard to the reality and value of man and of the sublimest flowers of his culture."

The resultant integration of the aims of science, religion, philosophy, ethics, and art would then be accompanied by a transformation of social relationships and forms of social organization. Organizations of the "superripe sensate culture" do not represent absolute but only relative and instrumental values. "Purer and more familistic relationships" are Sorokin's prescription for the replacement of "compulsory and contractual relationships." There is a decided religious tone to his formula for the way out of our present predicament: "crisis — ordeal — catharsis — charisms — resurrection." The fine arts, together with the other major institutions of society, will participate integrally in this "resurrection" as well as in the preceding stages of the change-over. This ethical function of art is undoubtedly more important to Sorokin than its barometric function.

Conclusions

The growth of a new science of policy—the study of decision processes—as applied to large organizations like the modern corporation is on the verge of embracing in its multidisciplinary approach the uses of art as a sciential department of human activity.

In this chapter we have seen repeated instances of the *knowing* artist, not perhaps as an individual creator of a special form of expression in the arts but rather as a part of a civilization at a certain stage of its cultural development. Art can be an indicator in this sense; and the analyst of social trends is always on the alert for reliable indices.

The undeveloped status of the sociology of art is such that this kind of social indicator is still indeterminate. Yet many studies to date clearly indicate potentialities not to be ignored by policymakers in both public and private sectors. The current efforts to "promote" culture by aiding artists and underwriting the so-called cultural boom, however, have very little to do with the necessity we are under of giving more serious and studious attention to the arts. We may need the artist as much as the scientist and the engineer. We probably have neglected to note the scientific aspects of that need.

This still leaves one far from a proper assessment of art as a path to knowledge, and especially of knowledge useful to large organizations. Granted that the artist has special sensors of use to social analysts. But corporations, as organizations, are not well equipped to take the artist's feel for social trends into their productive processes. I refer here in particular to those staff functions that have to do with long-term trend analysis. They are ill-equipped to do so because of their own stringencies as well as the stringencies of the artist.

Corporate trend-analysts, as well as those in the public sector, labor under culture-bound traditions of "conventional wisdom": the disparateness of Art and Science, puritanical assumptions about the nature and functions of Art, mutual intolerance of artists and scientists for each other's way of reading Truth and Reality, and a general visual and tonal illiteracy in the population from which the major decision-makers are drawn.

It may be that the most useful way to overcome this artistic illiteracy and to persuade an upcoming generation of corporate executives (as well as those in government) that art must be taken seriously is simply to hammer away at art as a path to knowledge. Realization of the complementary nature of Art and Science will be slow in coming, but it can be hastened if we remember Whitehead's observations that "Art has a curative function in human experience when it reveals as in a flash intimate, absolute Truth regarding the Nature of Things," and that "the service of Art is even hindered by trivial truths of detail."[41]

Long ago John Dewey reminded us that "the first intimations of wide and large redirections of desire and purpose are of necessity imaginative." Art is "a mode of prediction not found in charts and statistics." Rather it "insinuates possibilities of human relations not to be found in rule and precept, admonition and administration."[42]

CHAPTER V

Art, Business,
and the Moralities

The executive function of "moral creativeness" has been called the highest expression of responsibility, and responsibility—the most constant aspect of leadership—is the hallmark of greatness in the leadership of the modern corporation.[1] This idea is pertinent in considering the peculiar interplay of forces that occurs when business enters the realm of art. The interrelationship of ethics and esthetics, of the Good and the Beautiful, is an ancient philosophical inquiry. Less explored is the three-way relationship among art, business, and the moralities.

Executive Responsibility and Conflicting Codes

We consider the *moralities* in the light of Chester Barnard's observation that a responsible man is one whose private code of morals controls his conduct in the presence of strong contrary desires or impulses, but that in a contemplated course of action he is usually confronted with *a conflict of codes*. His code as a churchman may conflict with his code as a citizen; his code as an artisan, scientist, or professional, may conflict with his code as an organization man; his code as a good parent protective of his family may conflict with his codes derived from other sources, and so on.

In making this observation, Barnard did not assume that one code is necessarily, universally, and intrinsically superior to the others, or that there is a fixed hierarchy of codes. He simply defined responsibility as "the property of an individual by which whatever morality exists in him becomes effective in conduct." Of special interest is his further comment that there are wide variations in the number of codes that govern the conduct of men. The principal factors that govern this number are the number of organizations to which persons are attached and the variety of their physical and social activities. An executive position brings to a man a complex morality, demands a high capacity of responsibility under conditions of activity, and necessitates "commensurate general and specific technical abilities as a *moral* factor." But, even more than this, an executive position requires "the faculty of *creating* morals for others."[2]

Barnard's observations on the nature of executive responsibility, were not made with the corporate-arts relationship in mind, but they are relevant to the closer collaboration of art and business. A new code seems to be emerging to further complicate the executive task— *a code of corporate esthetics.* Moreover, the leaders of the great corporations have the task of *creating* such a code for the guidance of others, both within the organization and those outside who press their demands on a company. It is usual, for example, to hear that business has a responsibility to support the arts. It is not so usual to hear why this is so, aside from the irrelevant assumption that the modern corporation is a repository of wealth and ought to be the contemporary parallel of a rich Renaissance patron of the arts. The contemporary corporate executive has a far more difficult ethical assignment with respect to esthetic action than the Renaissance patron had.

The nature of executive responsibility in the modern corporation is a far more complex matter, not necessarily because the conflicting codes are more numerous today, but because they are different in content. There are not only the organization codes to which the corporate executive should conform—codes that inhere in the structure and processes of his own company—but codes inherent in the company's external relationships.[3] The scope of these external relationships has grown to embrace many areas that, only a decade or so ago, would have been regarded as extremely peripheral. But now these external relationships are of major significance to the profitability, and even the survival, of a company. Corporate relations with the arts symbolizes one of these new external relationships.

The corporate-arts relationship raises two kinds of responsibility issues: (1) issues that arise generally from the number and complexity of codes, and (2) those which arise specifically in the interplay of business and the arts. Before we turn to the second question, which involves the old problem of ethics and esthetics in a new corporate context, we must pause to examine the implications of the first one. In the conflict of moralities—always demanding but now more so with the introduction of a new esthetic code—what executive requirements arise from the necessity of *creating* a code for the corporate-arts relationship?

Moral Creativity

The duty to create moral codes for others is undoubtedly a distinguishing mark of executive responsibility. Conflicts of codes are inevitable. These conflicts must be faced constantly in the struggle to maintain cooperation among men in order to promote the total organization effort. One way out of a conflict situation of this kind is to find some concrete, correct action that violates no established code. But the creation of a more general rule, of a new moral code for those within the organization, was for Barnard sometimes the only way out and was in fact the outstanding executive function. It is a method of conflict resolution that requires imagination, invention, and innovation in finding new detailed purposes of action that are consistent with the general objectives of a company.

In the search for more comprehensive statements of the general purposes of a company, so as to accommodate new codes, corporate leaders today have to consider carefully the external social, political, and economic norms and processes that affect the internal collaborative effort. The educational process is an example.

Corporate concern for the educational process in society affects the recruitment of adequately prepared personnel, the development of products and services, the public's acceptance of a fruitful system of corporate capitalism. The nation's educational objectives and effectiveness of the educational process are now generally recognized as having a direct bearing on a company's destiny. The effect has been to create a new code of corporate conduct vis-à-vis educational institutions and the education community generally. It is a code not limited to corporate financial support but extending to many kinds of relationships with educational institutions at all levels and touching disciplines in the liberal arts as well as scientific and technical fields.

Corporate relationships with the scientific community offer another example of the necessity of executive responsibility for the creation of new codes. The aggressive advancement of new knowledge through pure and applied science is more than an educational process. It reaches out into many kinds of organizations and sectors of society with which corporate relationships are often of vital importance. Companies concerned with advancing the frontiers of knowledge in special fields of science must create new codes governing the right to know, to inquire freely, to have access to data that others want to withhold, to preserve proprietary information, and so on. The creation of new codes is a requirement of executive function that increases with the augmentation of knowledge.

The introduction of new purposes of corporate work, including now the esthetic purpose, complicates the executive function. Executive responsibility means reconciling all of the various codes under general corporate purposes. The resolution of conflicts of

118

codes really necessitates the creation of more widely conceived general objectives; this way out, as Barnard clearly saw, involves a species of executive moral creativity. The function of moral creativeness becomes especially difficult with the addition of a substantive area such as esthetics, which seems to many businessmen quite remote from the world of affairs.

Creating a Corporate Esthetic Code

When he is confronted with a conflict of codes of corporate conduct that have almost equal validity or power, an executive hopefully will avoid either paralysis of action, which leads to frustration, or conformance to one code, thereby violating the other. Instead of these undesirable outcomes, one wants a new kind of action worked out imaginatively to meet all the requirements of the situation so as to threaten no established code but rather to strengthen the old ones while pointing policy in more promising directions.

The relatively new code specifying corporate financial support of education, for example—although simply rejected by some companies as contrary to received legal and economic principles and accepted by others as a concession to external pressure but regarded as really violative of the old codes—has been developed by a third category of companies imaginatively and constructively to implement established corporate objectives. In this third category of companies, furthermore, efforts have been made to revise the law of corporate powers to provide the requisite juristic structure for corporate support of education. The purpose has been not to depart from good business practice of profitable operation and to convert the corporation into a philanthropist, but rather to reconstruct the general purpose and powers of corporate entities so that managerial action might extend to strengthening the educational sector of the corporate environment as a matter of business judgment.

Something of the same process of evolution is now occurring in the emergent code of corporate esthetic action. For some, any move in this direction will be resisted; there will be no company action at all in a corporate-arts interplay even to examine the case, and the result will be frustration, blockade, a loss of decisiveness in dealing with the issues as they inevitably arise in this area of corporate policy. There will also be a good deal of emotional tension both within the management and the community of artists. In other companies there will be too ready an attempt to placate the artistic community and its promoters for reasons of expediency, followed by a sense of guilt that the more traditional codes have been violated, and by a loss of confidence in management. Finally, in the leader group of companies—probably a minority, but also probably including in prominence some of the great institutional businesses—executive managers will find new paths that neither violate the established corporate codes nor duck a relationship that requires imaginative and constructive effort in unexplored terrain.

Any proposed new code of corporate conduct makes demands on executive leaders that men of weak responsibility or limited capability cannot carry. When they are overloaded, and especially with proposed new codes that further heighten the condition of complex morality inherent in large organizations, their response is a measure of their mettle. It is normal to require executives to live with what Barnard called a "conflict of moralities." The codes men live by are never singular, simple, and completely consistent with each other, and in large companies the resolution of conflicts of this kind is standard operating procedure. But new codes generate special stresses. On the technical side, they demand knowledge that has traditionally been alien to business management; and on the side of expanding external relationships they demand new organizational components with specialized staffs if the executive is not to be overwhelmed with the new relations.[4]

This principle applies with special force in the case of a new esthetic corporate code. The new code will be a set of norms for corporate relations with the community of the arts and for conduct of company operations in accordance with esthetic conceptions and standards that most executives have never examined. Many thorny philosophic issues arise, some of which must be firmly rejected as irrelevant, while others must be met head on as a matter of corporate policy concerning relationships with artists and art institutions.

A basic question involves the moral purpose of art, a kind of purpose that is heartily denied by some artists and estheticians but which has been a philosophical "staple" since Plato. In present terms, it will be argued that corporate rectitude (and who will deny that a corporate purpose is to do the right thing?) has its esthetic dimension; that a company must at least adhere to the community's standards of Beauty as well as those of Goodness; and that today a company is expected to do more: to promote the national cause of Beauty in the arts.

Here, of course, another thorny issue arises—is Beauty the aim of art, or is that aim something else? What is the real function of the arts? Is it a corporate function in any practical sense? If the pursuit of Beauty seems too remote for the practical businessman, what about the pursuit of Truth, both in its moral and metaphysical dimensions? We have considered the latter dimension in an earlier chapter. Here we turn to the moral one.

Today a new kind of corporate institution has become so intimately tied into the societal process that the artistic values stressed in a nation's goals inevitably appear in corporate objectives. In our society today there is a reach for new values, including those values esteemed in the arts. The reach now has the dimensions of a national moral purpose. It is this societal involvement at a time of cultural upsweep that necessitates careful attention to the moral aspects of an esthetic corporate code.

Art and Eros are associates in a world that the corporate executive is urged to understand. The ethical function of art, as philosophers have seen it, is worth more than passing notice. Art, it is said, can save us from the "meaningless dynamism" of an automated "pseudo-culture." Art is called upon to help bridge the chasm between the "two cultures." These are some of the issues that now knock at the doors of executive suites as the corporation faces the arts in dead earnest and not merely as a dilettante.

Eros and the Arts

Late in his life, and even before the Second World War, Sigmund Freud asked whether mankind was headed for self-destruction or preservation. Would men overcome the frightening derangements of communal life caused by the human instinct of aggression and self-destruction? Or would their vast powers of subduing the forces of nature now be used to exterminate the species to the last man? We now know that this latter choice is possible. This constant awareness of Thanatos seems to cause a prevailing mood of apprehension, a dejection of spirit. Yet Freud, who always was aware of the "eternal Eros"—the other of the two "heavenly forces" competing in the breast of man—hoped that this Eros would put "forth his strength so as to maintain himself alongside his equally immoral adversary."[5]

The dilemma has been stated many times before and since. It has become more awesome with the advent of the nuclear space age. But troubled men have stated this fundamentally ethical problem in ecological terms long before the age of mutual terror. They have asked what we must do to preserve an environment that will not only sustain mankind but also assure us of progressive moves toward civilization. In the past when mankind had not yet learned either to live with itself or with its natural environment, the question was one of human ecology as well as biological adaptation in the more primitive sense. But now we seem unable to keep pace with our technics. Wise men had seen that this was so long ago. Today, everyone realizes it for, in the nuclear age, it is a lesson with awful impact on the masses of men. How can men be made equally aware of the eternal Eros, the other immortal adversary?

For the answer to this question one might turn to the moralists, the theologians, the contemporary sages of public philosophy. However, it is doubtful that these are the only sources of useful response nowadays. In fact, they are possibly not even the most dependable sources. Nor does the House of Science seem to be a promising source

122

of such wisdom. Science does not yield knowledge of the Good. Its purpose is otherwise directed to the nature of the universe stated in ethically neutral terms. So, in the greatest age of science in the history of man, we stand before Freud's basic issue, still searching even more anxiously than before—for the key to the riddle. Art may have some answers.

It is not surprising that artists express their anxiety more vividly than anyone else. The Absurd in art is one response to the hard riddle.[6] It is no solution, but the sensitivity of the artist provides us with useful clues. Esthetic statements of the anxiety of our age may not satisfy the logician. However, they might bring us somewhat closer to an understanding of our dilemma. We have learned that exactitude cannot always be expected even of the scientist. Fuzziness of esthetic statement in art may not be directly comparable with probability in science. Yet, not a few scientists find parallels here. As we have seen in earlier chapters, art is a way of knowing, an ally of science. Is it also a possible way of access to moral truths?

The relation between ethics and esthetics is suggested in the assertion that art, as a social institution, has moral dimensions, despite frequent efforts to deny this. In the great ecological drama of Eros versus Thanatos it is natural that the great corporations, like great artists, should engage in the search for preferred outcomes. The search for answers brings these two salient institutions—art and the corporation—into some kind of alliance. It is an alliance with several dimensions. The corporation is already deeply involved in the search for scientific truth and the dissemination of knowledge through educational institutions. But the involvement of the corporate institution in art's ethical implications is a step beyond this concept.

Consider certain issues that currently confront corporate policy-makers with increasing urgency. The problem of corporate ecology, especially for large companies that operate nationally and transnationally, raises issues in which Eros and Thanatos are almost baldly pitted against one other. Danger lurks in a natural environment that we have too long neglected as a presumably inexhaust-

123

ible resource for clean air, fresh water, food and fiber, a bountiful ecosystem that we have unbalanced. The "natural beauty" that we now seek to preserve in a hesitant national effort is really a long, and in some instance almost a disastrously, neglected ecological goal. Abroad, the dangers to national security and to the precarious non-system of jerry-built order in the international arena warn of threats to corporate survival, to say nothing of prosperity. Yet, at the same time, there is the amazing, pervasive, crescent vitality of peoples and cultures and the creativity of man that beckons one on and says that, with insight, we will find the way out of our labyrinth. The insight of the artist may be as important to us as the sight of the scientist.

Here the creative urge in the corporate institution can be allied with the creativity of the artist. We see it superficially in the growing use of art as embellishment in the world of commerce and industry. But the more interesting manifestation of the new alliance is not here but rather in the laboratories, the studios, the workshops where the talent of artist and scientist now receive more and more encouragement. In our nuclear age, against the terrifying threats of Thanatos there are also the life-giving and life-bettering forces of a defiant Eros. Business institutions now are called upon—and in the best companies they initiate the call—to assert this vitality in various ways. The new mandate goes beyond mere productivity and profitability in strict economic terms. It is a thrust for new values. And among these new values, clearly apparent in corporate policies today, are esthetic goals closely allied with ethical aims.

The danger of mixing art and morals is obvious. The ideological-esthetic controversies of communist regimes can be found, in reverse, in other societies supposedly free. The cruel scythe of the brutalitarian who commands that there be only a sanitized art of ideological purity is more terrifying than the quieter imposition of codes of artistic and intellectual orthodoxy on this side of the wall. In both cases, however, there is an alleged moral purpose in the standards imposed upon artists and other intellectuals. In both cases, the imposition can have a deadly effect on the creative mind. Art may ennoble a civilization for all time, as with the Greek *polis* at the height of its cultural development. On the other hand, official art is not always so noble. Nor can one be sure that organized standards, whether in public or private sectors, for esthetic creativity will always be a benign influence. On the contrary, there is strong likelihood that they will be baneful. The chilling potentialities of Organization Art make it essential for us to pursue the question of the ethical function of art.

The Ethical Function of Art

"Beauty is the highest expression of morality." Frank Lloyd Wright's maxim is indicative of a long and noble tradition. Not that the Beautiful is superior to the Good, but that the two are universals so intimately related that one cannot sensibly be discussed without reference to the other. Art is said to be a "window of reality."[7] It helps us to glimpse a reality beyond the realm that we are normally aware of. It is an ally in the search for Truth. Art has also long been allied with the formation of character, with the search for the highest ethical values, especially in the educational process. From the standpoint of corporate policy on the corporate-arts relationship, the ethical function of art is even more important than art as a way of knowing. Yet the two kinds of search are so bound together that only artifice can separate them.

In Eastern philosophy, perhaps more than in Western thought, the ethical dimension of art is notable. In the Shingon doctrine, for example, introduced into Japan in the ninth century, art was regarded as one of the noblest ways of reaching perfection in the Buddhist sense. In the West, where many have looked upon objects of art as merely decorative or useful for nonesthetic ends, it is hard to grasp this Eastern concept of the artist's task. The Shingon artist translated the invisible forces of the universe into visible material. The training of the hands with chisel and brush was a nobler, less egoistical, kind of yoga. It was a kind of union with the divine. Calligraphic writing in China was regarded as expressive of the

125

character of the wielder of the brush. Among the canons of painting laid down in the fifth century by Hsieh Ho, the first was that a masterpiece must exemplify life-motion engendered by spiritual harmony. In the Meditation School of early Chinese Buddhism, "penetration of the Buddha-mind" as the way of enlightenment was, and still is, in part an esthetic exercise.

In neo-Confucianism, the "investigation of things," basic to the realization of principle, depended in part on art both for objective observation and intuitive understanding. Chinese architecture under this influence expressed an imperative: special regard for the spirits of earth, water, and air, a search for harmony with the underlying creative forces of nature and not an attempt to dominate it by man-made constructions. In the *Li Chi*, or Book of Rites, an ancient literary classic, a section (perhaps a later interpolation) is devoted to the ethical, ritual, and symbolic aspects of music. Painting, a branch of handwriting, was the preeminent art of the Chinese. There the emphasis was always on the contemplative life, on the principle of balance.

Artistic influence from central and western Asia reached China in connection with the introduction of Buddhism from India. Religio-ethical influences of Hinduism, through art, on the rest of Asia, were profound and extensive. The equal legitimacy in Hindu theory of the instinctive, moral, and spiritual aspects of man is no mere scriptural matter; it was pervasive in the life of the East.[8] The art of right living was intimately associated with the arts, as in the observation of ceremonial purity at the periodical festival of a village deity and the reverence for finely presented figures of the gods.

In the arts of both the East and the West Benjamin Rowland, Jr., has distinguished between traditional and nontraditional types of expression. Traditional art is especially important for the ethical and religious life of a people. Nontraditional art may fashion the creative works of painters, sculptors, architects, and industrial designers for utility or an intrinsic esthetic value. But in traditional art even the slightest articles of everyday use may be shaped for more specifically magical or religious purposes. With appropriate sym-

126

bolism an *objet d'art* may reveal certain supernatural powers that are believed to govern the terrestrial order. Rowland calls such art *magic* because its purpose is either "to give man control over the great powers that he represented in symbol or to enable him to apprehend the infinite, as displayed in a tangible icon or diagram."[9]

Realistic representation is not sought in symbolism; rather the artist and the beholders of his work in a traditional society need only to recognize the essence of the thing portrayed. There may in some cases be rigorous rules prescribing for the artist the material, the technique, the laws of proportion and measurement and of color and arrangement, even under the stern supervision of a priestly class, that he must follow for the conceptualization of the forces, the gods, or other things symbolized. The "unrealistic" distortions of human figures and other objects in such art may seem quite irrelevant, or even highly appropriate, to the traditional artist and his associates. The idea is not to record the outward appearances of nature but rather, as Rowland observes, to utilize the natural form to represent the inner spirit, thus paraphrasing a Chinese esthetic axiom, "He paints the idea and not merely the shape."[10]

The ethical function of art, thus illustrated from other cultures and earlier times, has contemporary and permanent relevance. Art symbolizes and articulates feeling, as S. K. Langer has reminded us, because we have to understand feeling to keep ourselves oriented to society and to nature.[11] She speaks of art as having an intellectual and biological importance adding up to a moral value. Symbolized and objectified feelings on a *total* gamut are a necessity in a mature and self-aware civilization. A serious function of society, in its several departments, is to provide for artistic expression along this total spectrum, for only in this way can man follow the Greek prescription of the good life: Know Thyself. Self-awareness through science and discursive logic alone is not possible.[12] It is especially from this point of view that a corporate esthetic code may be regarded as an important aspect of corporate policy—a code of corporate conduct, that is to say, which specifies certain discretionary courses of executive action concerning the arts.

Art and Corporate Ethics

The norms of corporate conduct are sometimes externally determined, as in the case of legal obligations of directors and those to whom they may delegate authority. But they are also self-generated, and this applies especially to a corporate esthetic code. There are some obligations to act or not to act in pursuit of esthetic goals. But generally it is up to each company to decide for itself what it will or will not do to help or hinder the advancement of the arts for esthetic purposes. It is highly debatable what the esthetic ends of art are. When the estheticians disagree, there is surely no prescribed corporate doctrine of Beauty or of any other value that may be assumed for art. Yet there may be a corporate ethical obligation to take positions on specific issues concerning a company's relations with artists, the community of artists, and art institutions, or with others outside the company on matters that involve esthetic value.

The question of esthetic value, like all axiological issues, is one of much philosophical complexity.[13] One of the major problems is whether ethical and esthetic values are mutually exclusive, and if not, how they are interrelated. We shall assume here, with John Dewey, that one of the functions of art is "to sap the moralistic timidity that causes the mind to shy away from some materials and refuse to admit them into the clear and purifying air of perceptive consciousness;"[14] that a moral function of art is "to remove prejudice, do away with the scales that keep the eyes from seeing, tear away the veils due to wont and custom, perfect the power to perceive"; and that art can indeed be more moral than the moralities.[15]

Esthetic norms may, in other words, run counter to some presumably decisive mores. At times we seem to depend on the artist to "keep alive the sense of purposes that outrun evidence and of meanings that transcend indurated habit."[16] Because the artist is capable of this, there is always the tendency to suppress him when he ques-

128

tions the received dogmas. He is denounced as immoral, unpatriotic, antisocial, counterrevolutionary, guilty of left- or right-wing deviationism, and so on. But, as Dewey observed, it is in character for the creative mind to reach out and seize any material that stirs it so that the value of that material may be pressed out and become the material of a new experience.

It may be popularly thought that in this clash between art and certain of the moralities, business will always be allied with the status quo, and that the corporation as an institution cannot be expected to foster the arts without great discrimination, implying an overly moralistic attitude. This is undoubtedly true of some businessmen. But one is reminded of Schumpeter's view of the function of the enterprisers: to reform, to revolutionize, to innovate; capitalism is not stationary, is by its nature a form or method of economic change, is involved in a process of industrial mutation that "incessantly revolutionizes the economic structure *from within,* incessantly destroying the old one, incessantly creating a new one."[17] He called this the process of Creative Destruction, an essential fact about capitalism. There are interesting parallels in the creative processes of artists and entrepreneurs.

Art Versus "Meaningless Dynamism"

Too much may be claimed for the morality of art; but the danger is that there will be insufficient recognition of its ethical value. It is said that poets, rather than scientists, technicians, and statesmen, will have to lead mankind out of the chaos and bewilderment of contemporary life because only the poet can "see around the unknown curve to guess by means of intuitive wisdom what the unborn thing we call our future will grow into."[18]

It is trivial to quibble about the word "only." We seek guidance wherever we can find it, and that is as true of corporate policy (or should be) as it is of personal choices. In an age of high science and superb technics the artist is apt to be underrated on this score. We may even find it good to seek guidance from those who, with Blake, held Art to be "the tree of Life" and denounced Science as "the tree of Death." Or from those who insist that economics and art are strangers. Or from those who insist that the Two Cultures are irrevocably opposed and mutually exclusive, and offer the humanities as the only road to freedom. From all of these dissenting notes one gathers a general complaint that art is neglected in a society that claims to be a great society.

But there is more to the complaint than this. And the further elements of the bill of particulars sometimes point straight to the modern corporation as the dominant instrument of our industrial era. It is said to be an era on the verge of disintegration, an era of directionless and meaningless dynamism. Lewis Mumford charges that it is one in which most of the creative energies have been canalized into the Machine—"a systematic organization of scientific discovery and technical invention that, under the pressure of excessive pecuniary gains and exorbitant political power, has transformed the entire existence of the Western World."[19] In this insensate dynamism, he says, there are no goals, only ceaseless expansion and inflation, breaking down the continuities of history and leaving the human self, so dependent on the past, with a loss of both continuity and identity. The discovery of human beauty in ancient religious esthetics is contrasted with the deformation, even the desecration, of the human form in our own day.

Reviewing the work of Sigfried Giedion,[20] Mumford deplores that path of the modern movement in art which moves in the direction of "non-sense, cultivated perversity, self-destructive dynamism, countering the rigidities of mechanism and automation with the psychotic freedom of purposeless 'happenings' and intentional nothingness." He allies himself rather with that other path of the modern movement indicated by Giedion, "toward recovering and reaffirming those values that contemporary art, in its first youthful rebellion, in its healthy effort to break down an overfixation upon a limited portion of the past and upon overrefined technique, had too peremptorily denied."[21]

Mumford, of course, does not extend his condemnation to the modern corporation per se, but in his demand, with Giedion, for continuity, for "respect for the human constants" not only in art but in our culture generally, and for repudiation of mechanization and industrial efficiency as ends in themselves, there is an implicit norm for the most influential of modern forms of organization, of which the corporation is undoubtedly outstanding. Giedion had declared in 1948 that mechanization, as envisaged and realized in our epoch, is "the end product of a rationalistic view of the world." Mumford regards this as far from complimentary on Giedion's part. He credits Giedion with seeing that "mechanization was already beginning its sterile intervention in organic processes, toward the result that 'death, generation, birth, habitat' would all 'undergo rationalization, as in the later phases of the assembly line.' "[22] And he quotes Giedion's final chapter in *Mechanization Takes Command*, a chapter interestingly entitled "Man in Equipoise," in stating the necessary remedy: "To control mechanization demands an unprecedented superiority over the instruments of production. It requires that everything be subordinated to human needs."[23]

Just as Le Corbusier had made a *volte-face* in his design of the Ronchamp church—defiantly turning his back on all the dogmas about mechanization, rationalization, and modern form that he had espoused earlier, and seeking inspiration in the remote beginnings of art—so Giedion returns to the eternal elements of beauty as against the modernist deformation of it. We must find our way back, Mumford declares, to the great human constants, the only safeguards against the directionless and meaningless dynamism of our humanly empty world "in which a power-seeking science belittles every human expression that does not lend itself to profitable scientific manipulation, in which automation releases us from the joy of work, and in which computers take over the rational functions of mind—leaving its growingly irrational contents to be dealt with by sedatives, hypnotics, tranquillizers, hallucinogens, and general anesthesia, collectively administered and—by 1984, perhaps, officially controlled."[24]

Art, Business, and the "Two Cultures"

Mumford's view may seem too gnarled and negative. Yet, it holds out an affirmative promise for the moral role of art, while sternly rejecting much of its modern manifestations. The clash between art and other institutions of modern culture,[25] however, is often taken in absolute terms, as though the humanities—of which art is a part of this confrontation—were somehow the St. George against the modern dragon of Science. In this confrontation, the modern business corporation is apt to find itself caught in a struggle that it had hardly wanted to engage in. But the engagement cannot thereby be avoided. A part of the interplay between the corporation and the arts today is this alleged antithesis of the Two Cultures.

The more reasonable view is to accept with gratitude the developments of science and technology, as well as the call to humane values that we have been fortunate enough to inherit. Science and technology free us from ignorance and superstition, help us to come to terms with our environment, and explode myths that impede the road to a better way of life. On the other hand, the vision that elevates man in mind and deed comes from the humanities. Science and technology can lead either way, upward toward that vision or downward to total destruction; the fearful effectiveness of the means they provide only serves to underline the importance of clearly envisioned ends.

Yet goals that once were dismissed as visionary now seem attainable through science and technology. The major organizational instruments for attaining these goals are the state and the corporation. The modern state is being mobilized for this purpose, and not only for limited policing and protective functions. It is to be expected that the corporation will also be drawn into the service of the goals sought by the humanists and the idealists. The corporation cannot avoid the challenge, inasmuch as it possesses many of the necessary means.

"Two cultures" may have become a trite phrase; but the indicated conflict has not receded and will persist. C. P. Snow introduced the theme in the fifties.[26] It reflected, and sharpened, an academic controversy of long standing, perhaps more marked in British than in American universities. The issue was not limited to ivory towers on either side of the Atlantic, however. Sir Charles's theme was that intellectual life was being split into two camps, the scientists on one side and the cultural traditionalists on the other. Here were not only two hostile camps, but worse, belligerents practically without intercommunication, with little understanding of each other's culture, and with hardly any use for each other. The literary men were said to be quite ignorant of science, unaware of its importance, and even contemptuous of the scientist. Yearning for a long-lost glorious past, they were resentful of the strongly future-oriented scientific mind that spurned the heritage of art and literature.

This part of the argument had a familiar ring in general academic controversy. But Sir Charles went further; he pleaded for closing the gap between the two cultures because of the critical period the world faces today. The dangerous chasm between rich and poor nations, he said, now demands the recruitment and training of vast numbers of scientists and engineers, of managerial specialists and others capable of undertaking the vital mission of bridging this chasm. Western education, and especially British education, was in Snow's opinion in need of drastic alteration to meet this pressing need. The literary intellectuals in academia, he said, with their great influence on the whole sweep of nonscientific culture, stood guard at the ivy-covered gates against such academic *aggiornamento*.

Some sociologists, especially in the United States, rejected Snow's argument as simplistic dualism, insisting that they saw the need for revision clearly enough but rather in terms of the clash of *three* cultures. Sir Charles rejected this suggestion on the ground that all those, including the sociologists, who "naturally had the future in their bones" and had common attitudes, common standards and patterns of behavior, common approaches and assumptions, were on his side regardless of their disciplines. They were poles apart from the others who, with a total incomprehension of science, radiated their baleful influence on all the rest. And the polarization was sheer loss for everybody.

Sir Charles conceded that the culture of science did not have much to do with art, with the exception of music, and had little interest in nonscientific literature. The literary side was also impoverished, pretending absurdly that the traditional was the whole of "culture," and neglecting that great scientific edifice of the physical world, "in its intellectual depth, complexity and articulation, the most beautiful and wonderful collective work of the mind of man."[27] He deplored the literary culture's failure to grasp the cultural significance of that edifice. An intense literary and nonscientific specialization from early through advanced educational levels precluded any such understanding. He referred to the literary intellectuals responsible for this situation as "natural Luddites" who were at war with the scientific revolution just as their antecedents had been against the industrial revolution. Nor did he excuse a comparable benightedness among the scientists themselves: pure scientists and engineers often totally misunderstood each other. The conservatism of the latter was a hindrance to progress; but so was the "dimwittedness" of many pure scientists about engineering and applied science, which they too often dismissed snobbishly as occupations for second-rate minds.

In view of all these dangerous fissures in the academic mental structure, Snow demanded a radically new educational strategy for Britain in order to meet the requirements of the scientific revolution. It involved the necessity for careful estimates of a nation's needs in four categories: (1) "alpha plus" scientists; (2) a bigger substratum of alpha professionals to do the supporting research, the high-class design and development; (3) a third stratum in the thousands upon thousands to do the secondary technical jobs—some with major responsibility in the human jobs; and (4) "politicians, administrators, an entire community, who know enough about science to

134

have a sense of what the scientists are talking about." He knew, he said, that education was not the only remedy for the gap between the rich and the poor, "but without education the West cannot even begin to cope."[28]

In his "Second Look," Sir Charles responded to some of the criticism that greeted his first edition.[29] But he restated the original thesis quite as forcefully as he had at the start.[30] He hastened to add that the chasm between the two cultures in the United States was not nearly so unbridgeable as it was in Britain, and commented on the "resilience and inventiveness of American higher education." In both countries there was, he admitted, more concern for the problem he had raised in the social science disciplines and among the social historians than he had been aware of. A "third culture" was conceivably on the way, one more on speaking terms with the scientific culture. But he hardly relented in his urgent demand for an educated understanding of science, and this for strikingly humanistic reasons. He made a plea for more general understanding of molecular biology and the sciences of the higher nervous system. This might point the way out of "the facile social pessimism of our time," the "egocentric chill" that stresses our tragic solitariness as individuals.

The great stir over the "two-cultures" issue in intellectual circles may have had little reverberation in the world of corporate affairs. But the influence will eventually be felt. Those who attack "purblind science" are too often inclined to align themselves against the world of business (with its high dependence on technology) as a potential and covert, if not an overt, enemy. The designation would be shocking to most businessmen who do their best to support liberal arts colleges from which they graduated and have no wish to attack the arts. On the contrary, there is a slowly growing corporate support of the arts, both through direct financial aid to cultural centers, for example, and through augmented use of good art and architecture for industrial purposes.

In the United States, moreover, the confrontation has never been as acute as it is in Britain, partly because of our more varied educational systems, from state to state and as between public and private institutions. Yet even here there is a modified version of the basic conflict that Sir Charles describes. It is a conflict inherent, perhaps, in the nature of the scientific and technological revolutions that have transformed the modern world in a half century. The accusations of Giedion and Mumford indicate that this is not merely a British phenomenon.

For corporate leaders in the United States these currents and countercurrents of esthetic debate relate to corporate policy. A company does not like to be aligned in the public mind with antihumanistic movements. The dread influence of "meaningless dynamism" ought not to be ascribed to the modern corporation without good cause. The charge can be forestalled by corporate esthetic codes that make sense both from the business standpoint and to those in the antiscientific literary camp. Such codes must be realistically grounded. It is hazardous to suppose that this is merely an academic debate that touches few people in the mass. Ideas have wings. And the negative reaction to some aspects of corporate capitalism is not always due to writers and winged ideas.[31] A corporate esthetic code must be more than public relations whitewash. It has to be backed up with corporate action. The question is, what kind of action?

Art and Corporate Paideutics

The wiser course of action for most corporations is to base their new esthetic code not on vague and generalized ethical doctrine, on the one hand, or on transparent expediency, on the other. They would do better to move from familiar to unfamiliar ground, approaching esthetic policy on the basis of educational policies already developed. This is not the only approach to a corporate esthetic code, but it can be useful. Philosophically, the educational aspects of art have the most respectable auspices; and the tie between the institutions of art and culture, as instruments of education, and the corporation is already being made in many communities, if only through the medium of the donative power.

136

Corporate financial aid to education has been recently the most glamorous, if not the most significant, facet of a long-standing corporate concern for education. But the corporation as educator suggests far more varied, more interesting, and more promising facets of the relationship of business and academia. Among these facets is the esthetic dimension of corporate paideutics.[32] It is a relatively unexplored and unutilized aspect of corporate educational policy. In many companies, of course, it is not even yet recognized that there must be an important branch of corporate work devoted to education. The arts, as part of this effort, are the more remote from ordinary executive attention.

But we are now reaching a stage in the development of corporate external relations and the changing conception of corporate social responsibility where no responsible executive can afford to give the matter due attention. The impetus is of two kinds. To seek out and prepare men for executive positions requires attention to educational backgrounds of potential candidates for promotion; it is becoming more and more evident that narrow technical training is not enough. A broad education in the liberal arts is increasingly a requisite for the successful candidate; at least some exposure to the arts, in the sense that we have used the term in this book, is an essential part of that education.

But there is another kind of motive that drives business toward a more conscious and systematic concern for the arts in education. Financial support of education, begun on a large scale only during the past decade or so by the major corporations, was initiated as an emergency measure to help institutions in distress. But in the process of developing corporate policies to meet this presumably temporary and interim need, pending some long-range solution of the financial problem that was never well articulated, corporate leaders here and there did formulate an educational-support rationale that occasionally approached philosophic depth. The concept of education, the nature of educational goals, the breadth of the educational venture as a human effort, the need for continuity of this effort—all these considerations have led the more intellectually and esthetically aggressive executives to new avenues undreamed of in the first steps of corporate educational support.

The place of the arts in both these approaches to corporate paid-eutics—the education of corporate personnel, and the gradual establishment of organic corporate relationships with educational institutions—is one of the more exciting elements in corporate esthetics. It not only leads to the inspiring association with artists; it opens up new possibilities of dealing creatively with Barnard's "conflict of moralities." Education is, after all, essentially a moral pursuit, as all the great philosophers of education and of ethics since Plato have realized. Modern educators like Dewey, Whitehead, and Read have stressed the value, even the necessity, of introducing the arts into education (at all levels, at all ages of man) if its highest aims are to be realized. As the corporation gains institutional stature, the corporate responsibility for internal and external paideutic action necessarily embraces the arts. It has already been indicated in an earlier chapter how essential the arts are as a way of knowing. There is now a corporate responsibility, in the development and carrying out of educational policies, actively to introduce the arts.

To the value of art as a way of knowing truth in the sense of reality orientation, there may well be added its further value for truth in the ethical sense. Corporate policy can embrace the arts in educational programs on both grounds. The moral value of art is always an arresting issue; for the corporation the negative side of the matter deserves attention. Bad design, tasteless industrial architecture and urban planning are cases in point. The responsible corporation will take a stand on these matters, particularly when civic standards in the corporate environment are at stake. Yet the positive potentialities beckon. Beauty can help to liberate us from our prisons of ugliness. And whether or not beauty is the center of value-theory in art, there are several esthetic values that can claim our allegiance and release us from that obscurantism that makes life grimmer than it has to be.

If all this seems to make of art a mere utility, or to lead to a facile conclusion that art is a necessary part of education only because of its ethical purpose, we can at least avoid a narrowly moralistic view of that purpose. Alfred North Whitehead's two caveats are in order: "the concept of Art as the pursuit of Beauty is shallow"; and "Goodness must be denied a place among the aims of art."[33] But these statements, made within the context of the Whiteheadian metaphysics, must be taken together with his further view that Art has a "curative function." Its curative function in human experience occurs "when it reveals as in a flash intimate, absolute Truth regarding the Nature of Things."[34] Art also "heightens the sense of humanity," and incidentally serves society in that adventurousness which Whitehead prized.

The wonder of the human adventure is revealed more clearly in the humanities, and above all in the arts, than anywhere else. To open men's minds and hearts to the spirit of this adventure is a service above value. That is why art cannot be omitted from the scope of education. William Faulkner, in his speech of acceptance of the Nobel award, said that he labored as a writer to help men endure by lifting their hearts. In art, there may well be, as Whitehead said, a commingling of Beauty and Evil; but there has always been difficulty in drawing the lines among such absolutes.[35]

Art, Architecture, and Business Morality

Of the many ethical aspects of art with which corporate policy is concerned, hardly anything exceeds in importance the question of architecture. The subject is a large one; nevertheless it can be indicated by the insights of Le Corbusier.[36] The great Swiss-Gallic architect, convinced that machines would lead to a new order of work and of leisure, warned that entire cities had to be constructed or reconstructed, in order to provide even a minimum of comfort. Delay would endanger the balance of society. For society was unstable, "cracking under the confusion caused by 50 years of progress that have changed the face of the world." With the single-minded purpose of a zealot, Le Corbusier declared that this was not only an urgent problem but *the* problem of our time. His case, now that he is gone and we have all had time to think things over, will be increasingly examined.

In the book that contained his credo, *Toward a New Architecture*, the great "Corbu" exclaimed: "Architecture or Revolution!" Building, he insisted, is at the root of social unrest—or rather bad building and inadequate building. He readily conceded that man now lives in a new and better world that produces useful things. But man was still living in the old hostile environment. This environment— his lodging, his flat, his house, his street, his town—all rise up against him as useless hindrances against his following the same path in his leisure that he pursues in his work. They bar him from following in his leisure the organic development of his existence: "to create a family and to live, like every animal on this earth and like all men of all ages, an organized family life." Society in this way helps to advance the destruction of the family while watching, terror-stricken, the consequent destruction of society itself.

Le Corbusier believed that machines would lead to a new order of work and of leisure. He was no hidebound traditionalist. On the contrary, he hoped to liberate architecture from the tyranny of "style," to get away from freezing old habits in steel and stone, to turn architecture into a tool for making technical and social change a change for the better. When he made the famous remark that a house is "a machine to live in" his figure of speech was resented, but widely misunderstood. Wolf van Eckhardt's translation of the idea is that we must mass-produce elements of the house so that the poor man can live as decently as the rich man, that we must properly state the problem of the house in terms of modern needs and modern technology just as engineers must properly state the problem before they can design an airplane or an automobile. The traditional house, declared Le Corbusier, takes no account of man and is conceived as a furniture store. And today's city repudiates the existing layout in which the congestion of buildings grows greater, inasmuch as it is interlaced with narrow streets full of noise, gasoline fumes, and dust. The windows of the house open to this foul confusion. The great towns, he insisted, have become too dense for the security of their inhabitants. Yet they are not sufficiently dense to meet the new needs of modern business. He wanted a city of towers in which large numbers of people could dwell in "sun, space, and silence," the arterial roads running well away from these towers and separated from them by parks. For all this "the plan is the generator; without it, poverty, disorder, wilfulness reign supreme."[37]

Frank Lloyd Wright, no lover of cities, was nevertheless, like Le Corbusier, an exponent of the larger ethics of architecture. There are more examples of his work to be seen in the private than public sector of the United States, so little was he inclined to design public buildings. His views of "organic" or "usonian" architecture have been incorporated in some company structures, however, perhaps because the executives of these companies caught a glimpse of his ideals.[38] Wright insisted on a certain "continuity" that he found missing in most of our architecture today, a continuity that unites the interior and the exterior of a building, provides a repose due to unity and gives enjoyment of the environment.

The understanding of nature was Wright's key to this unity; in nature one found the pattern that was the wellspring of inspiration for the architect—the "nature pattern" that one sees everywhere in the poetic forms of flowers, trees, animals, and in music. "Pattern" for him was "the interior expression" of nature; architecture was the structure of patterns of materials and humans. He said that he was a follower of Paraclesus: bricks and stones were "alive"; the artist had to bring out the significance of this natural material. But the creative artist, as an interpreter of natural patterns, he insisted, would not disdain the machine; he would *use* the machine and not permit it to be destructive and murderous. In fact, he added, *the machine has to be in the hands of the creative artist* to prevent its being a destructive thing.

Perhaps Wright, Le Corbusier, and Mies van der Rohe, and other great architects of our time do not have the answers to the great questions of ethics that architecture turns up. Perhaps, as

Mumford has suggested,[39] contemporary architecture is in a state of irresolution and division that merely reflects the state of the world itself, that the school headed by van der Rohe "builds air-conditioned Ice Palaces for virginal Show Queens," and that headed by Le Corbusier "constructs romantic grottoes where the Tristans and Isoldes of our age may quaff not on love potions but nuclear poisons in murky solitude." Yet, a survey of the hopes and fears of modern architects from William Morris to Walter Gropius establishes the point we make here:[40] to build is to make ethical as well as esthetic choices. The modern corporation, one of the major builders, cannot avoid these ethical choices.

As Barnard observed, though not necessarily with architecture in mind, corporate leadership involves conflicts of moralities. This is especially true of the construction of industrial plants and a company's role in the planning of plant communities. A new science of *ekistics*—a comprehensive attack on making the man-made environment work better, the joint effort of architects and other professionals, including the scientists—has been called for by Constantinos A. Doxiadis, a famous Greek planner.[41] The necessary collaboration will also include top executives in the great corporations, and the real estate and banking firms that can sustain or veto the best plans of Doxiadis's "ekisticians."[42] It must include, furthermore, a reasonable public policy.[43] The corporation cannot do it all, but it can encourage the right public policies and support the right educational programs.[44]

Conclusions

Although nothing in art reveals so clearly as architecture the ethical dimensions of esthetic problems, similar themes can be found with respect to all the arts. They are themes of great significance to corporate executives searching for clues to sound codes of esthetics for guidance of company policy in relationships with the arts, and with all external interests where esthetic standards are involved. This is true for painting and sculpture, for the dance, theater, music, and the other performing arts, and for all, indeed, that falls along the wide spectrum of the arts as indicated in an early chapter in this book.

In assessing the ethical aspects of the arts, in fact, it is always hazardous to limit the discussion to one or few of them. That is why the more comprehensive approaches of Whitehead, Langer, and other philosophers is to be preferred to dissertations that are grounded on only one or two esthetic disciplines. This is especially important for the student of corporate-arts relationships, which cannot safely be blue-printed on the experiences of a specialized branch of the arts.

Nor is it safe to take either of two extreme positions in approaching the question of corporate esthetic codes (the plural is used because there are many autonomous companies that would not brook dictation, even if there were a single universal esthetic standard to which all could repair) : first, that all art must advance the Good— as one conceives it—or it is not good art; or second, that Art and Morals are disparates, that the artist has no moral purpose and cannot have if he is to be a good artist.

From the standpoint of corporate policymakers there is at least the question of indirect benefits to the corporation in any wise program of support for the arts, and this is an ethical—and not an esthetic—issue for the company. Utility is a norm that cannot be escaped in corporate policy, whatever may be said of utilitarianism and hedonism as abstract ethical norms. Also, the pursuit of beauty, the improvement of artistic expression, or any other goal of the artist has to be related in some practical way—that is to say, in philosophical terms, some ethical way—to the business objectives of a company.

It may well be that corporate objectives, in our age of institutional companies that seek greatness, have become less exclusively "materialistic" and more "idealistic" (question-begging terms) and that the esthetic aims of a company belong in the latter category. But why must one assume that the business corporation is per se indifferent to and even hostile to art? And why must it be conceded that an interest in art dilutes business purpose? Is there not a complementarity here that has been all too little explored—to the great disadvantage of both artist and businessman?

CHAPTER VI

The Corporate Reach
for New Values

The arts and the corporation, as institutions, are both evolving at so rapid a rate in this country that contemporary observers are likely to miss the significance of the change. The arts and the modern corporation have both attained new stature in recent decades.

A cultural renaissance is not merely reflected by current trends in the growth of cultural centers all over the nation, the enactment of legislation seeking candidly to beautify the environment and to support the arts and the humanities, and a boom in the sales of good records, concert tickets, art materials, and so on. Something is stirring that has long-range significance. The institutional structure of the arts is undergoing basic change and no one can predict the profound effect this change will have eventually on the tone of life in the United States.

At the same time, there is an evolution of the business corporation into a major, responsible, social institution. As we have indicated, this development, when it meets and crosses the path of the other development—the evolution of the arts in our society—the concurrent institutional changes are almost certain to be productive of a new chapter in American culture, one that could not have been predicted from the separate study of these institutional trends. Here, we shall make a brief survey of the corporate institutional development, and then go on, in later chapters, to show how the intersection of this trend with the trend in the arts may be expected to affect both of these institutions.

The Corporation of Tradition

The corporate institution of today, as compared with the corporation of traditional juristic and economic lore, has undergone a remarkable evolution. It used to be said that "commerce is piracy without manners." The modern corporation is no pirate. It has manners. How, then, can it be an instrument of commerce? The critics of commerce and corporations tend to see in business only the buy-cheap-sell-dear formula. The Robber-Baron age of the older capitalism is over. Yet critics too often assume the business corporation is motivated only by a ruthless drive toward maximum profit. An "artificial person" that can do everything but make love,[1] the business corporation is caricatured as an instrument cunningly contrived to be only a more mannerly pirate. Although corporate managers strive for a benevolent public image, the attempt is not always successful. The traditional "soulless" corporation has now been replaced by the figure of the "soulful" corporation that looks out, not only for its own good, but for the community good as well.

Yet contemporary corporate benevolence is suspect not only by the critics on the left. On the far right there are other critics who deplore the emergence of the social-minded corporation. These ultra-conservative critics think corporations ought to tend strictly to the single business of making a profit for its owners. They denounce corporate philanthropy and the diversion of gross receipts to any other purpose than necessary business expense. They reject the idea of any corporate-arts nexus.

146

These left- and right-wing critics of the modern corporation have a losing case. The great corporations do not follow the blueprints set for them in the literature, either of the conservative economists or the critics on the left. The policies adopted by the largest of the corporate leaders of the business world often fly in the face of the received dogmas of both classical economics and classic socialism. Indeed if one goes back to Adam Smith, Marx, and Marshall, the classical views reflected suspicion and even hostility toward capital combinations of the corporate type. Yet the great corporations of today have evolved to their present institutional position as though their directors were quite oblivious to the autonomous classical rationales.

It was less an unawareness of economic doctrine than the pressure of events that determined the trend of corporate institutional evolution. That course has been set less by economic theory, political diatribe, or legal lore than by demands made on the corporate institution by society. The corporation was legally an "artificial person,"[2] to be sure, but it was also a natural response of intelligent men to the ecological conditions of Western society.[3] A remarkably ingenious device from a legalistic point of view, the corporation as an institution of human cooperative effort was altogether natural and endowed with the vitality that is generated by common purposes. And since the corporation as a human institution necessarily reflects human attributes in the content of its policies, made as they are by men who must take the longer view, as in steering a ship, the "soulful" quality of corporate policy is hardly to be wondered at.

We should not be astonished at the emergence of the socially responsible corporation. This emergence was implicit from the start if the corporate idea was to take hold and not go the way of so many discarded social institutions in human history. The corporation is the servant, and not the master of men. To persist in the fallacy that it is the servant *exclusively* of the "economic man" would have doomed it as a viable institution.

The corporate device certainly fits beautifully the needs of cooperative effort among seekers of profit from pooled investment. But this is no adequate description of the great institutional companies we see today. The goals of these companies are so varied and so complex that they defy description in terms of single goals such as "profitability." Their goals are multiple and often reveal a great deal about the complexity of the managerial minds that guide their policy processes. It is often a very human quality that scarcely fits the mold of classical doctrine of the right or the left.

Yet we must take note of the fact that the vast majority of business companies still fit a different and more conventional mold. The corporation of tradition is still with us in large numbers, and in some respects it still influences the preponderant opinion in the business community. It is true that these companies are influenced by the great institutional corporations, and that even among some of the smaller ones a high degree of social responsibility evidently controls company policies. Corporate giving, for example, has often been more generous among medium-sized and smaller companies than among the largest, even though the large corporations are more capable of making big and decisive moves that break new donative paths. But by and large, the incorporated business of the United States is mainly profit-oriented. Companies in this category run into the hundreds of thousands. The great institutional companies are numbered in the hundreds. Their goals of profitability, however, are supplemented by a complex of objectives.

In the traditional corporation, directors' powers and responsibilities, derived from sovereign concession, are to be used solely for serving the property interests of the company's stockholders. There are, of course, secondary and tertiary responsibilities to creditors, to employees, to customers, to suppliers or vendors, and perhaps to a few others. But the primary responsibility is to those who have invested in the enterprise. In the traditional view much is made of the concession theory: that the right to act as a body corporate can be conceded only by the state. The original justification for this remarkably authoritarian doctrine was that, otherwise there would arise great corporate entities to threaten the power of the King in the form of "lesser common-wealths in the bowels of a greater, like

148

wormes in the entrayles of a naturall man," as Thomas Hobbes, the seventeenth century philosopher colorfully put it.[4]

In the beginnings of Anglo-American law concerning concession, however, the real reason for the sovereign's claim to monopoly over the creation of corporations may have been quite different. It is undoubtedly true that in late medieval England the monarchs who strove for national unity had to deal sternly with stubbornly independent towns, guilds, and ecclesiastical corporations that stood in their way. But the king's lawyers also had discovered that certain royal words and phrases were highly salable to towns enriched by trade and commerce. His charter could grant the right conferred by phrases such as: the right "to be forever corporate," to have fictitious personality, and to be "one perpetual community incorporate in word and deed." He was in a position to drive hard and fisty bargains with these thriving towns,[5] aided and abetted by his lawyers who had learned much from the Roman and canon law brought over by the Normans.

The idea of corporate personality is especially interesting because it winds up in the United States in the Fourteenth Amendment. In the Church, where abbatial rule was monarchical and monks were dead men in the law, the *ecclesia* or *abbatia* succeeded to all property rights, for example, the abbot being the mere transitional carrier of a *persona ficta* which was the continuously succeeding right-and-duty-bearing unit; the majority could bind the rest as in a modern stock company, and suit was brought by and against the fictitious *persona*. "Person," as a corporate entity, had already become a word of art, primarily as a result of the work of the medieval jurists, who in turn had learned from Justinian's lawyers how to think and speak of *collegia, sodalitates*, and *universitates* as collectivities capable of enjoying proprietary capacity within the range of private law.

The lawyers of ancient Rome had found the way, through such words and phrases, to distinguish sharply between the collectivity and its members. The *universitas* had separate rights and liabilities of its own; its property was not the property of the individual members; its responsibilities were not theirs. Even the Roman state, despite its numerous fiscal privileges peculiar to a public body, was treated—in the form of a *fiscus*—like a private person capable of holding property under the *jus privatum*.

This development in the ancient law had little or no relevance to the world of Roman business affairs;[6] corporateness was an instrument only of public entities, such as municipalities, and not, as in the modern world, of private business. As the historian Rostovtzeff has remarked, Roman law never mentions the kinds of stockholder companies so familiar to modern economies simply because they did not exist; joint capitalization was not the rule if, indeed, it ever occurred.[7] The Roman idea of corporateness served public bodies only.

In medieval England, the kings who seized on the corporate idea, backed up by the powerful premises of concession theory, had no thought whatever of forging an instrument for commercial use in what we call the private sector. It is true, however, that corporate autonomy already had its deep roots. When the English kings tried to palm off the essentially alien idea that boroughs had no life of their own except by royal grace and command, they ran into trouble. For, there was a strong Anglo-Saxon tradition that communal ties had deep native roots and grew not at all from the mere sowing of royal seeds.

There was resistance to the idea that, for example, the "borough of Holborn" was an entity only by royal concession, to be distinguished clearly in law from the "burgesses of Holborn," when as a matter of fact the five points of corporateness, allegedly permitted the borough only by charter, were not new at all. These five points were perpetual succession, the power of suing and being sued as a whole and in the name of the corporation, the power to hold lands, a common seal, and the authority to issue by-laws.

The greater boroughs had these corporate qualities as early as Edward I's reign. But the idea that only the king could secure these corporate rights through a charter granted by him and containing the magic words was a new doctrine that had irresistible sanction behind it, not only by reason of royal force, but through judges who, according to Goebel, subtly concealed the source of their concession theory and bootlegged canonical lore into the English law "under the guise of native brew."[8] The alchemy of this lore was useful in converting the raw fact of a borough's native corporate life into the refined and more secure symbolism of the royal charter that had to be sought and bought.

Along some such path of legal development, still not clear in all its historical details, there appeared at last the incorporated as distinguished from the unincorporated body, and the licit as distinguished from the illicit. It is a curious fact that the modern business corporation, grown as a legal entity from these alien authoritarian roots, has become in fact a highly autonomous and self-governing body. The concession theory is given the customary lip service. Corporate autonomy, at the same time, has been supplied with the constitutional and statutory safeguards against intruders. The potential intruders include not only persons in the private sector of the economy, but also legislators in the public sector. The history of the fencing off of the latter type of intruder on corporate autonomy is a separate and fascinating chapter in American constitutional law.[9]

The story begins with the pregnant words of Marshall and Story in the Dartmouth College Case in 1819, when the distinction was drawn between public and private corporations, the latter being thus protected against state legislative encroachment on its internal government. The story proceeds through stages of constitutional interpretation and amendment, with the aid of helpful legislation, to our modern conception of the corporation as a major social institution, essentially in the private sector although with certain social responsibilities. In the American view, the *privateness* of the business corporation is due, not only to the fact that it employs private capital as its financial basis, but just as importantly to the doctrine that the corporate charter, though a grant of the "sovereign" by unilateral state or federal legislative action, is a species of contract to which the incorporators, and even the corporation itself, are parties.[10] It is a contractual relationship that has the blessing, in constitutional law, of constitutional clauses that throw a cloak of immunity around corporate enterprise: immunity from undue tampering with the corporate sector by legislators.

Although it seems anomalous that a corporate creature of the state, being in law a fictitious person, should have rights that are enforceable against the sovereign creator, and that this "person" should have rights against state and federal governments, enforceable in the courts under the due process clauses of the Fifth and the Fourteenth Amendments of the federal constitution, these are constitutional principles that are never in doubt. They form a secure basis in the legal fabric of the nation for a corporate economic system that has been responsible for much of the nation's growth. Nowadays, when these constitutional protections are taken for granted, ridiculous sectarian attacks (of splinter groups who attack the Fourteenth Amendment as "unconstitutional" and void) never come to anything. There may never have been, as alleged, a "conspiracy" of corporation lawyers and "Black Republicans" just after the Civil War to put that amendment over to help business as well as the freed men. Nevertheless, it would take more than a conspiracy today to nullify the due process and equal protection clauses of that amendment. They are too valuable as protectors of corporate autonomy, as well as a vast complex of private rights beyond the corporation.

The corporation of tradition and the newer socially responsible corporation of today rest firmly on such legal bases. But that is not the only, or perhaps even the main, foundation stone. Quite as important is the conception of the rights of property. This is as basic a conception in our constitutional system as any; nor is it entirely a legalistic conception. The law has been influenced by it rather than the other way round. Yet the trend of the law reflects historically the force of the idea that property must be respected by governments as well as by private persons. The federal constitution and state constitutions all show this concern for property rights as against the legislative and executive organs of political democracy.

152

The danger of impaired contracts, cheapened money, and other malignant measures affecting the rights of creditors and similar interests, enacted by the state legislatures after independence and before the framing of the constitution, had been a principal cause of the constitutional convention in 1787. In Hamilton's *Federalist 78* it is explicitly shown that a strong Supreme Court, with powers of judicial review of state legislation, was thought necessary to prevent injury to "particular classes." In both state and federal courts there were important decisions during the decades before the Civil War which notified legislatures that acts bearing too harshly upon existing property rights would be disallowed or so construed that this unfortunate effect would be avoided.

After the Civil War, this doctrine of vested rights was greatly strengthened by the words of the Fourteenth Amendment and by judicial interpretations of the words. The courts became major protectors of corporate enterprise as against reformist legislation aimed at regulation. On the other hand, there grew up another line of decisions which strengthened state, and especially federal, legislative power to intervene in the economy on behalf of the public interest. This trend was the dominant one during the New Deal period of the thirties. There were further waves of regulatory legislation in the Fair Deal and the New Frontier periods, and for the proponents of the older, pre-New Deal judicial dispensation, these developments were lugubriously deplored as antibusiness.

But it should be noted that all this has not meant the decline of corporate autonomy, nor the demise of the corporation of tradition. The traditional conception of the corporation was in fact underlined in New Deal securities legislation, which sought to protect the property rights of stockholders and creditors more effectively. This legislation posed no antinomy between the corporation and the public interest. Rather, it emphasized the importance, in corporate capitalism, of positive public action to preserve the rights of investors against arbitrary action of *corporate governments* in much the same vein as earlier judicial action had intervened to protect corporations against public government.[11]

Whereas this legislation introduced some new dimensions of public policy concerning corporate capitalism, it did not depart from traditional respect for the rights of property.[12] On the contrary, the purpose of contemporary securities legislation has been to throw new safeguards about those rights. Other legislative trends may have affected basic change in the "old-style capitalism"[13]—a "free enterprise system" of laissez-faire vintage—but the law of corporations was not changed in any fundamental way.

There has been no statization of the economy. The principle expounded in the Dartmouth College Case a century and a half ago that the internal government of a private corporation is to be relatively free from legislative intervention, has never been superseded by the totalitarian and authoritarian "corporative" systems such as one sees in fascist regimes. The prospect of such a revolutionary change in our system of political economy would be appalling to most Americans, whether in business or nonbusiness sectors.

Emergence of the Modern Corporation

What has changed is management's conception of itself as the governmental body steering the corporate ship. It is a conception not forced upon the corporation by legislators or by any external authority. The concept of corporate governance as entailing a new set of responsibilities,[14] different from the simpler and more limited responsibilities of the traditional corporation, has come from business leaders themselves. In some respects, the new view of corporate responsibilities runs counter to the concept of the corporation that underlay the early New Deal securities legislation. There the chief managerial responsibility was to stockholders. Now it is a diffused responsibility, with concern for a good many more kinds of contributor-claimants on the corporate usufruct. This aspect of the new corporate governance is of particular interest in considering the corporate-arts nexus, though of course it has far wider ramifications.

Concurrent with the development by management of a new con-

154

cept of corporate responsibilities has come an interesting trend in state legislation, a "new look"[15] in corporation law that widens the scope of corporate powers.[16] There has also been a trend in the judicial interpretation of corporate powers that works in the same direction. The total effect is to give renewed emphasis to the established doctrine of corporate autonomy while laying to rest, at least for the big publicly-owned companies, the concept of the traditional corporation. This apparently paradoxical evolution is not so strange to the student of social structures whose vision is not confined to strictly "political" or "economic" institutions. So long as the corporation is regarded narrowly as a profit-seeking business unit in a self-regulating world of rational and competitive "economic" men, on the one hand, and the state as a system of power in relation to the "political" man, on the other, the place of the modern corporation in the entire social structure at a given time is undiscoverable and unstatable.

The corporation is a complex social institution in which both governmental and economic functions are carried out, and without which mixture of functions, in fact, our mixed economy would not work at all. The corporation of classical tradition presumably had no governmental functions, but belonged exclusively to that hypothetical world of the economic man. It was a corporation dominated by a single kind of unquestioned and monolithic property interest: the property interest of the shareholder. Corporate managers were the instruments of this interest and of no other. The single-minded devotion to profit-maximization of the traditional corporation's directors and executive managers, undistracted by any other considerations, such as the "public interest" and the "demands" of labor, may never have found pure expression in any company. Nevertheless, it was and is the ideal goal of the traditionalist in economics and corporate mythology.

The reasons for dilution of this pure ideal in the world of business realities are many. Foremost is the nature of the executive function in all large organizations. The executive function goes on twenty-four hours of the day and every day in the year amidst ever-changing circumstances that do not conform to simple theoretical models. The modern corporation is an institution that exists *in* society, is an integral part of the warp and woof of society, stands there as a target of innumerable demands on its superb organizational and capital capabilities, is drafted into service for all kinds of societal functions, and most important of all, is run by men who are themselves deeply involved as citizens in the ongoing adventure of humankind. Under these conditions, the neat separating out of the economic man and the traditionally conceived corporation is an impossibility.

When all has been said, however, we observe that the corporation of tradition is still very much with us, even if it is overshadowed by the great institutional company as a prototype of the "new capitalism."[17] The corporation of tradition is to be seen mainly in the lower echelons of the mixed economy. Or, if we prefer to avoid hierarchical and vertical gradations, it appears near the far end on a scale that divides the wildcatters from the great institutional corporations that we are most concerned with here. In the evolution of modern capitalism there has been room for a wide variety of organizations, together with the individual enterpriser, which provide "supply" for the economy. The very pluralism and flexibility of the system— if it is a system—is a source of strength.

A further source of strength is the pragmatic way in which this so-called capitalist system has responded to the economic and political needs of western countries that have avoided doctrinaire solutions. The corporation of tradition flourishes side by side with the big, new modern corporation of institutional significance in the political economy. Proprietorships and partnerships abound in the total matrix. The entire pattern—if it is a pattern—might be called the "new capitalism," which is better than a homogenized old-style capitalism or a statized economy under socialism.

Those who go by the book may have difficulty grasping the contours of this somewhat confused pattern, and sometimes one falls into the error of seeing the interests of the capitalist and the public in fundamental conflict, as though a clear antinomy is obvious in the nature of the system. But, in fact, there is a place for collaboration as well as conflict, for the visible hand of the social-minded business executive as well as for the "invisible hand" of the supposedly self-regulating economy of classical doctrine.

A more realistic picture of the structure of our "new capitalism" has been offered in a provocative schematic spectrum of companies designed by Armand G. Erpf, an investment banker of wide experience in analyzing corporate securities.[18] It provides a picture that is highly useful to one who seeks an understanding of the reach for new values in the world of the great institutional corporations. At the same time, the Erpfian spectrum indicates quite clearly why it is a good thing that not all of the corporate structure of our economy is describable in terms of such major companies. In the corporate-arts interplay it is important to make certain distinctions. We are talking about a highly variegated corporate world when we speak of "the corporation." Although our main concern is with the relationship between the great institutional companies and the arts, it is necessary that, in laying out policies for their own special kinds of interrelations both the artist and the corporate executive pause to reflect on the exact nature of their own enterprises.

Art and business are both species of ventures, involving, in Whitehead's term, adventures of ideas. But the nature of the venture is not the same in a great institutional company as it is in the little enterprise or the wildcat operation. Nor is the venture of the architect in designing a great urban complex the same as that of the painter at his easel, unimpeded by institutionalized requirements of form, color, composition. A realistic spectrum of companies, like the more catholic spectrum of arts as indicated in an earlier chapter, should aid policy makers both in business and in the arts to approach the corporate-arts relation with greater chance of success.

The structure of our capitalist society involves roughly half a dozen layers or types of companies which fall into two general categories. In the first category there are companies that can be designated as "public corporate capitalism" or "democratic capitalism" as distinguished from nineteenth century bourgeois family-owned personal capitalism. In the second category, one finds that true private capitalism most people have in mind when they speak of our economy in terms reminiscent of Adam Smith, a capitalism that does not at all fit the realities of the first category, but which, nonetheless, still exemplifies a large number of the business units in this country. Within each of these major categories of companies there are gradations. The nature of the corporate-arts nexus will vary remarkably from one end of this spectrum to the other. To generalize about that nexus on the basis solely of one kind of company is to invite ridicule from the managers of another, for the conditions that apply to one group will seldom apply to another.

Public Corporate Capitalism

In the first category of *public corporate capitalism* the differentiating mark is in the separation of ownership and control as among the stockholders, the management, and the directors. This is the characteristically organizational type of corporate business in which the executive managers and directors have to go before the stockholders at least once annually to justify their stewardship. In this general category one finds the very large institutional companies. The question of social responsibility weighs heavily in executive decision-making. The criterion of profitability is not the sole test of good business performance in such companies. And because there are other criteria than profit, it is in these companies that one is more likely to find attention given to such issues as the corporate-arts nexus, not only as a matter of social responsibility, but more broadly as a facet of the institutional company's "fit" into a society moving toward higher cultural goals.

Yet this broad category of publicly owned companies contains some that are not so institutionally and socially oriented. Three subtypes can be distinguished, each with its own attitudes toward the arts. Doubtless there are further subdivisions that would be meaningful, but no attempt is made here to draw the lines more finely. The three major subtypes include: (1) the great multibillion-dollar corporations; (2) large companies in the range of perhaps several hundred million dollars in market value to a couple of billion; and (3) medium- to large-scale, professionally managed, service-type corporations.

To some extent the attitudes of managements toward the arts in all these companies may be expected to vary with size of assets. A rough-and-ready basis for classification, it is nevertheless relevant because the emphasis, in general, on social responsibility as compared with profitability has seemed to be in inverse ratio to size. There are notable exceptions, of course, but this rule of thumb may at least be used tentatively.

1. The great multibillion-dollar corporations have become institutions of the land. These are the old-line, long-established companies, many having had their origins in the activity and burst following the Civil War, and then again around the time of World War I. We all know these companies. They encompass the railroads, steels, automobiles, mass retailers, oils, communications, copper, and many manufacturers. These are the huge companies characterized by a large number of stockholders, in many cases more stockholders than employees; professional management teams, many echelons deep; boards of directors, usually culled from outstanding names and increasingly owning minor or negligible percentages of total shares outstanding. Such directors tend to think of themselves as trustees and conservors, and are no longer doers or creators.

These companies, because of their size, must operate under bureaucratic procedure, and to the extent that they are big, they are subject to the threat of antitrustism. Social pressures are upon them to stabilize employment, and they proceed cautiously in the development and unfolding of their long-term plans. Perhaps because of their gigantic size and the dominance of their position in their respective markets, perhaps because many phases of their operations are mature, their growth rate is more consistent with the growth of the country as a whole than superior thereto. The upsurge of business from 1946 to 1958, during a period of shortages the world over, engulfed them in an atmosphere of dynamism that in many cases was temporary. In any event, whatever the bold and aggressive developments in one or another of their many activities, the impact has to be related to a multibillion-dollar base. The shares of these companies, with important exceptions and leaving out the revaluation of the postwar decade, move in price occasionally, gradually, and in general not as dynamically as newer segments of the economy.

2. Next, there are large-sized companies, many of which moved out of the private sphere in the last few decades and represent the corporate organization outside the heavy segment of our industrial structure. It is perhaps possible to characterize them as more aggressive, not yet the full target of government antipathy. A number are growing faster than the economy as a whole.

3. In a third layer, there are companies largely of the service type, many of which represent new industries as far as the market place is concerned but old in their activity or history; some are new institutions in their particular fields and are not infrequently dominant in their respective markets.

These three types or layers constitute our public corporate capitalism. At these strata of the capitalistic structure of our economy one would expect to find characteristic tendencies and tensions of management concerning corporate-arts relationships. There is concern about social responsibilities, insofar as these responsibilities seem to call for support of the arts, but at the same time concern about what the stockholders think of new departures in external relationships, and especially in fields that may seem to some quite unrelated to business. Next, there is the development among professional managers, especially younger men with widened cultural horizons, of keener interest in a "great society" and their companies' part in the "cultural boom," but at the same time the pull of their economic interests in other directions.

Finally, there is a willingness in the larger companies to push out the frontiers of managerial discretionary authority into unexplored terrain—whether for social-responsibility reasons or out of sheer venturousness and "business statesmanship" notable in the new breed of big business executives who find this outlet for a place in the sun.

Private Capitalism

Turning now to the second broad category of *private capitalism*, three subtypes are discernible: (1) enterprises in the more traditional sense of the term; (2) ventures; and (3) wildcatters.[19] All three of these types of companies fit more clearly into the older genre of capitalism than the public-capitalistic companies we have just described. We may designate the characteristics of these private-capitalistic companies briefly: the enterprises do have public stockholders, professional managers and directors, but there is no such separation of ownership and "control" as one sees in the first general category of companies. The ownership, the direction, and the management are all much more coincident. The driving hand of a management-ownership is much more evident. Tension between managerial concern about social responsibility and stockholder reluctance (real or imagined) to move into new areas of corporate activity is absent. The ventures are a group of companies in which capital and management combine to explore or exploit a business concept or concession. Here, again, there is not the separation of ownership and "control" that one finds in the general areas of public corporate capitalism. Public stockholding is not so widespread. Finally, there are the wildcatters who engage in radical speculation and have little or no interest in those external corporate relationships that characterize the great institutional companies.

In the enterprises, ventures, and wildcatters one sees the ferment of private capitalism. Here is the field for bold exercise of intuition, for adventuresomeness, and for agility. Risks are recognized and undertaken with the aim of becoming bigger, stronger, and finding a firm position in the industrial structure either through growth or combination. Ultimately, many of these companies find safe harbor as divisions of the great institutional organizations who, for one reason or another, have not moved into their areas.

These three subtypes of companies in the category of private capitalism engage in activities that are distinctive, but they blend into each other and their borderlines are blurred. A mark of distinction might be their relative degree of fragility. In all three, however, the private stockholders, to a large extent, ride along on the coattails of the dominant managerial ownership who determine the policy, constitute the decisive force, and have no qualms as to the predatory pursuit of their profit objectives. For this reason many investors prefer such managements if their objective is speculation, while other investors, of a more conservative bent, may lean toward the companies in the general category of public corporate capitalism.

Implications for Corporate-Arts Relationships

It is frequently said that today's corporate managements go their own way regardless of the will of the stockholders—those "ultimate owners" of corporate capitalism who seem to have less and less to say about the use of their money by corporate governments. The probable fact is, however, that there is equal concern of management about the preferences of investors and the financial community. But the differences among the six subtypes of companies mentioned above constrain corporate executives to different kinds of policies in their external relations. The differences affect the corporate-arts relationships of these companies in interesting ways. These differences are best seen in historical perspective.

In the multibillion-dollar corporations, and even in many of lesser size, the corporate concept has reached a high stage of maturity. In these corporations, the principle of perpetuity prevails; there is a strong desire to maintain personnel and talents intact; there is a constant search for new outlets for the company's energies and resources, the replenishment of its depleted or obsolete assets. In line with this concept, the modern corporation attempts to create a continuing institution that has stability and growth, that can assure more or less constant employment, and where the equity constitutes a gradually rising reservoir of value for the savings of the nation. When such an institution has achieved adequate strength and stand-

162

ing in the economy, it has access to capital markets—whether from retained earnings or from its ability to issue capital stock that will be sought by investors—so that it can undertake new enterprises.

Stock certificates for these major corporations represent institutions that in many cases comprise a segment of the country, or of the society in which we live. Such institutions are manned by officers of merit with broad managerial staffs two and three echelons deep in key functions. They plan and undertake long-term programs of capital expenditures to maintain, to renew, and to expand their corporate activities. They undertake research to keep abreast of developments, to create new values, to improve old values, and to obtain optimum efficiency. The modern corporation thus has a strength and continuity that frequently, if not generally, was absent in older enterprises, where the mortality rate seems to have been much greater.

The mature giants no longer benefit from an appreciable per capita expansion in demand for their products. From the investors' point of view they must be distinguished from some of the electric utilities that can serve as a standard in judging other equities, and from established growth leaders operating in industrial and other competitive markets and that register sustained growth rates ranging from that of the average utility up to the phenomenal near-15 per cent of one or two outstanding cases.[20] All of these companies, together with some smaller companies that are institutions in their own particular fields, fall into the general category of public corporate capitalism. Investors can assess them somewhat differently from those enterprises, ventures, and wildcatters that are the true private capitalism of the nineteenth century type.

Whereas the great corporate institutions have won their race, the speculative private-capitalism companies are often striving and struggling to hack their way upward. These more venturesome companies cannot be satisfied with the sedate rates of growth of the institutional corporations, whose safety and impregnability stand in decided contrast. Nor can they afford "the luxury of cultural uplift," as a manager of one of these marginal operations once put it, that seems to the venturer the only reason for a corporate relationship with the arts. They do not have that sense of security against the chaos of the market which the great institutions more nearly attain. Nor do they have the advantage of planned operations in known areas of administered prices and markets. Their exposure to the risks and perils of business is different both in degree and in kind. Therefore, one must not expect them to approach the corporate-arts interplay with the same measure of enthusiasm.

The large number of business units in the general category of private capitalism, leavened by the yeast supplied to the entire economy by enterprises, ventures, and wildcatters, is an impressive reminder of the continued vitality of a competitive system that tends to rule out the cultural activities of company managements. If, on the basis of nineteenth century models of the economy, we were to assume a continuance of corporate shunning of the arts except for narrowly expedient aims, there would be little point in a protracted consideration of the corporate-arts interplay. But the emergence of a new kind of modern, scientific corporate capitalism, bearing the stamp of the great institutional companies, opens up new horizons for this interplay. With their extraordinary stability, these great institutions can afford to try out new paths. With their staffs of specialists they can explore the potentialities of the term "corporate enlightened self-interest" in this particular field of company external relations. With their access to available new knowledge, and their capacity to enlarge the store of knowledge, concerning the cultural ecology of institutional growth and survival, these companies can soberly engage in the search for new values that would be generally foreclosed to companies in the category of private capitalism.

There are of course important exceptions on both sides of the line. The purely private capitalistic sector sometimes turns up outstanding examples of companies that make imaginative forays into the field of corporate external relations, especially in the development of the arts and culture. On the other hand, the great institutional companies are sometimes the most conservative, and their managers seem never to grasp the opportunities open to them, as potential leaders, to become standard-bearers of the new capitalism.

The corporate reach for new values today is to be seen, however, mainly in the general area of the great institutional companies that have established foundations or have undertaken to push out company operations into new fields. This reach, it should immediately be added, is not away from the proper area of business activity, but rather an enlargement of the vision of the businessman to encompass functions that had been hidden from view by outmoded economic doctrines. The growth rate of the economy depends to a large extent on this widened vision on the part of corporate management. Among labor leaders, politicians, publicists, and academicians, it has gradually been realized during the past few decades that the forward movement of the economy depends on the private as well as the public sector, and, perhaps as importantly as any, on that intermediate sector described here as public corporate capitalism.

Opposed to the nostalgic pull of both the politics of an agrarian age and the economics of mythical systems, the executive leader of the great institutional company must face the future in terms of new patterns for the political economy as a whole. The older rural ideas and orientations have begun to dissolve in the face of an urban age —both in politics and in economics. The dominance of the rural point of view in politics will disappear as our representative system of government—thanks to recent Supreme Court decisions—is brought up to date. The dominance of the enterpriser-with-blinders in the economy will disappear as the voice of the public corporate capitalist comes to be heard and respected more and more in the marketplace.

A recent survey by the National Industrial Conference Board provides confirming evidence of a trend that has been evident for some time: The nation's leading corporations consider public affairs to be an important responsibility of management.[21] Over 80 per cent of the more than 1,000 firms surveyed had a public affairs function, embracing such activities as relations with legislators, political and economic education, community relations, and corporate philanthropy. The top issues that the companies regarded as "urgent" were inflation, taxation, and labor relations; near the top came a host of socioeconomic problems, including air and water pollution, poverty, civil rights, and urban renewal. Only a small minority of the companies said it was not their business to solve the nation's problems but simply to produce and sell goods.

These trends point to heady reconsiderations of the long-debated issue of social responsibilities for the businessman. So far as the corporate-arts relationship is concerned, this translates into the problem of corporate responsibilities in the interplay between the world of business and the world of the arts. For this reason, we must turn next to the question of corporate responsibility.

CHAPTER VII

The Dialogue and Dilemma of Social Responsibility

It is widely assumed that when one talks of the relationships between corporations and the arts the focus of attention should be upon corporate responsibilities. The usual assumption is this: the bigger the company the bigger its responsibilities to the practitioners and custodians of the arts. And it is often assumed, too, that corporate responsibility to the arts is but a subfunction of the general "social responsibility" of the modern corporation.

All of these assumptions are subject to serious challenge. An intense dialogue has been in progress for some time on the nature and even the existence of an alleged social responsibility for the business corporation. It is important that this be understood both by the arts and corporate communities, and especially their leaders who will formulate the policies for future corporate-arts relationships. In this chapter we shall look at some of the major issues involved in the contemporary debate about corporate social responsibilities. With these issues in mind it will be possible, later on, to discuss more realistically the future of the corporate-arts nexus.

Responsibility Is Shared

In the first place it is necessary to view the responsibilities of large companies—and we are mainly concerned with large companies here—in the context of other economic forces in society as a whole. Corporate economic power is undoubtedly a major consideration in any assessment of corporate responsibility to society. Yet it has to be remembered that there are two other important forces at work: (1) big government, and (2) the complex of small- and medium-sized business units that flourish in our political economy and constitute a substantial part of it.

The federal government alone is so vast an economic force that its responsibilities in matters that are usually regarded also as corporate "social" responsibilities are bound to be extensive. If we add the economic impact of the state and local governments, the total of this public-governmental economic force far exceeds the economic impact of the private sector. But let us take the federal impact itself, and regard it from the perspective of a decade.[1] A decade ago the federal government took over 20 per cent of the national income in taxes (this included social security), spent one-fifth of the national income, controlled the money supply and interest rates within certain limits, regulated foreign trade, set the laws on patents, bankruptcy and labor-management relations, and redistributed purchasing power through veterans' payments, social security disbursements, and, indirectly, unemployment compensation. In addition, there were the direct effects of specific federal programs such as housing, highway construction, oil exploration and imports, shipping, farm production, communications, small business financing, atomic energy, medical and other scientific research, slum clearance, and so on—all carried out by a complex of semigovernmental and

168

semiprivate methods through contracts, subsidies, guaranties, direct financing, grants, staff assistance, tax benefits, technical advice, and many other means. The defense budget alone then ran to over $40 billion, of which nearly half went to procurement, and that was before escalation of the war in Southeast Asia.

The small- and medium-sized business sector of the economy is a force that has also to be reckoned with in any serious discussion of the social responsibilities of the businessman. America's small business concerns are a main source of our economic strength. There are more than 4.5 million small businesses in the United States, and they make up more than 95 per cent of our business population. They account for about 40 per cent of our business activity and provide employment for some 30 million of our people.[2]

"Small business" as defined by administrative action under the Federal Small Business Act and the Small Business Investment Act may look like big business to some artists. By administrative action, the Small Business Administration (SBA) in Washington generally applies a limit of 250 employees in classifying manufacturing concerns for the purpose of obtaining financial assistance, but it applies annual sales or receipts of $5 million or less for wholesalers and construction concerns, and $1 million or less for retailers and service trades. For the purpose of bidding on government procurements and sales it generally applies a limit of 500 employees for manufacturing concerns and $5 million in annual receipts for construction concerns. A limit of $5 million in assets, $2.5 million net worth, and $250,000 in net income after taxes is applied in classifying concerns for the purpose of obtaining assistance from small business investment companies.[3] These definitions are binding only as they relate to the activities of the SBA; other agencies, public and private, may apply different criteria. However, SBA's definitions provide useful guides.

By way of contrast with small business is the big business reflected in *Fortune's* annual directories of the 500 largest industrial corporations.[4] The smallest of these in terms of net sales for 1955 amounted to over $55 million, and in 1964 over $97 million. The smallest in terms of assets stood at $14 million in 1955 and $7 million in 1964. The largest in sales in 1955 was General Motors at $12.4 billion; in 1965 it was again General Motors at almost $17 billion. Number One in assets in 1955 was Standard Oil (N.J.) at $7.1 billion, and in 1965 it was still Standard Oil (N.J.) at almost $12.5 billion. The large publicly held corporations with which we are mainly concerned here have thousands, sometimes hundreds of thousands, of stockholders and are not, generally, closely held by a few. In absolute terms, size is not always the distinguishing characteristic of a company with notable "social" responsibilities; it is often a relative matter, a question of social context. A "small business" in a small community may still be the biggest business unit there, and will be looked to for responsible action in community affairs, including cultural activities.

But when we speak here of the large corporation we think mostly of the type listed in *Fortune's* directory and referred to by some writers as the "endocratic" corporation which, of necessity, is governed not by its numerous stockholders but by its executive managers. The responsibilities to society, as distinguished from managerial responsibilities to stockholders, employees, customers and suppliers, is one that may or may not be acknowledged by the endocratic management. And because the endocratic management is not, as it is in most small businesses, a corps of principal proprietors, the self-assessment of social responsibilities is determined by different criteria than those that influence owner-managers.

We shall pursue this question later on; here we simply note that it is on the whole the group of a few hundred biggest companies that fit this endocratic pattern.[5] They do control a large part of the corporate wealth of the national economy. Yet, it would be misleading to assume that when one talks of the "social responsibilities of the businessman" one refers only to this particular economic force in the political economy of the nation. The other two main forces in the economy—big government and the sector of small- and medium-sized business units—are also responsible for the cultural development of the nation. So when we talk of shared responsibility for the state of the arts and the humanities it is well to keep all three economic forces in mind.

The Public or Social Responsibilities of Large Companies

Having drawn these distinctions we now turn to the central issue: the public or social responsibilities of the large, endocratic corporation. Companies in this category are still essentially in the "private sector" and enjoy a certain freedom of action that is not allowed the governors of the public sector. Yet freedom of action in the private sector of the economy is qualified by the necessity of acting responsibly with the public interest in view.

The public or social responsibilities of the businessman have long been recognized in principle by leading companies. Specification of the content of these responsibilities, however, presents highly debatable issues. What are the criteria for good corporate performance under the heading of social responsibilities? How does one go about the drafting of substantive requirements of managerial action in this elusive area of running a business, and what methods of appraisal are to be used?

The difficulties are partly terminological. "Public" and "social" responsibility both are verbal indicators with connotations that may lead far astray as practical guides for managers of very large corporate enterprises. These terms have to be made applicable to the work of managing businesses that are manned with hundreds of thousands of people who conduct company operations in many foreign as well as domestic jurisdictions, that are financed through widely dispersed share ownership, that get their supplies of goods and services from a wide range of small business as well as large corporate vendors, and that serve customers of many kinds including not only the individual and family end-users of their products but large and small distributors and dealers and also governments.

Basically, however, the difficulties of drafting the public or social responsibilities of large companies lie deeper than terminology. There are profound philosophical issues that have never been resolved, and perhaps never can be. Between extreme laissez-faire assumptions, on the one hand, to extreme collectivism, on the other, there is a wide range of philosophies of economic production and distribution. Economic units at both ends of this spectrum have characteristic social responsibilities.

In the middle zones, where one must locate our "mixed economic" system,[6] business corporations fall clearly within the private sector, but they vary greatly in the roles they play in the economy and, more broadly, in the political economy of the nation and the world. Their social responsibilities also vary. Some of the largest companies are virtually indispensable, for example, as suppliers of the goods required for the defense of the Free World and the security of the United States in particular.

But quite aside from their service to the protective function of government, to which these companies make their vital contributions through private-sector operations, the general fabric of civilized society today is dependent upon them to a high degree. If they were not there they would have to be invented. The invention of such organic entities is obviously an impossibility. The great corporations have grown up in response to social needs. Their functions, and their consequent responsibilities, are related to these social needs. Realistically, they are not to be regarded simply as the lengthened shadows of profit-seekers.

Yet the goal of profitability, especially long-term profitability, is basic to all of these great enterprises in our economy. The profit motive necessarily influences all other objectives, including objectives subsumable under "social responsibilities" of business. This is not to say that the substance and content of social responsibilities have always to be derived from and subordinated to the goal of profitability. "Social responsibilities" that specify responsibility to society as against a company's interests may, in fact, interfere with the pursuit of profit.

172

"Public" or "Social" Responsibilities?

It is better to speak of the *social* rather than the public responsibilities of large companies. The agencies of government have public responsibilities. Public officials are responsible to the public in fairly specific ways that have been defined through years, even centuries, of procedural development. Responsible government means responsibility exacted by constitutional systems, through devices such as the separation of powers and judicial review, periodic elections, a free press, legal norms of correct official conduct, and so on.

In the private sector there is a different pattern and technique of responsibility, particularly in the private economic sector where market forces are heavily relied upon to bar irresponsible conduct. Business companies are private, and not public, corporations. And despite a growing insistence that they have a quasi-public status in some respects, it is basic in our jurisprudence that they are not agencies of government. It is better to avoid terms that imply that business companies are public or quasi-public agencies.

On the other hand, it is now fully conceded by most business leaders that large corporations have a social status that carries with it both great influence and great responsibility. In our plural society consisting of many decision centers we firmly deny any totalitarian claims that the sovereign may absorb the private sectors into the public sectors. But, at the same time, we recognize the indispensability of organizations in the private sector as supporters and invigorators of a society of free people. The privateness of the private sector of a plural society is in itself a public good. The big corporations are a part of this indispensable plural structure, together with noneconomic organizations in education, religion, science, and other spheres of civilized life. All of these organizations have *social* responsibilities that are based on our conceptions of human freedom and dignity, and on the conviction that a viable democracy depends on the voluntary acceptance of these responsibilities.

So far as large corporations are concerned, there is a clear responsibility, over and above those specific obligations to immediate claimants, to sustain and strengthen the plural societal environment of a free people, and to do this voluntarily in accordance not merely with norms pressed from the outside, but more importantly with self-generated and rationally constructed policies of company responsibility to society.

The Meaning of "Responsibility"

Responsibility as *enforceable obligation* has but limited application in this view of the corporate role in a plural society. All companies have certain enforceable legal and contractual obligations to four main groups: their stockholders, their customers, their employees, and their vendors. It is taken for granted that corporations will obey the law as responsible legal persons and that those who act on behalf of the corporation will be held to legal accountability. All this is elementary. However, it does not get to the heart of the matter of social responsibility for large companies.

The more significant areas of corporate social responsibility lie in the undelineated zones of inchoate law, of uncoded public expectations, and of incipient demand. The relationships of a company with its stockholders, its customers, its employees, and its vendors include in any realistic analysis the potential as well as the actual members of these groups. A company has some responsibility to anticipate the requirements of all these people.

It is convenient to examine a company's social responsibilities under the four headings of these primary groups. But one must always remember that this is only a matter of logical convenience and not of necessity. A socially responsible company deals with people as human members of a free society and not merely as economic integers. For business purposes strictly confined to annual profit-

174

ability, productivity, and like measures of business performance the legal, contractual, and ordinary business relationships with members of the four groups can be laid down in company policies on stockholder relations, on marketing, on employee relations, and so on. But policies of this sort do not exhaust the issues in undelineated zones of responsibility for pointing a company in the general direction of man's best aspirations.

A company remains indifferent to these aspirations at its peril. One does not have to wait for legislation to realize that urban ugliness, water and air pollution, and other disfigurements are a threat to the culture that sustains a free way of life. There is a growing feeling in the United States that business corporations should aid in meeting these problems. Stream pollution may involve violations of law. There may be no law requiring a company to beautify its buildings and grounds. Yet to ignore the incipient esthetic norms that are becoming more and more an integral part of civic duty would be a failure of corporate social responsibility, irrespective of sanctions.

Here a caveat is in order. The social responsibilities of a corporation do not demand responses to all public expectations. The public may expect too much. Its desires may be transitory. Imaginative and constructive business leadership may, in the public interest, teach the public to want what it now regards as unnecessary. The social responsibilities of a corporation cannot, therefore, be defined in terms of merely passive adaptation to the public demands on business.

Prudent business leaders do not ignore public expectations, even if they seem to make unreasonable demands. There can be a reasonable response even if there is a negative answer. To ignore public aspirations, when cooperative corporate effort is called for, is to invite criticism for insensitivity to the new social dimensions of the modern corporation. Obdurately to resist just demands is to court failure in the objective of long-term profitability. Yet, to meet all public expectations indiscriminately can be equally costly. Managers must be prepared to listen attentively, and then to act on the basis of judgment that not only balances demands against resources, but more significantly, also balances short- and long-term advantages to a company in accepting certain social responsibilities.

At some point in this process of balancing interests the crucial question has to be faced squarely: are there any corporate responsibilities owed to society that must be accepted even though they are ultimately costly and do not really contribute to the goal of long-term profitability? In other words, are there some social responsibilities that have to be accepted simply because great enterprises have to be run by executives who think greatly and act greatly as heads of major social institutions?

The situation is entirely different in the case of very small ventures, wildcat companies, and marginal firms run by men who look no further than profit for their immediate claimants. The requirements of survival, the norms of ordinary business, the mechanisms of the marketplace, may permit the men who run such businesses only the most elementary gestures in the direction of social responsibility. More is expected of major corporations that are in fact among the institutional bulwarks of society.

Corporate greatness, whether or not it is well-founded in economic theory, is a fact of economic life. The age of the Robber Barons and the Muckrakers is gone. The public has become accustomed, instead, to new corporate images based upon performance of a high order. Nor is this merely the result of large benefactions in the form of corporate giving. It is more significantly the result of a sharp upgrading of the standard of living due in large part to the productivity, innovations, and imaginative extension of services by private enterprise. The public expectation of corporate greatness is due, further, to the active participation in public affairs by outstanding business leaders who are almost always top executives in big corporations.

Public, or social, responsibility on the part of corporations has in this way come to mean to most people far more than reliability and accountability for the performance of standard and customary business functions. It means that many socially responsible companies have done more than could be expected of them in the meeting of

176

the minimal legal, contractual, and customary requirements of a business unit in the economic system. The socially responsible company today is one whose leaders conceive of their company as a vital social institution, an essential part of the fabric of a civilized society and contributing—along with good business performance—to a common effort to achieve the higher goals of a free country.

Responsibility and Corporate Ecology

The base line of this generally esteemed corporate effort is clearly economic: a business objective of profitability for the ultimate purpose of meeting the elementary obligations to the company's immediate claimants, its shareholders, its employees, its customers, and its vendors. But the economic implications actually reach much further. Additionally there is the long-term goal of corporate *continuity* as a profitable enterprise, and continuity in terms of survival through periods of adversity as well as those of prosperity. A major element in the assurance of this continuity is full recognition of corporate ecology on the part of a company's executives: a recognition that the ecological factors of continued success must be constantly assessed accurately and followed up with certain courses of corporate action that reach far out into the corporate environment.

The ecological approach to corporate social responsibility means more than planning for a company's long-term success. It means a calculated willingness to assume big tasks and to be venturesome in more than a purely entrepreneurial way. The movement of business corporations into the mainstream of philanthropy for community health and welfare services during the first World War was an example of this, and so is the extension of corporate giving to higher education and the support of cultural institutions in recent years. The rationale for corporate support in these areas has not always been satisfactory from the standpoint of classical economics and the older jurisprudence. But new executive thinking has emerged to meet the new demands on the business structure. Service to the nation in time of war and for national security is another example. Defense business, though profitable in some cases for short periods, has been comparatively unprofitable and burdensome in many ways; yet corporations that had become part of this special fabric were willing to accept this responsibility.

The ecological approach to corporate social responsibilities suggests certain criteria that might be used to appraise company performance. How, for example, do executive managers deal with such incipient public issues as the industrial befoulment of the air and of our waterways, the degradation of urban areas, the problems of urban and interurban transportation, the constitutional reconstruction of our weak state governments, the appropriate policies for capital investments abroad, the requirements of an international monetary system, the role of multinational corporations in the fabric of regional and worldwide trading structures?

All of these issues indicate social variables that will sooner or later affect the profitability, perhaps even the viability, of some of the largest companies. The reality-oriented company will sense these variables in advance of public demand for action and make an effort to forestall damaging attacks on the company. The socially responsible company will go one step further; it will feel the necessity of attacking the incipient problem, and will make appropriate advance moves. These moves will often be collaborative, through such voluntary organizations as the Committee for Economic Development. But they will also be company-by-company, sometimes on a highly individualistic basis and motivated by the desire to benefit the public through imaginative new programs that others have not thought of.

Corporate Interests and the Public Good

The public issues that call for corporate social responsibility do not have to be invented. They press for solution from every side. The socially responsible company does not ignore such issues as they arise nor attempt to sidestep their implications for business planning. At the same time, the apparent rivalry of company and public interests has to be faced candidly. This can be denied on several grounds, not all of them sound.

The most conservative position is that company managers must not attempt directly to serve the public good at all, for two reasons. First, their posited prime responsibility is to stockholders and others who stand in a direct business relation to the company, not to the general public; the public interest is presumed to be protected by the invisible hand of market forces, where the public's representatives in government do not suffice. Secondly, the public good is held to be best promoted through the undiluted pursuit of self-interest by business units in a competitive system; the public interest, in this view, is in part an indirect by-product of the individual efforts of profit-seekers in the private sector of the economy, and where such efforts do not suffice it is the duty of governments to act marginally to advance the public good. In this general conservative position it is denied that there is really a conflict between corporate and public interests, and it is sometimes bluntly asserted that corporations have no social responsibilities whatever.

Modifications of this position are encountered in economic literature and in the unarticulated premises of some corporate executives. It is urged, for example, that while profitability and not promotion of the public good is the essential goal of a business unit in our economy, the public good is in fact sought indirectly in two ways: a profitable operation is per se one that satisfies public wants efficiently, and in any case it is impossible for long to reach the goal of profitability without due attention to public expectations of company social responsibilities. It is also sometimes urged that a company frequently does things in its own interest—good architecture, for example, for good public relations—that automatically redound to the public benefit.

These and comparable arguments for the presumed identification, or at least parallelism, of public and corporate interests are vulnerable on several grounds. A profitable operation, even in the long term and under competitive conditions, may not be of sufficient public benefit to fulfill public demands on the business that it assume certain social responsibilities. Moreover, a company in pursuit of self-interest, may very well serve the public good, even by action that deliberately ignores any calculus of public benefits that might result, but the benefits to the public will not necessarily be in the right amounts nor in appropriate directions.

Self-interest, so the counter argument goes, will lead a company to act so as to enhance the value of a social variable (identified in the corporate ecology) only so long as the resulting gain to the company exceeds the additional cost it incurs through this action. Self-interest alone thus offers no motive for a company to include the public good in its calculations of profitability, whether for the long or the short term. The argument here is that the profit motive will not lead to optimal corporate outputs of social goods and that private efforts have at least to be supplemented by government action in order to bring social goods to their optimum level. The most extreme argument is that government action for this purpose is indispensable and that corporate action cannot be relied on at all.

These considerations cannot be dismissed as irrelevant. Yet the fact remains that concurrent private and public action is constantly relied upon in our plural system to advance the public good. This joint effort (it is more than concomitant action) is inherent in the system. Growing managerial attention to corporate social responsibilities may not meet the requirements of certain kinds of social and juridical theory concerning the nature of the modern corporation. But the answer is better theory and not managerial retreat.

Obviously, society cannot rely *solely* on private action, motivated by self-interest, nor *solely* on government action to meet the requirements of social goods and the public interest. The great corporations cannot be expected to, nor would they elect, to accept the guardianship of the public interests or any considerable part thereof. That would take them beyond their fields of competence and experience; it would also place a burden on their motivation which they cannot reasonably be expected to assume.

On the other hand, it is incorrect to assume that the motivation is

180

always (and narrowly) economic in a company that diligently and extensively concerns itself with the social variables that impinge directly and indirectly on the company as a profitable enterprise. It is true that prudent management requires attention to these variables. The welfare of the community (using this term broadly to cover at times very large areas and numbers of people) influences the company's input of supplies, its costs, its operating efficiency, its markets. For these reasons alone it must accept many of the so-called social responsibilities that are in fact obligations to act responsibly as stewards of the firm.

Good corporate stewardship today demands a reach of thought into the corporate environment that exceeds anything we have known before. But social responsibility involves even more than this. It demands an awareness of the potentialities of great corporations as constructive social institutions in their own right, contributing to the public good *in their own ways*, independently of their service to society as profitable producers of salable goods.

The qualifying phrase is used advisedly. It is of the essence of our plural system and the corollary of corporate autonomy that every company will be free to see the nature and dimensions of its own social responsibilities uniquely. It does not have to accept any external dictates on this issue. There is much room for imaginative innovation, for creative thought and action. For the same reason, initiative and voluntary effort are required at high executive levels. The great dangers are timidity and inaction, the bars of dubious doctrine, and willingness to follow the crowd.

The Content of Corporate Social Responsibilities

A company has certain responsibilities to society, independently of its direct business responsibilities to its customers, its stockholders, its employees, and its suppliers. Its social responsibilities derive from its long-term goals of duration and growth as a profitable enterprise serving national and international markets, and from its intention to maintain a position as a leading institution in a plural society where business organizations in the private sector must share with the public sector the work of continued progress toward the highest goals of civilization.

Social responsibilities can be considered under two main headings: (1) the communities and other groups of people to whom a company's socially responsible actions are addressed, and (2) the substance of these actions in terms of the mutual interests and benefits sought.

Two categories of groups are of special importance in considering a company's social responsibilities: first, those with whom it has immediate business relationships and for whom the company assumes certain responsibilities over and above those that arise directly from the business ties; and, second, other societal aggregates and organizations that constitute vital elements in the corporate environment because of their specialized functions in the public and private sectors.

The first category of groups primarily includes the company's shareowners, its customers, its employees, and its vendors. The usual appraisals of business performance at the executive level and in product departments require attention to company relationships with each of these groups, but more particularly with respect to short-term results and not to long-term implications for the status of a company as a major institution in American society. For the purpose of appraising company performance in this respect under the headings of these several relationships it is necessary to formulate different criteria. These criteria are derived from a consideration of the substantive issues that arise in such relationships over the long run.

The second category of groups includes an open-ended list of communities, associations, organizations, and activities in the corporate environment—immediate and remote—all of which impinge in some significant way upon the operations of the company. The zone between significant and less noteworthy impingement is a matter of managerial judgment, but the tendency to be too restrictive has to be avoided. The social variables that influence the company's input supplies, its costs, its operating efficiency, its markets, and above all, the attainment of its long-range objectives, are many and complex. A fully scientific understanding of the interactions involved in company external relations may never be achievable, but as new knowledge is acquired in this elusive area the company will redefine its list of groups and activities covered in setting up the criteria of socially responsible company action.

At the head of the list in the second category stands organized society in the form of public governments—local, state, national, international, and foreign. A dependable system of law and order under norms of justice is a prerequisite for a company's corporate life and continued prosperity, both within the United States and beyond our frontiers where the company operates under other flags and the protection of treaties and other international arrangements. The business community, functionally and not necessarily geographically defined, is probably next in order of importance. Relations with the financial community, with competitors, and with businesses in allied fields involve other kinds of social variables that affect the long-term development of the enterprise. Company relations with educational, charitable, scientific, professional, and cultural organizations have long been regarded as important because these relationships indicate certain social variables that affect the attainment of company objectives. These variables are, in fact, the chief clues to the content of a company's social responsibilities.

Identification of the Relevant Social Variables

The social variables that affect the attainment of company objectives are numerous and include causal factors over which a company has no control. Reciprocally, there are numerous societal consequences of company action which seem beyond social or company control, at least in the present state of knowledge in the social sciences. On the other hand, there are certain variables on both sides that can be managed to some degree by rational policy. A company's impact on society can be influenced to a considerable extent by principles of corporate action designed to benefit simultaneously the company and those with whom it has direct and indirect relationships. The company benefits sought are, in general, long-term benefits. A major objective is company continuity, growth, and long-term profitability. Another objective is public recognition and acceptance of the company as a major social institution known for its wise and timely response to public expectations addressed to leading business corporations.

Wisdom in response to public expectations of a company's social responsibilities means selectivity among the many demands made upon a large company and the careful calculus of cause and effect in the corporate ecology. On some matters a company can do little or nothing to influence the course of events for the dual benefit of company and society; on others much can be done, but at costs that have to be weighed against other possible uses of limited resources. Reasonable balances can be struck in such calculations only if some systematic attempt is made to survey those variables in the corporate environment which merit attention in the planning, executing, and appraising of the company's social responsibilities.

The Boundaries of Social Responsibilities

A company's social responsibilities are not boundless. They are delimited both by the boundaries of company action that can be planned and executed effectively for the purpose of attaining the common and mutually desirable goals of the company and related societal groupings, and by the nature of the objectives of a large business corporation. These limitations ought to be understood and made as explicit as possible by a company's officers and managers.

As to the boundaries of action that can be effectively planned and executed, overly optimistic social theories of cause and effect are to be avoided, whereas at the same time every effort can be made within the company, as one aspect of socially responsible action, to push out these boundaries through internal studies and research as well as supported external research.

As to limiting business objectives, a corporation-for-profit has immediate and prior obligations to its shareowners, creditors, employees, and vendors, that must be met before assuming less direct commitments. These prior obligations do not exclude other kinds of obligations that arise from incipient and emergent social norms, but it must be expected that certain public expectations addressed to the company will be assessed by the company both in terms of available resources at its command and the extent to which the relevant burdens need to be shared in our plural society with other sectors, public and private.

This assessment is a managerial responsibility of the company itself, requiring decisional procedures and patterns that, although devised so far as possible to afford due consultation with external groups, must preserve the autonomy of company action. The reservation of authority and commensurate responsibility for company action at executive levels, under policy concerning company social responsibilities and the appropriate delegation of that authority and responsibility to subordinate levels and components, is implied in this autonomy.

The locus of managerial authority for defining the scope and content of a company's social responsibilities *within the company* is a subject that does not in itself fall under the heading of such responsibilities. In other words, the company is not socially responsible for its internal decisional patterns for defining these responsibilities— an issue of some importance in free and plural societies where autonomy in the private sector is a crucial social variable.

The philosophical, political, and legal significance of these comments is that for purposes of public comment and for guidance of those who draft substantive social responsibilities it must be understood that these responsibilities are *unilaterally* determined by a company and are not under any circumstances to be regarded as subject to bargaining with external groups and interests. In some respects, a company's social responsibilities fall into an intermediate zone between strictly enforceable obligations and unenforceable but desirable norms of ideal action.

There is of course a sense in which unilaterally accepted social responsibilities are at length enforceable by the discipline of the balance-sheet and by the market mechanism broadly conceived to include public opinion and attitudes. But no prior agreement is assumed as to the substance of these responsibilities beyond the internal agreement based on good decision processes by management. Obligations that rest on a company by reason of prior commitments of a contractual character may have a corona of nonobligatory social responsibilities, as in the civilized treatment of employees not called for specifically in collective bargaining agreements, but these outer obligations are not necessarily the result of bargaining.

These outer obligations should not be misunderstood. Such social responsibilities do not descend from on high, ineluctably, as though commanded by a brooding omnipresence in the sky that no manager dare disobey. Their substance cannot readily, if ever, be deduced from great ethical principles that bind corporations and businessmen generally. Large, diversified, geographically extended corporate operations often reach into many different kinds of communities, cultural milieus, and social situations. The requisite autonomy of action for components within such companies to meet these varying conditions and situations has its counterpart in the needed autonomy —both for the company as a whole and for its component businesses—in defining social responsibilities.

Because the content of these responsibilities can be derived neither from external bargaining nor from soul-searching alone, the task of definition becomes essentially one of specialized corporate ecology: the science of a company's adaptation to the human conditions prevailing in the places where it does business and hopes to do business profitably for a long time. The unilaterality of decision concerning the content of the company's social responsibilities does not, obviously, preclude extensive collaboration with outsiders of many specializations in the process of refining a corporate ecology; such collaboration is indispensable. The important thing is to avoid the extremes of social-responsibility content that merely restate known and established corporate obligations, on the one hand, and elaborate moral platitudes and ethical abstractions, on the other.

A further limitation on corporate social responsibility inheres in the dynamics of our society. The rapidity of change in contemporary science, technics, and politics—especially in the international arena —necessitates reservation concerning definitive statement of a company's social responsibilities. Caution is indicated, both in stating publicly responsibilities that may soon be anachronistic, and in precluding others that may emerge in full clarity tomorrow. Corporate giving, for example, as straight philanthropy, in support of some community institutions and activities may very well be justifiable as a social responsibility to neighbors on an emergency basis. In the long run, it is more than dubious as a settled social responsibility, requiring instead a quasi-investment rationale, perhaps, or some other basis that permits the formulation of criteria for good managerial business performance. The social responsibilities of a big company that is itself dynamic cannot resemble a Decalogue of duties, fixed for all time and all places.

Some Major Substantive Areas for Corporate Policy

With the boundaries of corporate social responsibility in mind, and given the dynamic character of contemporary society—which makes a Decalogue of responsibilities meaningless—we can now list some of the major substantive areas that currently engage the attention of corporate executives. The list is not exhaustive, but only suggestive. The purpose here is to indicate to those who may overestimate the importance of corporate-arts relationships the other areas that compete for consideration. And it is important again to underline the distinction between direct business responsibilities of companies to those persons and groups with which a corporation must maintain business-oriented relationships, and social responsibilities that have a less direct and even a remote logical connection with a company's business objectives.

Strictly speaking, action undertaken by a company for other-than-business purposes, such as a completely altruistic social policy of aiding others regardless of company gain, is the only kind of action that belongs logically under the heading of corporate *social* responsibility. Yet it is generally recognized by company executives that there is a zone of common objectives that embraces both profitability and the social good. Corporations that rank as major social institutions are governed by men who pursue both types of objectives simultaneously. Compromises are often called for, but this does not vitiate the principle of common objectives. Politics in a democracy also requires compromise of interests, including the give-and-take of public and private interests.

For these reasons it is not surprising that the substantive areas of corporate social responsibility often appear to be the same as those which engage the attention of public policymakers. For the purpose of checking and balancing the power to govern in society as a whole, there must be clear lines of distinction between public and private sectors of authority; but that does not mean a hard and fast line between the fields of interest open to private and public governments, respectively.

Education, for example, is no longer a matter of interest exclusively to local governments and to educational institutions. A soundly conceived and financed educational system is indispensable to survival as well as the necessary foundation for a civilized and cultivated society. Education extends from infancy through old age, embraces many new disciplines and techniques not recognized in classical pedagogy, and requires the collaborative efforts of all societal sectors. The responsibility for seeing to it that there is an educated population was held to be solely individual and private under Spencerian laissez-faire. Then it became a heavily public responsibility in modern nations. Today, it is a universal responsibility, and one from which corporations cannot escape. Business leaders have formulated this responsibility in broader terms than taxation; there is growing corporate support of education, not only through donations but also through in-service educational programs that reach far beyond technical training into humanistic and scientific fields of learning.

It is true that corporations, as a whole, have a long way to go in formulating their educational objectives adequately. In many cases there appears to be less creative thought on the problem than a follow-the-leader mentality on the part of executive management. If one leading company decides to support higher education with matching grants, others follow the patterns already set instead of thinking through the problem from its premises. The appropriate premises relate to the potential value of education in strengthening the kind of society of free men in which corporate enterprise can flourish for a long time to come; and that kind of society is not one exclusively devoted to the consumption of the things that industrial corporations produce. It is a society of high culture, characterized by balanced advancements in the arts and the sciences as well as the immediately useful technologies. This larger view of education, and of corporate support for it, was adumbrated in the *Smith* case, to be discussed in the next chapter.

The more deeply company thinking gets into the true nature of education, the more these premises approach the Platonic sweep of the subject, and the closer corporate enterprise is brought into the mainstream of life in a truly civilized society. In this larger view of education, the corporate-arts nexus takes its proper place and not merely that of a peripheral and accidental field of corporate policy.

Science and technology are special fields of theoretical and applied knowledge that increasingly attract the attention of corporate policymakers concerned with social responsibilities. The development of science and technology is, of course, a major concern of certain kinds of corporate enterprise which require the fruits of such knowledge for engineering purposes. Even so, it would be difficult to name any kind of business today that can be indifferent to the advancement of such knowledge. The essential issue, so far as corporate social responsibility is concerned, is whether such knowledge can be gained mainly by internal or external company action.

Even those big companies that can sustain their own laboratories, however, realize that the advancement of useful knowledge demands a vast common effort that cuts across all boundaries of private and public sectors. There is, in short, a corporate responsibility to back up those public policies that ensure the advancement of knowledge and oppose the obscurantism of anti-intellectual forces that are always endemic in human societies, none of which are very far removed from primitive superstition. A corollary responsibility is the support of freedom of association and expression among scientists and technologists, as against the authoritarian controls of some contemporary regimes abroad and among our own private governmental sectors. The advancement of scientific and technological knowledge for the common good depends, too, on the revision of certain secretive and censorial practices in our own system of public government, not all of which are justifiable under the heading of national security.

The *protection and improvement of democratic society* is another major area of corporate social responsibility, increasingly recognized in the executive suite. The essential premise here is a goal value concerning the worth and dignity of man as a human being, together with reaffirmation of governmental organization and procedures calculated to move toward that goal. No company is bound in law or ethics to defined and partisan ways and means of reaching the goal of democracy, and none can be denied the right to stand firmly and openly on chosen ground in this respect; the right of political action is embedded in our system.

On the other hand, the right to remain aloof is questionable. This is especially true of corporate inaction concerning private property rights, closely allied as these rights are with the goal-values of the American version of democracy. The modern corporation has been attacked as an organizational device that dilutes and dissolves the traditional property rights of individual stockholders, partly

190

through the separation of ownership and control, and partly through the proliferation of pension and investment funds. The charge raises basic issues of corporate governance as well as issues of public policy such as corporation law and the laws on security markets. Fundamental problems of democracy are involved here. But they are also involved in the question of corporate political action—the direct participation of a company in campaigns and elections and in the policy processes of legislatures and administrative agencies.

The subject is too complex to be explored here at length. But it is relevant to our present discussion in two ways: (1) the practitioners and custodians of the arts, in looking to the modern corporation for increased interest in the arts, do well to observe other aspects of corporate external relations that engage the time and energy of company executives; and (2) when corporate action at the level of public government is expected on behalf of the arts, it should be remembered that there is a whole range of public policies that demand corporate attention. From the side of the arts, this means that one must compete for attention with many other social forces and that it is wise at times to ally with some of these other forces.

The *conservation of natural and national resources* is still another area of corporate social responsibility of growing importance. The basic premise here is ecological. Within the past few years the question of physical survival has tended to press to one side the question of attaining a higher culture. With the upward population curve, the pollution of the environment, the spectacular augmentation of capabilities of human self-destruction, and the depressing failure of earthlings to institute a preservative system of global law and order, or even viable regional ones, corporate executives are faced with the urgent necessity of co-action for survival. The need for public policy based on sound human ecology has never been clearer, and the formulation of that policy demands corporate attention. From the point of view of creative people in the arts, and indeed of all who produce and hand on the fruits of high culture, it may be distressing to be shunted aside in the face of this ecological crisis.

THE CORPORATION AND THE ARTS

Yet it is not impossible that within the arts lie some of the crucial answers to man's adjustment to a habitable and hospitable environment that promises to be less ugly and forbidding to the senses. This suggests an area of collaboration for the arts, the corporation, and public governments, as in urban planning, the design of better housing, the reduction of noise, the provision of access to the performing arts raised to a high esthetic level, and the better education of the senses for aural, optic, and kinesic appreciation of all the arts.

It is evident from this summary view of corporate social responsibility that the modern corporation has deep involvement with many other social institutions that would have been regarded as completely alien to the business world a few decades ago. It is still true that those who take the most conservative position on corporate social responsibility, even going so far as to deny that it exists, would make profitability for the owners the sole purpose of a company and subordinate all external corporate relationships to this one objective. But this is a doctrinaire position that most business leaders cannot afford to take. The executive managers of large industrial corporations in particular have to face the fact that their external relationships in practice are based ultimately on a corporate ecology —explicit or implicit—that comes down to something that looks very like social responsibility, whatever name may be attached to it.[7]

Conclusions

Whether one looks at the span of groups with which a company has to maintain working relations or at the substance of external relationships in general, and whether one thinks of these relationships as bilaterally or unilaterally determined, the net effect is to require definite company policies in an increasing number of fields that are not the same as the orthodox ones. Manufacturing, marketing, accounting, engineering, finance—these are the established and traditional "sound" areas of business activity. But new ones have encroached on the old tight preserves: community relations, relations with labor unions, public relations, government relations, corporate giving, and, in the case of multinational corporations that must operate in foreign jurisdictions, a whole array of societal contacts to secure a company's status abroad and to improve its chances of building a profitable enterprise there.

Yet the demand for profitability and productivity alone are not sufficient stimuli to account for managerial action in all of these new external relationships. The fact has to be faced that very large companies are going to be run by men with no small vision and that as men of some stature they will expect the corporate institutions they represent to measure up to rather high standards of business performance. Business performance today is measured by criteria that simply do not fit neatly into the picture of the "economic man" of the dismal science of classical economics. The measure of good business performance introduces both ethical and esthetic norms, just as good civic action does. It may be shocking to the traditionalist to see that term "esthetic" in this context. But it has to be there. Esthetic as well as ethical norms now govern public policy; there is no reason to doubt that they will also govern corporate policy—at least in the big institutional companies.

The dialogue concerning corporate social responsibility then turns out to be a logomachy that has little relation to the facts of corporate life. There is no dilemma for the leaders of most institutional businesses; there is no necessity of choice between being a good business man and a good citizen. The hardline executive who dismisses as irrelevant all policy proposals that have no obvious and immediate payoff in this year's profits may do very well as a leader in wildcatting companies, which have their place in the economy, but not so well as leaders in the great institutional companies, or even those in the smaller ones that hope for status. The social responsibilities at one end of the spectrum of companies have to be distinguished from those at the other end. What it takes to be a "good corporate citizen" is a relative matter. Size is not the only criterion; the nature of the business, the fit of the business into its hinterland of supply and markets, the long-range intentions of its owners, the demands made upon it by national security and human ecology—all of these factors enter in. But surely the 500 biggest companies in *Fortune's* annual directory are all candidates for public inspection as to their social responsibilities, and especially those that have stayed on the list for a decade. These organizations seem to have contributed something of value or they would not have survived.

Yet survival alone is not the key to good citizenship. The further element of concern for others, not as sheer altruism but as a brainy philanthropy, is also relevant. Whether philanthropy can be both altruistic and self-seeking is the subject of the next chapter on corporate giving. It is important, for the assessment of the future of the corporate-arts relationship, that we look closely at this aspect of social responsibility.

CHAPTER **VIII**

New Dimensions of Corporate Donative Power

Whereas it is incorrect to identify the corporate-arts relationship solely with corporate financial support of the arts inasmuch as the nexus is far more extensive, it is nevertheless true that this financial aspect of the subject immediately leaps to mind for most people. There is justification for this, both in the recent trends of corporate giving and in the potentialities of corporate support for moving the country toward a more balanced "high culture." In science and technology we are well along the road of corporate support, but in the arts and the humanities we are said to lag.

What can we reasonably expect from the corporate sector of the economy by way of financial aid for the arts? To properly answer this question one must take a look at the development of corporate giving, the present status of public policy, and especially tax policy, as an encouragement of corporate donative policies, and the role of corporate giving in the whole picture of American philanthropy. In this way we can attain a more realistic approach to corporate support of the arts, and we can dispose of some popular myths in this area at the same time.

195

Trends in Corporate Giving

In the short period of three decades, corporate giving has risen to substantial proportions: about one per cent of taxable corporate income, or about $500 million annually—roughly 8 per cent of all American giving. Contributions to community health and welfare programs, and more recently higher education, represent the traditional areas of giving. But now there is a discernible trend toward support of civic and cultural purposes, including support of the fine arts and the performing arts.

As in the past, there is hesitancy on the part of corporate managements about new directions, as well as a marked absence of fundamental thinking on the entire philosophy of corporate giving. As the totals of corporate contributions edge closer to the permissible 5 per cent limit of taxable corporate income sanctioned by federal tax law, corporate managements are, as one leading business magazine put it, "hunting for some crystallized corporate policy," "groping for words," and "reaching for vague concepts," admitting for the most part that they "play it by ear," with a "wary eye on their corporate neighbors." But to paraphrase Shakespeare, they were not wont to be so dull.

Despite its brief history, corporate giving has deep roots in our social system. Its rise to prominence is traceable to many factors, including changes in the nature of corporate enterprise, increased corporate concern for community relations, the impact of wars and depression on charities, the growth of the body of law relating to corporate donative power, the federal policy of stimulating corporate aid through tax exemption, the American belief in a plural society comprised of strong private sectors, the development of a new and sounder rationale for corporate support programs, and the emergence of the donative function as a significant aspect of corporate external relations.

Insofar as the law is concerned, there no longer exist any serious barriers to broad-range donative power, exercised with reasonable discretion by boards and managers. But the demise of the old rule against gifts and the end of the old insistence upon showing direct benefits in return for valid contributions do not automatically relieve managements of their basic responsibility, both as corporate decision-makers and as corporate citizens of the community. Donative actions must always be based on an articulate policy that relates to the long-range goals of the business enterprise.

The major issues that must be faced in the articulation of such a donative policy—with special emphasis on giving to the arts—are suggested here. However, it is impossible to make a rationale for corporate support of the arts, or anything else, without first looking at the entire canvas, as it were, of corporate giving in the United States, from its early beginnings to the present.

This is especially true because we have now reached an important turning point in the development of corporate donative policy. Increased public and private pressures for more corporate support in more and more substantive areas now confront corporate boards with the necessity of taking a more comprehensive and better reasoned approach to the entire subject. It is said, for example, that corporations ought to provide much more cultural support.

Does this mean giving less to other types of donees? Or does it mean a steep increase in total corporate aid? Assuming that the theory and practice of corporate donative action as we know them today remain stable, the time has come once more for a thorough review of its philosophic bases to arrive at sounder operational principles to guide boards and managers.

Early Stages of Corporate Aid

Fifty years ago, business giving was mainly restricted to the personal philanthropy of proprietors and company presidents in closed corporations. As the distance widened between the owners and corporate operations, as stockholders multiplied into the millions and professional managers took over the reins, events contrived to replace the older personalized philanthropic giving.

The railroads had early anticipated the new pattern in aiding numerous YMCA's as havens for their trainmen. The "Y" expanded its appeal to other industries in annual community drives for funds. During World War I, the American National Red Cross and other organizations undertook fund-raising drives systematically directed at attracting corporate support. Those wartime drives provided essential services that the federal and local governments were not equipped to handle. "War Chests" were followed by "Community Chests." New York law soon authorized corporate contributions to war charities (some of the corporate gifts were large for the time).

Charles Evans Hughes, the noted jurist, regarded such corporate contributions as appropriate "for the maintenance of the very foundation of corporate enterprise itself"—a formulation of principle that heralded a new philosophy of corporate giving.

In the post-World War I years, however, corporate giving dropped off, even during the prosperous years before the Great Depression. After 1929, the federal government moved in massively with emergency relief operations. But the private health and welfare agencies were needed more than ever before. These agencies made urgent appeals for corporate support. As taxes rose to meet heavier federal burdens, private agencies were gravely endangered by the prospect of a new graduated corporation tax that threatened to seriously reduce corporate contributions. Tax exemptions on charitable gifts had been granted individuals in 1917 to promote contributions for war purposes. Obviously, corporate tax exemption was now a necessity to save the private-sector agencies. Under the vigorous leadership of Frederic R. Kellogg, Newton D. Baker, and others, and on behalf of the community chests and other private agencies, Congress at length extended the principle of tax exemption to corporate contributions.

The Five Per Cent Limit

The Federal Revenue Act of 1935 ushered in a new era in corporate giving. Its now-famous 5 per cent clause permits corporate net income deductions up to that amount for contributions to charitable and educational organizations. For the past three decades, corporations have had an unprecedented opportunity to raise their sights and to make innovations in contribution policies and practices.

The new law also afforded a substantial economic opportunity because the combined effect of the high corporation income tax and the 5 per cent clause offered large "charitable bargains." For example, with the tax rate at 52 per cent or higher, as it was in 1952, the federal government would forego $5.20 for each $10 of corporate contributions that actually would cost the company only $4.80. And in the higher tax brackets the cost would drop to 18¢ on the contribution dollar. The corporation income tax rate was lowered to 50 per cent in 1964, and lowered again in 1965 to 48 per cent. Even so, there are still real economic advantages to be gained for the corporate contributor under the 5 per cent clause.

From the standpoint of recipients of corporate support, the 5 per cent clause saved the day. Although total corporate contributions, as reported in U.S. Treasury "Statistics of Income," were rather small in the first years after 1935—only $30 million in 1936, for example, or 0.39 per cent of corporate net profits that year—by 1945 they had reached $266 million, or 1.24 per cent of net income. This figure was not exceeded until 1951 when the amount was $343 million. The peak was reached in 1953 with $495 million, and it has declined somewhat since. In 1962, however, about 1.2 per cent of taxable corporate income was contributed for a total of $595 million.

Clearly, then, the 5 per cent clause has been an incentive to the support of vital private-sector institutions that might otherwise have eroded away, with consequent weakening of the entire social structure. It has also created some formidable policy headaches that need to be eased, especially now as we approach the fourth decade of the 5 per cent era, and as corporate giving shows every indication of taking off in new directions, into civic and cultural areas.

Corporate Giving and American Philanthropy

Now consider the relative impact that corporate giving has on American philanthropy. In the first place, corporations are far from being the major pillar of American philanthropy. The great bulk of philanthropic giving in this country has always come from individual living donors and bequests. Corporate giving, albeit a vital new factor of growing importance during the past four decades, still comes to less than 10 per cent of the total. The American Association of Fund-Raising Counsel has estimated that philanthropic giving in 1965 was derived from the following sources:[1]

TABLE I

Philanthropic Donors in 1965

Individuals	$ 8,662 million	76.6%
Foundations	1,125 "	10.0
Bequests	780 "	6.9
Business corporations	733 "	6.5
	$11,300 million	100.0%

These figures fail to take into account the fact that some foundation gifts originate with business corporations. Nor do any of the standard tables show the full scope of corporate support in non-cash aid, which is substantial. It should be noted, too, that the recipients of most American philanthropy are not the usual recipients of corporate aid. The Association's estimates for the distribution of philanthropic giving in 1965 is shown in Table II:

TABLE II

Recipients of Philanthropy in 1965

Religion	49%
Education	17
Welfare	13
Health	11
Foundations	4
Civic, cultural, and so on	4
Other	2
	100%

Can one assess the actual and potential role of business corporations in the total picture of American philanthropy?

The answer is complicated by the ambiguity of the term "philanthropy" and the changing status of the modern corporation as a major social institution. For, philanthropy, strictly speaking, is giving for the love of mankind and, presumably, not for business-transactional purposes. It is questionable whether the corporation ought to be counted among the philanthropists at all, although it is clear that fund-raisers will place them in that category, like it or not. Yet, with the vast diversity of purposes shown in the entire range of American philanthropy, as contrasted with the relatively limited objectives of corporate giving, it seems almost as though we were talking about two different things. Nevertheless, there is an important common denominator: giving is overwhelmingly directed at strengthening the private sectors of our plural society. On the whole, this voluntary financial aid supplies the main undergirding for most of the reputable and indispensable private institutions that stamp their high character on our free society.

The quality of life in the United States would be very different from what it now is were it not for the great philanthropies that have pioneered ventures now routinely accepted as essential public services in the fields of education, health, and welfare. Nor has the arrival of the welfare state made this kind of philanthropic pioneering obsolescent. Having satisfied some of the basic needs that cried out for attention most urgently several decades ago, we are proceeding to satisfy others that seem as urgent today. This exploratory motive and elevating spirit tend to push the frontiers of giving outward.

Although this viewpoint may be fine for society as a whole, it is not necessarily that of corporate managers who are the stewards of business enterprises. What is, and should be, the scope of their "philanthropic" activities, if any?

Changing Patterns of Corporate Donative Policy

The National Industrial Conference Board—one of the best sources of statistical information on the patterns and trends of corporate giving—has found in its recent survey that the traditional support areas of health and welfare are being shared increasingly by educational and cultural types of contributions.[2] It should be mentioned that the Board's figures are merely estimates based on sample surveys that do not cover the entire field of corporate enterprise. However, NICB's figures are the best we have, so we must take off from there.

The Conference Board's 1965 survey covered 448 companies, which gave 0.68 per cent of their pretax income to various types of donees during 1965. The bulk of these companies are manufacturing firms with a heavy concentration of electrical and nonelectrical machinery makers, fabricated metal firms, and chemical and allied companies. Most of the nonmanufacturing companies are from banking, finance, and real estate. Though some of these concerns are of modest size, the majority controlled assets of $100 million or more. Table III shows the survey's breakdown of the 1965 company contributions dollar:

TABLE III

Corporate Contributions Dollar, 1965

Health and welfare   41.5%

Education   38.4

Culture (cultural centers, performing
    arts, symphonies, little theaters, li-
    braries, museums, and the like)   2.8

Civic causes (municipal and community
    improvement, good government)   5.8

Other (religious causes, groups devoted
    solely to economic education)   9.2

Nonidentifiable (because the donee is
    unknown)   2.3
                                                    ‾‾‾‾‾‾‾
                                                    100.0%

Comparison of these figures with those of former years shows a decided shift in corporate emphasis toward the support of cultural organizations and activities. The Board began these studies in 1955. Corporate giving was then predominantly for health and welfare. In 1962, for the first time in the series of surveys, company gifts budgeted for education exceeded those for health and welfare. Funds allocated to civic and cultural purposes also figured more prominently than before. On average, companies in 1962 set aside 17.2¢ out of every contribution dollar for other causes than health, education, and welfare. About 5.3¢ went mainly to cultural and civic projects.[3] This level represented a high point for these cultural and civic types of contributions; earlier surveys had averaged only 3¢ for these categories. In the cultural-civic sector, the performing arts accounted for about two-thirds of all projects in 1962. This shift in corporate giving toward cultural and civic projects is not yet a strong trend, but it is a significant one.

Corporate donors must seek valid criteria of selectivity that they can adopt to help determine appropriate support areas. The objectives and patterns of corporate support are not fixed; they are

203

changing and will continue to change. Will the response be in reaction to initiatives urgently pressed by others, or will the response reflect considered analysis on the part of corporate leaders?

In the relatively short history of corporate giving on a large scale, one hesitates to draw sweeping conclusions. But it is hard to escape the impression that many contributive practices have merely been responses to pressures and are all too often precedent bound. A special study of corporate support of the performing arts recently undertaken for the Rockefeller Brothers Fund[4] revealed that there was a general hesitancy on the part of corporations to lend broad support to the arts—even though many corporate executives wanted to do so— because there was no precedent for it. And yet everywhere in American business today we see signs of the corporation as art dealer and art patron and of the corporation as cultural ambassador. Moreover, executives are lending a growing amount of their time, talent, and influence to the support of the performing arts.

The need for a viable theory of corporate giving and for guidelines to future policy is evident in the experience to date. As a basis for such theory and policy, a more detailed analysis of the legal bases of corporate donative power is in order. Following this legal review—which applies to *all* types of corporate giving—we will again take up the involvement of the corporation with the arts.

The Juridical Basis of Corporate Donative Power

The first question that must be answered by any company proposing to support any charitable, educational, or cultural activity is whether the financial aid falls within the powers of the corporation. This is a legal question concerning corporate donative power, i.e., the power of directors to give money for certain purposes. The extent of a corporation's power to engage in philanthropy depends upon the law of the state that grants the corporation its charter and gives it legal existence.

The most conservative legal position is that a business corporation has nothing to give away. "Corporate philanthropy" is said to be a contradiction in terms, if by "corporate" we mean corporate enterprise for profit. The common law rule of "direct benefit" requires some reasonably calculable benefit to the corporation for any funds disbursed to anyone other than stockholders. The husbanding of resources for profit-making is said to be the primary goal of a corporation. This view precludes any philanthropy that diverts the corporate usufruct into the hands of outsiders. Unavoidable business expense for the support of certain charities (community funds, for example) can be justified, but outright gifts for the disinterested purpose of benefiting mankind—the hallmark of philanthropy— cannot be upheld.

This position, with its antecedents in nineteenth century laissez-faire capitalism, has both a distinguished lineage[5] and a surprising degree of minority support today.[6]

Yet within the past decade we have seen a salient legal trend in the opposite direction. There is now a strong legal precedent in favor of the corporate donative power, seen primarily in the statutory law of the states. Most states now authorize corporations to make certain kinds of gifts, thus modifying the old common law rule.

The statutes in question are called "permissive" legislation because they authorize (but do not direct) corporations to make the kinds of gifts defined by these statutes. The permissive character of the legislation underlines two significant facts about the donative power: (1) corporations, as creatures of the state, have only the powers conferred upon them by their creator; and (2) the powers thus conferred are in the nature of quasi-governmental powers exercisable in the private sector and hence are to be exercised according to the discretionary judgment of the government organ of corporations. The only states that do not now have permissive legislation of this kind are Arizona, Idaho, Montana, and South Dakota.

Increasingly, the liberal legislative approach to the question of corporate donative power is shown in federal, as well as state legislation. Congress amended the National Banking Act to grant the donative power to national banks. Since 1939, the Internal Revenue

Code has authorized the deduction of charitable contributions for corporate income tax purposes up to 5 per cent of taxable income. In addition, we have a series of judicial decisions affirming the constitutionality of these statutes and upholding their applicability in cases where dissident stockholders have tried to prevent directors from exercising the donative power.

Thus, in the case testing the action of the Union Pacific Railroad in creating a charitable foundation and making a donation to it, the court refused to apply Utah's new permissive legislation, but it had no difficulty in upholding the gift under a liberalized interpretation of common law principles.[7]

The leading New Jersey case, *A. P. Smith Company* v. *Barlow*,[8] upheld a corporate contribution to Princeton University, not only under New Jersey's permissive legislation, but also under the state's common law principles.[9]

This combination of permissive legislation, plus a changing view of the application of common law have led one commentator to remark that it is now clear, in the United States at least, that "the business corporation may love mankind."[10]

How is one to explain this remarkable trend away from the older, more restrictive view that circumscribed corporate donative power?

Doubtless there is a growing need for corporate support of activities that had been previously supported by wealthy families and individual gifts. The tax bite on inherited wealth and on personal incomes has thrown the burden into new quarters, whereas in the meantime, the demands of charitable, educational, scientific, civic and artistic organizations and activities has grown apace. A society committed to the principle that human affairs should be governed, so far as possible, in the private and not the public sectors, has confronted us with the necessity of replenishing the sources of private support, and even of extending the resources on a vast scale.

A modern, civilized society moving rapidly toward higher goals of spiritual as well as material content—and determined to do so without unduly enlarging the powers and responsibilities of the public sector—is naturally on the lookout for ways to make optimum use of private reservoirs of wealth and power in this task. It is not simply a question of corporate wealth being an obvious target for fund raisers. The deeper significance is that the corporation acknowledges the imperative to be in the forefront of certain fund-raising efforts that strengthen the corporate environment.

Nor does the new trend mean acceptance by businessmen, legislatures, and judges of "vague concepts" of social responsibilities. Admittedly, many corporate executives do attempt to feebly rationalize the new trend, placing exclusive emphasis on the social responsibilities of corporations. This does not mean to say that such responsibilities do not exist, but rather that the true basis for business prudence and law in corporate giving has always been a careful consideration of justifiable corporate *powers* and not corporate *duties*.

The problem has always been, and still is, essentially one of finding a reasonable basis for the donative power. For, in all constitutional governments, both public and private alike, the meaningful theoretical questions are not just questions of limitations on the power to govern, but also questions about the adequacy of powers granted. With respect to the donative power, then, it is not surprising that in an age when corporate powers to govern business enterprises are expanding to meet the needs of large organizations confronted with complex ventures, the power to spend in new areas is being pressed by the most venturesome.

In sum, the trend toward legal sanctity, as well as the blessing of business leaders for corporate donative power, is best explained in terms of the larger picture of constitutional evolution. Modern governments, both public and private, must do things that previous governments were not asked to do; they must now be given powers to meet these expanded requirements. In public governments, this pressure has resulted in a vast increase of activities, and hence of powers, in national capitals, sometimes without the necessary restraints on the uses of those powers. But in every case, a centralizing tendency is noted. The same is true in the private sectors. In both cases, the reaction against centralization of power has been, on the whole, a vain plea to turn back the clock. Instead, what one must recognize is the necessity of keeping up with the times while assuring that the powers inevitably centralized are exercised with good judgment and accountability.

The growth of corporate donative power, as a reasonable, and even indispensable, part of the governing powers of corporate boards is thus intimately related to trends that transcend the evolution of business. The legislation and judicial precedents now firmly supporting corporate aid to health, welfare, education, and cultural organizations seem to reflect a determined effort in the United States to sustain a viable *plural* society—a society of vital autonomous organizations in nonbusiness as well as business private sectors.

Donative Issues and Answers

On the basis of past trends and present prospects of corporate giving in the United States, and in view of the juridical foundations of corporate donative power, it is possible to frame some tentative answers to a number of key questions.

1. *Is corporate giving philanthropy?*

If it is, then the history and philosophy of philanthropy should provide invaluable guidelines for corporate donative work. If, as it seems more reasonable to assume, corporate giving is not philanthropy at all but a special use of corporate assets for prudent expenditures that will benefit the payor as well as the payee, then we need a different set of principles.

2. *Is donative policy essentially investment policy?*

Donations are not necessarily an improvident use of corporate assets. Gifts may have "goodwill" value, for example. But corporate donative practices have now so mounted in volume and expanded in range of purpose that the old formulas of "business expense" have become grossly inadequate. They provide neither an acceptable rationale nor any reliable criteria for donative policy. Simply to authorize managers to make giveaways at their discretion for "business purposes" is to retreat before the most insistent external pressures. On the other hand, investment as an outlay of money for income or profit is too restrictive a concept that can be applied only loosely even to expenditures for basic research or institutional advertising. The measure of return introduces different criteria.

3. How to estimate anticipated benefits from corporate donations?

Some way of stating the anticipated value to a company of its corporate donations is required, and these anticipated values need to be related to its *business* objectives. Otherwise, one deals with *philanthropic* practices that require different criteria for action. In evaluating contemplated gifts, the purposes of these donations need to be spelled out in some detail to specific company objectives in such functional areas as engineering, research and development, manufacturing, marketing, employee relations, finance, legal corporate work, and community and other public relations. In each of these functional areas the donative objective can be stated operationally so that any proposed donative payments can be justified reasonably. The anticipated benefits cannot always be stated with quantitative precision, and a judgment type of decision will ordinarily be needed.

4. Is "social responsibility," as currently conceived, an adequate criterion for estimating corporate benefits to be expected from corporate contributions?

Probably not, for two reasons. First, most of the contemporary arguments based on the alleged responsibility of business-as-philanthropist overlooks the basic fact that corporate support payments are both legally and economically justifiable as an exercise of corporate *powers* and not *duties*. Secondly, one may concede the necessity of recognizing, as a matter of business policy, a rising tide of *public expectation* that corporations should come to the aid of certain vital private sectors, without at the same time giving in to the argument that this demand creates either a duty or a power to provide the aid. There are much sounder ways to formulate a rationale for corporate donative policies.

5. *Is corporate ecology a more promising clue to a theory of donative policy?*

Donative practices always involve corporate external relations and, thus, the mutual adaptation of corporate and community action in all the functional areas mentioned above. Donative theory and practice are reasonably statable as *instrumental;* i.e., as auxiliary to the business activities of a company. Aid to education, for example, is related to the supply of new knowledge, educated and trained personnel, and creativity that are requirements of corporate enterprise. Because of the indirectness and the indefinite timing of returns from corporate contributions, a new kind of corporate ecology is needed to link cause and effect, to state conditions, and to provide indexes for measuring results.

6. *Does this mean the abandonment of the concepts of corporate citizenship and the ideal goal-values of business?*

No; it does mean, however, a more business-oriented conception of donative policy and practices, without at the same time reducing these to narrowly profit-centered and egoistic principles. "Enlightened self-interest," though not an unworthy principle, is not an operational one for those who have to formulate and execute company donative policies. The same thing applies to the "responsibilities of the corporate citizen"—a formula without operational content.

7. *What are the criteria for selecting the substantive areas of justifiable corporate support payments to external groups and activities that rely on voluntary contributions?*

Several unacceptable criteria can be eliminated: precedent; keeping up with the corporate Joneses; responses to the biggest external and internal pressures (as to the latter, for example, the preferences of company officers who have their pet philanthropies); selection of

210

"tax bargains" from the Internal Revenue Service's list of eligible donees. The kind of problem managers face in selecting the right area for corporate support is exactly the same as that of any other problem of business policy: what are the objectives, and what are the most feasible means of reaching the objectives? The answer is largely a matter of appropriate procedures fitted to the normal business functions of a company.

8. *What procedures for corporate donative policy and execution are most likely to turn up the right answers to question 7?*

Briefly, those procedures that most effectively relate donative transactions to normal transactions in every functional kind of company managerial work, and at the critical decision-making desks bring to bear the relevant knowledge required for getting the right answers. As in the law, where the substance of Justice is often hidden away in the interstices of procedure, so in corporate donative practices an exposure of faulty donative procedures will be a necessary first step toward sound substantive policy. If a comprehensive view is taken of donative policy as instrumental to *all* kinds of functional work in a business enterprise, this will necessitate that policy formulators examine every facet of corporate-community relationships, taking "community" in the broad sense indicated in the preceding paragraph.

9. *Given the best procedures for donative policy and practice, what are likely to be the substantive fields for action in the immediate future and in the long run?*

Good procedure will reduce this speculative question to more manageable subissues; but it may be suggested tentatively that the traditional major areas of health and welfare will rather rapidly be new foci of corporate aid. Education may be here to stay, but the kinds of corporate educational support are likely to undergo rapid change. The new demand for aid to "cultural" projects requires the most careful examination; the corporate response should not be simply a retreat before overwhelming pressures. Companies that think through their donative policies will meet every new demand with positive programs of their own.

10. *What should be the dimensions of a company's positive program of corporate support?*

The answer is certainly not a jerry-built program that shows signs of giving in to transient (but apparently irresistible) external and internal pressures. The answer has to be made on the basis of sound premises about a company's roles in the community, interpreting "community" to be coextensive with the entire economic, political, and social structure required for the company's continued and successful business operations, and "roles" as the part the company must take in all the external relationships thereby indicated. The correctness of this view of company policy has never been doubted in strictly financial ties with a company's environment. Now that the corporation has become a major social institution (even in the case of relatively small companies that survive and prosper as integral parts of a corporate-enterprise system), the other kinds of community ties must be similarly matured. In corporate donative policy there is a unique opportunity to develop a comprehensive rationale for these ties.

CHAPTER IX

The Future of the Corporation and the Arts

The Basic Tie

The probable future interplay between the corporation and the arts cannot be described principally in terms of corporate charity. It is said that corporate support of the arts will grow. Undoubtedly it will. And undoubtedly it should. There is enough evidence of a trend toward corporate support of cultural institutions generally to warrant the guess that the arts are going to be supported more and more. There is also ground for accepting the trend as sound policy, both for the corporation and for the arts.

But it is doubtful that the arts can or should rely mainly on corporate support for the growth they need in this country. Nor is there any reason to expect that corporate boards and executives will ever come generally to the conclusion that this growth is a primary responsibility of corporate enterprise. The fact is that the corporation-arts nexus based primarily on corporate donative action is and will long remain a very minor one. The more promising and exciting forms of art-corporate interplay lie in other directions.

It is not to be expected that the interplay between these two major institutions is adequately described and its future conceptually projected from the viewpoint of the "social responsibilities of the modern corporation." Such responsibilities exist and among them there undeniably may be company obligations toward the community that involve artistic and esthetic considerations. But like the donative basis for the corporate-arts nexus, the social responsibilities argument is one-sided; it seems to make the relationship between artists and businessmen a one-way street, with no responsibilities and no gifts running in favor of corporations. The result is denigrative of the artists and of the arts, as though they had little or nothing to contribute and had always to be on the receiving end of a passive relationship. There are mutual responsibilities in the relationship, and there is the need for bilateral action grounded in mutual respect for unique capabilities on both sides.

There are further difficulties with the purely donative and corporate-responsibilities bases for the interplay of the corporation and the arts. The main one stems from the ego- and profit-oriented character of the corporation and the artist as business units in the economy. A company may deal straightforwardly with an artist or an artistic institution as a customer, a supplier, an investor, or an employee, as the case may be. The artist or the art institution may deal similarly on a business basis with a corporation. No corporate-arts interplay, in the sense that we speak of it here, is necessarily involved at all. As long as the relationship is a straight business deal, all of the normal economic criteria of profitability, efficient production, bargaining, and so on, apply. Such dealings need to be kept separate from nonbusiness relationships. A company may donate to Lincoln Center, but the donation involves a relationship that differs essentially from selling services to the Center or buying services from it.

In the public-responsibility and donative conceptions of the corporate-arts relationship, too, there are business considerations, and unavoidably so. A company's gift to Lincoln Center has somehow to be justified for legal, accounting, and other business purposes. The justification is required and must be spelled out; it cannot be carelessly and irresponsibly assumed by persons who act on behalf of the company. That justification, as we have seen, entails a rationale of business prudence. Somehow or other the company's board and managers must be prepared to show that the donated assets of a corporation-for-profit have not been profligately disbursed and, at best, that a return on the investment or the business expenditure can be reasonably expected some time in the future.

Elaborate mentations are available for contrary opinion—namely, that corporate giving can be economically sound and entirely altruistic at the same time and that corporate social responsibilities all run in the direction of society and never the other way. But it is far safer to assume that when artists are on the receiving end of corporate benefactions, some quid pro quo is or ought to be expected even though we are talking about companies in an economy attuned to the profit motive.

No matter how great a latitude is allowed for managerial discretion under the more sophisticated newer conceptions of corporate governance, there remains the basic question of prudent use of other people's money. Naive notions of "shareowner democracy" are not useful since a corporate board is collectively the legal owner of corporate property and not a simple agent or representative of the so-called "ultimate owners" who hold the shares. Corporate governance requires centralized control over the disbursement of funds. These are funds in which hundreds of thousands of investors have a real interest as profit-seekers or rentiers. The holder of a stock certificate has certain claims on the managers of corporations, and may approve of corporate giving not as a good thing in itself but only as a means to corporate business ends. In some of the more esoteric lore of the modern corporation, there is a strong tendency to forget this idea. The corporation has become a great social institution, not because it disregards these basic economic interests of shareholders for the "higher" things of life, but because its goals of profitability are made consistent with other socially valuable goals.

For these reasons, in speaking of the future of the corporate-arts nexus, we must always bear in mind the reciprocal economic benefits in the relationship. Yet it would be erroneous to let this economic mutuality occupy the center of the stage. It is an error to make economic self-interest the main theme, either by overemphasis or elaborate avoidance. There is elaborate avoidance in denying the cash nexus and in conceiving the corporation as some kind of altruistic deus ex machina that will somehow come to the rescue of the arts. The business corporation simply cannot perform such a life-saving function and still remain consistent with its central productive role in our economy. Certain companies, of course, may elect to do so. But for the general run of companies in the business world the corporate-arts relationship, for continuity, must be based on common goals of the artist and the executive.

Common Goals of Artist and Executive

The real tie that binds the corporation and the arts is to be found in their common goals. The corporate executive may take an incidental and peripheral interest in the world of art. Yet this will never engage his deepest interest unless he perceives the parallel aims of the two worlds of art and business. Nor will the man of art enter into that partnership of equals (without which the corporate-arts nexus can only be an uncertain and even embarrassing relationship) until he sees clearly and believes sincerely that this sense of mutual engagement prevails in the corporate world. Both sides are engaged in tasks that are teleologically related.

The common telos in business and the arts appears in probing certain current issues that stir modern man and modern culture deeply. On the surface, the corporate world and the world of the arts are disparate, or, at the most, at an arms' length relationship. The common goals appear, however, in specific issues. When we begin to examine the purpose, scope, and methods of education, to take a prime example, it soon becomes obvious that both executive and artist can and must enter the dialogue. The same holds true of the nation's aim at a high culture.

The long upward slant in economic growth is not unrelated to the pursuit of the nation's ecological and cultural goals. There may be in these goals a close and intimate relationship to which leaders in every sphere should give the most careful attention. If the rate of growth levels off or begins to decline, the effect on the arts and the cultural standards of the country may be profound.

We have attracted to our shores a remarkable array of talented men and women in the arts, as well as in the sciences, technology, and business. Many came because of the openness of our society. The way has been open to a flourishing life of art, of science, of culture generally, as well as of a higher material standard of living. Our "free society" has never been interpreted alone on Herbert Spencer's model of a rigorous old conservative-liberalism. It has meant to those who came, and to those who were already here, the grand opportunity to *make things* that they want to make, including things of beauty in all the arts, without let or hindrance from despotic and dogma-ridden authority. Rather, the accent has been on positive encouragement and optimism concerning untapped human resources of innovation and creativity.

Will the necessary and sufficient conditions for continued stimulus of creativity persist? The question is of profound importance to men of business and to men of art. They are, in fact, peculiarly on the same ground here, as we shall see, because of a common interest in what Etienne Gilson has called the "factivity" of art[1]—a term equally applicable to the corporate industrial world.

There are still other basic issues of the day which bring the world of art and the world of business together on common ground. There is a growing national concern about our total ecosystem. One of the issues is our adaptation, as a society, to the natural environment of land, sea, air, and space under conditions that arise and will arise as a result of rapid technological change affecting all of these elements. It has gradually dawned on us that survival depends on human respect for certain canons of natural and man-made beauty in our environment. The arts are not alien to this issue, nor do they enter the picture merely to embellish the scene. The artist now becomes an indispensable part of civilization's survival plan, to say nothing of his invaluable contribution to high culture.

The emergence of the affluent society raises questions of time, work, and leisure related to both survival and cultural advance. The corporation is deeply involved. We grasp for clues to solutions of the problem of leisure time in an age of automation. The arts acquire new significance as we search for new meanings of employment and production. The line between lay and professional practice of the arts becomes more difficult to define; the serious purpose of artistic production becomes more ambiguous. "Art for art's sake" is an ambiguous dictum at best, and it is no guide in a society that begins to take art seriously as a means to other than esthetic ends. Some companies build their own museums, hire industrial designers and architects to improve sales and public relations, create a corporate image that appeals to the more sophisticated public in the higher culture. The artist, on the other hand, moves from the garret into the marts of trade where art sells. Both institutions—the corporation and the arts—are affected by these changes in the interplay of economic forces.

But the clue to common goals does not lie in the cash nexus. Matters of art enter into the board room and onto the agenda of the directors' meeting on a great variety of corporate and public policies that touch art and business at the same time. Economic and esthetic considerations then become inextricably commingled. Directors and executives may have to take public positions on urban design, the elimination of automobile graveyards, a purification of waterways and the air we breathe, the reshaping of educational structures and institutions in plant communities, tax policies arising from more active pursuit of national goals at the cultural level, and other issues where esthetic values may become a decisive factor.

On agenda items of this kind, the man of art and the man of affairs must both compromise extreme positions and try to understand each other. They must learn a common language for the sake of drafting action-proposals. The artist must descend from the stratosphere and formulate his requirements as blueprints, designs, adoptable minutes, legislative bills; the corporate director and the legislator must raise their sights and widen their vision to take in the esthetic needs of the community. Both sides are likely to meet nowadays on the prosaic ground of facts and figures, economic analysis, and practical courses of action in corporate and public policy.

There is a common ground of procedure in these matters: both sides learn how to sit down together and consider at length and in depth the matters of common interest. There are important substantive matters, too, on which the man of business and the man of art have common goals. Among the most significant of these substantive issues is, surprisingly to many, the question of Alienation—the existentialist Absurdity of man's predicament in the modern world. It might be supposed at first blush that it is the artist who is the alienated one. But that is an erratic view. It is true that the language of protest arises primarily in art and philosophy. But is it not the businessman, rather than the artist, who has been (and continues to be) the most revolutionary force disintegrative of the old society and its orthodoxies?

Marx saw this clearly enough when he looked at the bourgeoisie of his day—a ruthless dissolver of the feudal fabric. The orthodox of both the radical left and the radical right (and even among some in the progressive middle) would have stopped the historical process of change, hoping, apparently, for more institutional rigidity. The corporate institution, far from pursuing this line, now actively threatens the old patterns, not least in its drive towards a world of transnational business for which the traditional political fabric is woefully inadequate. Economic enterprise, freeing itself so far as possible from political limitations, works as a driving impersonal force to crumble old and outworn social and political institutions.

Corporations today have powerful allies in science and the technology of the space age. A world community is being born through this alliance, despite the bar sinister of antique models of a Hobbesian world of nation-states at each other's throats. The clash of business and public policy is not exclusively a domestic issue. It appears more significantly in the international arena. And while there can

THE CORPORATION AND THE ARTS

be no doubt of the loyalty of business executives to the states of which they are citizens, it does not follow that their corporations are natural servants of national policy. Economic development and supply, in a world of scarce goods and especially in the Southern Hemisphere, will continue to depend heavily upon the partnership of state and corporation. But it is not a master-servant relationship. The corporation of democratic capitalism is a revolutionary force in contemporary society and not a static defender of the status quo. A common stereotype conveys the opposite impression, as though art and not business enterprise were the yeast of change.

In the world of art we hear much of the alienated poet, playwright, musician, and painter, as though these proponents of the Art of the Absurd were bellwethers. They are supposed to be harbingers of an age of cynicism and despair. But, as Isaiah Berlin has correctly put it, this is not an age of crumbling values and of the dissolution of the fixed standards and landmarks of our civilization. What we see, if we look more closely, is not the loose texture of a collapsing order, but rather a world "stiff with rigid rules and codes and ardent, irrational religions," both secular and sacred.[2] Among those who are the most intolerant, whose outlook is the most irrational, who would suppress and not raise the basic questions that attack ancient sanctions, we find the angry men of Alienation. There have always been angry men who questioned the ancient and accepted sanctions; but in the twentieth century Berlin points to an appallingly novel kind who suppress all questioning as sick. The cure for the "sick" questioner in totalitarian regimes, communist and fascist, is to brand him as an obsessive patient and then to administer treatment that will make the questions vanish utterly from his mind, like evil dreams that will trouble him no more.

The true artist, like the driving enterpriser, resists such treatment with all his might and main. Artists and enterprisers at their best are among the prime questioners of our time, along with the philosophers and the scientists. They have a common goal in opposing the authoritarian suppression of questioners and the totalitarian pretense of monopolizing all innovation. All this entails heavy responsibilities both for the artist and the corporate executive.

For the executive, it means an assumption of a protective role vis-à-vis art in its most trying mood, the mood of acute spiritual discomfort, and even rebellion, over the crises of consciousness of modern man and modern culture. The communist and fascist reaction to the despair of philosophers and artists has been to suppress the questioning and creative rebel that a free society will encourage in all of its spheres, including business enterprise and art. For both the artist and the business leader there must be cooperation rather than antagonism in allying with all the forces of society that can man the bulwarks of freedom at home and abroad.

The intellectual outlook characteristic of totalitarian ideologies —the suppression of issues, not by answering the great questions of the day but by classifying them as obsessions from which patients must be cured—is not absent in free societies. It is convenient, from totalitarian and authoritarian points of view, to stop men from hankering after democracy and individual liberty and from wondering whether liberty can be made compatible with coercion by the majority in a democratic state. It is thought easier simply to rid them of this *idée fixe* so certainly that it will never return to plague society's masters.

Both the artist and the businessman, for different reasons concerned always with this basic political issue, ought to be in league against the totalitarian state and the authoritarian personality to whom these suppressive tactics are so inviting. Collaborating in the name of real freedom the arts and business can be unassailable; divided they weaken the whole social structure.

The Corporate-Arts Antagonism

The engagement of the arts and corporate business has both positive and negative sides. There are common goals to be pursued; but

THE CORPORATION AND THE ARTS

there are also basic antagonisms. Some of the antagonisms of today are perhaps only the preface to comities of tomorrow. For, as businessmen and artists clash they also communicate with one another. Some of the antinomies may persist, however, because of the very nature of the relationship. The antagonisms should not be overlooked or avoided in any survey of the interplay of corporate enterprise and the arts.

To face the realities in this respect is to clear the air of cant and get to the root of nascent trends—some of them full of promise, paradoxically enough, because of the heat generated by current hostilities. The so-called materialism of the corporate business world as against the so-called idealism of the world of art and the humanities, for example, is related to the "two cultures" controversy. There are hidden truths in such controversies that need to be exposed by inquiry, just as there are superficial fallacies. There is a kind of dialectic at work here. The antipathies are not necessarily destructive. Out of the corporate-arts dialogue of hostilities there may yet arise a synthesis of great value.

The presence of some hostility can hardly be doubtful. It is there on both sides. The artist sometimes suspects the corporate world and openly charges it with anti-intellectual and antiesthetic intentions. In the world of business one frequently detects an air of contempt for the esthetic and an identification of art with dilettantism or even "dangerous radicalism"—dangerous, that is to say, to the free enterprise system and to conservative values. Businessmen, on the other hand, are not always credited with the highest motives in their support of the arts. One writer has openly charged the "immensely wealthy corporations" with setting up foundations just to "cheat the government out of tax money and assuage their do-good consciences."[3] In the world of business, the pleas of an arts-minded business leader for his colleagues' support of the cultural projects in their communities may be shrugged off with the observation that these things have nothing to do with business prosperity and that too much culture is in fact ennervating. The charges and countercharges are often born of ignorance and prejudice.

222

There is often a tendency to relegate the artist to an intellectual ghetto. That the community needs the arts and the artist and has certain duties toward them is not universally recognized in the corporate world of business. Maritain has said that the artist, the composer, the poet, the playwright expect from their fellowmen, as a normal condition of their own development, to be listened to intelligently, to receive an active and generous response, to meet with cooperation that involves a certain communion with others in society rather than this relegation to the ghetto. Maritain's plea is for more community respect for the spiritual dignity of art. In his view, a work of art conveys to us "that spiritual treasure which is the artist's own singular truth, for the sake of which he risks everything and to which he must be heroically faithful." He asks, as a first condition of the judgment of the work of an artist, a kind of "previous consent" to the artist's intentions and to the creative perspectives in which he is placed.

The felt antagonisms directed against the world of art by the world of business indicate that this previous consent has not always been established as a condition for progress in the arts. The failure to establish such consent may be due to other-than-corporate forces, yet the corporate world is not notably in the vanguard of counterforces in favor of art. Probably the indifference, rather than the hostility, of business to the arts is the more accurate picture. It is erroneous to make business per se the culprit.

There are certainly other social forces of a more acutely antagonistic nature. Max Weber wrote of the extreme coyness of the genuine virtuoso religions in confronting art because of "the inner structure of the contradiction between art and religion." Art has a certain "diabolic grandeur"; it becomes "an 'idolatry,' a competing power, and deceptive bedazzlement." The religious ethic of brotherliness stands in dynamic tension with any "purposive-rational" conduct that follows it own laws without regard to religious dogma.[4] Indeed, the artist's insistence upon independent esthetic values in their own right endangers the claims of the salvation religions, for then art threatens to take over the function of a "this-worldly salvation." Every rational religious ethic, Weber went on to say, must turn against this "inner-worldly, irrational salvation" offered by an independent system of esthetics.

The arts-religion antagonism is not always evident or present, but in any case it has no close parallel in the arts-business antagonism. Certainly the antagonisms are different both in degree and in kind, and they are not necessarily analogs. Yet there are similarities that deserve notice. Weber speaks of the tendency of men in our secular age to transform moral judgments into judgments of taste; an act may be in poor taste, for example, but not morally reprehensible or a sin. This shift in the forum of judgment from ethics and religion to esthetics has the grand advantage of cutting off further discussion since the available criteria are cloudy or conflicting. It is a shift that Weber regarded as characteristic of our intellectualistic epoch, satisfying certain subjectivist needs in such an epoch but reflecting at the same time a fear of appearing too narrow-minded in a traditionalist and Philistine way.

The esthetic mode of judgment, so to speak, thus has it over the strictly ethical or religious for the man who wants to ward off the shafts of criticism from puritans of every stripe, whether they be in the hidebound religious mold or in the secular antibusiness sects. Art and business then become silent partners as they both reach for criteria for good conduct based on taste and the mores. There are still other indices of the consanguinity of artist and executive, as in the mutuality of interest in industrial design, industrial architecture, and the many other alliances of apparently disparate disciplines.

The basic antagonisms still remain, however. We see the revolt of the irrational in art against the rationalism of bureaucratized industry (especially in the large corporation, as in big government and big unionism). We hear the cry of the Theater of the Absurd against the alleged dehumanization of this bureaucratic machine and the technological society it spans. We witness the rage of the artist when he is dismissed as an "impractical" dreamer by the "practical" man of affairs. The disjointedness of artistic presentations, as in New Wave films, stands in contrast to the orderliness of efficient and well-run organizations. The man of affairs is apt to brush aside, and show impatience with, the Absurdist and his artistic depiction of alienation, estrangement, and confusion in contemporary society. The artist, on his side, strives to state a situation that he equally deplores, but more candidly faces.

To be sure, didacticism in the arts is not always to be assumed, and indeed ought not to be expected as the essence of art. Artists are not necessarily telling us what we ought to do, or ought to take notice of, in the world around us. They may be seeking insight for themselves alone. But this very quality of introversion is likely to be anathema to the man of affairs. It is a rare business management that deliberately sets up laboratories for pure research and ateliers for the unadulterated and undirected esthetic pursuit of Truth. And when the artist is also a Man with a Mission, he is just as likely as not to espouse a mission that some businessmen abhor.

There are plenty of reasons for regarding the arts and the corporation as adversaries rather than allies and friends. Yet even the adversary interests may clash to produce new insights for both parties and fruitful results for society. There are antagonisms that can yield positive results. At the very least one has to warn against sweeping the antagonisms under the rug. Where there are signs of irreconcilable points of view—cases that are probably rare indeed—the antagonisms may arise at inopportune times to plague those who deny that there neither can nor should be any corporate-arts nexus. Somehow the difficulty that exists with both positive and negative implications must be resolved.

The Arts, the Corporation, and Education

Of all the contemporary matters on which consanguinity of interests, rather than antagonism, should prevail, the most important is education. Here the corporation and the arts have strongly parallel interests. And here there certainly can be no talk of disparateness, as though no corporate-arts interplay of interests can be realistically or rightfully entertained. This is true whether we are talking about the great aims of education in the Platonic sense, more limited aims in a time and a place, or the multifarious means to reach these ends.

Education in the great philosophic tradition of classical Greece —a life-long pursuit of knowledge approaching the ideas of Justice, Beauty, and Truth—is today a paideutic conception that reaches far beyond the schooling of youth, on the one hand, and adult education, on the other. Society is a comprehensive educational adventure, and all social institutions play their respective parts. Business and cultural institutions have integral roles in the educational process thus broadly conceived. The arts and the corporation meet on this common ground.

That business and education have common problems is no news. The schools and the universities not only prepare the young for business careers. They are in many ways professional training centers of the "knowledge industry" for a corporate age. These ways include the pressing out of frontiers of knowledge in the humanities and the arts, as well as in the natural and social sciences and engineering. And they include, too, the inculcation of respect for the heritage and hope of civilization, together with learning to use the tools that the race has found indispensable for survival and the good life. It is on these premises that corporate support of education properly rests. But, as we have often reiterated in this book, it is not primarily the matter of corporate financial support of the arts that we need to emphasize in the search for the true corporate-arts nexus; and that is true of education-corporate relationships generally. The fact is that the modern corporation is itself a great educational force in its own right. It has educational obligations and opportunities that can scarcely be stated with the limits of a corporation's donative policies.

In Plato's model of the Republic the legitimacy of all social institutions depends heavily upon their role in the education of citizens. Would this ancient wisdom apply to the modern corporation? The thought is somewhat alien to modern liberalism, especially economic liberalism, but it is a useful point of departure for examining the future of interplay between the corporation and the arts in an educational context. We can no longer think realistically of the business corporation as the lengthened shadow of the "economic man." It is far more than this, and not only because the real men who run corporations are more than facsimiles of the bloodless economic-man prototype.

A company's policies reflect a wide range of goal-values that have their source not only in the human disposition of its leaders but even more importantly in the whole community that uses the company's services. The modern corporation has evolved into the major social institution that it is today because of society's demands upon it. Men who can encompass the meaning of these demands and respond through organizational action in corporate form become today's business leaders. The others are left behind in the race for leadership in modern industry. The goal-encompassing capability of executive leaders in the great corporations includes insight into the educational potentialities of business institutions along with those associated with the more traditional business acuity. The modern corporation seeks legitimacy as an educator as well as a producer of commodities.

The corporate educator, however, may be thought of in many ways. A narrow view is that of the corporation as advertiser "educating" the consumer. A somewhat less narrow view widens corporate educational interests to take in educational institutions simply as sources of supply—the supply of manpower as well as technological and other resources in knowledge. Corporate educational work may go further to widen the investing public and make it aware of the virtues of "people's capitalism" and the availability of corporate securities. Finally, the somewhat restricted, but still somewhat more extended view, of corporate concern with education emphasizes the need for "sound" economic instruction in schools and colleges to indoctrinate the citizenry in the evils of socialism and the virtues of capitalism.

Without debating the value of any of these more conventional views of the corporation as educator—and they all have some value

—we have to use a much more comprehensive canvas here. While the approach through donative policies is not broad enough, those who have had to think through the problems of corporate support of higher education during the past decade or so know that this intellectual exercise does expose one to a vast new world of ideas. In the preceding chapter on New Dimensions of Corporate Donative Power it was evident that jurists facing this problem, as it relates to corporate gifts to universities, found themselves probing the fundamentals of corporate governance, of corporate ecology, and in particular of the legitimate role of corporations-for-profit in the advancement of education.

The old "direct benefit" rule has been retired with appropriate formalities, and in its place we now have a new rationale for donative power that places the corporation squarely among those institutions whose powers are exercised in trust for the entire community and not alone for stockholders, customers, employees, and suppliers as immediate elements in the business complex. In the leading judicial cases on donative power the corporation appears as a major social institution bound by inseparable ties to the community's educational purposes.

As the aims and the scope of education broaden and deepen, so does the community orientation of the modern corporation, and especially its rights and duties as educator. The place of the arts in education has been examined in previous chapters. There no longer can be any doubt, surely, that the arts are not the icing on the cake of civilization; they are a part of the staff of life. And as education comes generally to embrace the arts, to give them their proper role and recognition, the corporate educator will be drawn to the task of the larger paideia. This is a prospect that may frighten some executives, but assuredly it will galvanize others into action that can be enormously fruitful both for business and for the arts.

Illustrative of the point was the cross-fertilization of ideas among educators and artists at a conference in Lima, Peru, in 1964, sponsored by the Council on Higher Education in the American Republics (CHEAR).[5] The often-heated exchange of views there shows how difficult it has been to bring the arts within the ambit of university education, especially those arts which involve professional practice. There was sharp difference of opinion on the place of the creative artist in the university.

On this point a statement by Chancellor Franklin D. Murphy of the University of California at Los Angeles was enlightening.[6] He spoke from the standpoint of land-grant institutions that have responded to community demands on higher education, especially in many western states. It is in the land-grant tradition to put the universities to work, he said, for manifest and probable interests regardless of what these interests are, and whether or not they relate to the medieval curriculum. The university is a moving dynamic force that absorbs like a sponge those aspects of society that become important and imperative at particular points in our social and cultural history.

This has not always been true of universities in the European tradition. The land-grant tradition grew not only from that older tradition but also out of the soil of the United States. The chancellor observed that engineering—the application of science—was still not a respectable discipline in Oxford and Cambridge. Agriculture, based on respectable science from which some of the most interesting scientific discoveries have been derived, has been even further from the older tradition. But both these disciplines have been responses to real needs and at the same time appropriate for American higher education.

In the long-standing debate between the applied, on the one hand, and the theoretical on the other, Chancellor Murphy said that the land-grant tradition has accommodated the doers as well as the thinkers and the commentators. The debate has its medieval roots: medicine had become devitalized when only the thinkers and not the doers had a place in the medieval curriculum and application was left, for example, to the "barber surgeons" on the outside, and the return to the cadaver, the dissecting ward, the patient, the teaching hospital brought modern medicine to full flower and a proper discipline in the university. In other disciplines it has at times been hard

229

to convince the academic community that the *application* of science and the practice of professions, is as respectable within the ivy-covered walls as the contemplation of ideas. The problem is especially difficult in the fine arts, where it is more than theory versus practice; it is the *doing of* versus the *commentary on* art that raises hot issues.

A second basic problem raised by Chancellor Murphy was the verbal tradition in learning as against visual communication. The idea that scholarship and the learning process are primarily verbal has meant the downgrading of museums, theaters, the visual media —and he might well have added the audiovisual media of modern technology generally—in the learning process. The way we still hamper learners through persistent use of truncated and outworn teaching methods, together with the failure to develop their latent capacities through nonverbal techniques, has already been mentioned earlier in discussing the views of Alfred North Whitehead, Sir Herbert Read, and others who stress the need for esthetic dimensions of education.

The question is of growing interest to corporate executives, who have to rely heavily upon the academic tollgates for the recruitment of the men and women who will man the corporate institutions of tomorrow. Our almost exclusively verbal-oriented academic methods of instructing, grading, and selecting tomorrow's leaders will need to be drastically revised if Whitehead is right.

This does not mean that we must turn academia over to the artists. Nor does it mean that art should be abused and misused in the academic process. At the Lima conference, Theodore Roszak, an American sculptor, protested against the misuse of art as therapy for the maladjusted person; it might help neither him nor art. On the other hand, he strafed the faculties and course structures in the teaching of the arts. Roszak questioned whether we are geared to turning out young artists committed to the creative way of living and working in the welter of courses that fracture a student's time disastrously. This, he said, accomplishes little beyond turning out graduates that become simply more ardent museum-goers and augment a public that is overzealous for the arts for extraneous reasons. The social, personal, and vocational motives for this zeal have to be contrasted with a desire to experience what art is trying to do and say.

The ingrained conviction that it is immoral and a concession to the devil to live a rich emotional life, to explore beauty, to react to beauty, is a characteristic of American society with implications for education in the arts. Chancellor Murphy referred to this widespread suspicion that the arts are frivolous and beauty unimportant, as a possible explanation for neglect of the arts in universities. Roszak went further: the real block is the misunderstanding of art and of the artist, the kind of work he is trying to do; there is a superficial view of art as a dispensable luxury, and a failure to grasp philosophically that art is not an expedient but a necessity. Without this philosophical conviction, Roszak could see no possible institutional basis for the creative personality. He urged that there is a responsibility, resting by inference on corporate as well as other institutions, to provide an atmosphere where genius or creativity can be nurtured and can develop its potential and rightful place.

A corporate responsibility exists along these lines because it is often the business sector that calls the tune in many nonprofit institutions, owing to the make-up of their boards and sources of their supply. Here is one of the major avenues of improvement in the interplay of the corporation and the arts. In the year-by-year decisions of trustees of these institutions, concerning prosaic budgetary and other administrative matters that come before boards, the corporate executive has a duty and an opportunity to do something about the matters that Chancellor Murphy and Theodore Roszak were talking about.

They are basic matters in the corporate-arts-educational complex. And here we speak not only of the schools, colleges, and universities, but quite as emphatically of the museums and cultural centers that are increasingly taking on important educational functions. Again let it be underlined that we are not talking about corporate giving primarily, but about other and equally important policies where the two worlds of art and business intersect. The policy-making bodies of educational institutions are key loci of these intersections.

An example of the kind of question that a corporate executive may face as a member of a board or visiting committee of such institutions appears in the following statement made by President Grayson Kirk of Columbia University at the Lima Conference of CHEAR. He asked:

> Is the primary role of the university to duplicate what was done in the atelier and the conservatory, and to try to train superlatively the future performers, the painters, the sculptors, and composers or, if not actually the composers, the concert artists? Or is its primary role to follow the theory that there is an educational value to the ordinary student not only in studying art history and art appreciation, but in actually undertaking to do a reasonable, limited, amount of painting or sculpture even though he has no special talent? Should the university disregard these people and say that they should study merely art history or music appreciation, and then concentrate its activities on the select few because we all like to teach only the most gifted?[7]

He did not believe that the two different roles were compatible; the university has to choose the one that it will emphasize.

The issue was met by W. McNeil Lowry, director of the Program in the Humanities and the Arts at the Ford Foundation. He urged that there be no confusion as between two types of students—the potentially gifted artist, and the general student taking courses in the arts as an adjunct to his liberal education. A university could properly decide, he said, to accommodate both kinds of students, to have different curricula for different roles that the institution undertakes. But whatever it decided to do—take on both kinds and to pursue both functions, or to choose only one—a university should make that course of action quite clear to students, and to their parents and to others who support the students in college.

Lowry was critical of limiting courses in the arts to the gifted;

consistently, one would also cut off students in other disciplines—mathematics, economics, and so on—who never emerge as full-fledged practitioners in these fields. No one, he said, could rightfully be excluded from a field of study; academic freedom requires that we make no arbitrary attempt to contain ideas, personalities, the growth of the individual. On the other hand, he conceded that the curricular choice is a matter for each university to decide for itself.

In the training of the creative and performing artist it had been found, Lowry added, that teachers who are themselves creative artists want the spirit of the atelier and the studio, of an apprentice working with a master. This had meant the rigorous selection of the apprentices by the master—a condition that does not usually prevail in the university. There was, moreover, in the art school and in the conservatory more of the atmosphere of single-minded pursuit by students of their goal as creative artists without distractions of a liberal arts curriculum. Universities did not as a rule create this kind of environment in his opinion.[8]

That the large universities might eventually do so, however, was not denied by anyone in the Lima conference. President James A. Perkins of Cornell University pointed to parallels in the current problems that universities face in regard to the arts, and problems of a hundred years ago in science and engineering:

> If this was the beginning of the nineteenth century we might be discussing the proper role on the campus of science and engineering, not the creative arts. On any of our large campuses a person working on high energy physics has a completely separate environment, with students who operate in almost the same way as students in a conservatory. The area of the creative arts differs only in the fact that we are now going through the dreadful strain of adjustment that is needed to take the creative artists onto the campus, a process that we accomplished a hundred years ago in the field of science and engineering. The only lesson—a very hopeful one—may be that now in the 20th century we are rating the arts and creative artists so high as to force this dialogue

within the university. It may show the importance we are attaching to an area that was in second place in relation to other parts of human knowledge for almost 200 years.[9]

Art as a career of creative expression seems to require a different kind of preparation than art as a part of the culture that educated persons should be exposed to and even participate in avocationally as amateurs. Probably the complete university makes room for both kinds of education. As a matter of corporate policy it would be unwise to take too dogmatic a position on the question; yet as donors, corporations must always face the issue of objectives, and so must their executives sitting on boards of trustees in universities, conservatories, and museums.

For some companies it would seem too far afield to contribute substantially to the professional training of artists; to others this might fit precisely into corporate purpose. Companies that elect to support education, however, should seriously consider the integral place of art in liberal education and the special function of participative training in some of the arts in the educational process at all levels, from primary grades through the professional schools. To be sure, the businessman who sits on boards and committees that determine educational policies is not bound by corporate policies, but he is often there because of his status in the world of corporate affairs. This presents him with a special opportunity to impart to the corporate-arts-education complex a new spirit of concord among these elements of the equation.

The problem of concord arises at every level of education and in all of its many manifestations, formal and informal. Nor should it be assumed that the corporation's role is exhausted by considering the work of businessmen as trustees of educational institutions. Businessmen are also taxpayers and voters with local responsibilities, for example, concerning primary and secondary education in the public schools. The state of music education, to take but one facet of the problem, is hardly edifying. Curricular reforms of a basic character are required here.[10] The performing artists and the music teachers might join in the movement for a renaissance of the humanities and their inspiriting leaven at these critical levels of education; many seem now to stand by, inactive and ineffective.

Perhaps what is also needed is a better conjunction of effort among musicians, educators, and cultural centers now receiving so much public attention and growing corporate support. The financial elements of corporate support are good; even better would be corporate encouragement of the ties between these centers and the educators in all the arts. But the understanding of such issues requires deeper and broader policy studies of the corporate-arts-education complex than any company has yet essayed.

The guiding philosophy in such corporate policy has to be one that cannot be supplied by the accountants, the lawyers, the salesmen, and the advertising experts. It is suggested, but of course not formulated—for that has yet to be done in every company for itself —in two quotations from widely different sources. The first is by Robert Ulich on creativity: all creativity is a form of liberation, for "the creative man acts as a liberator when he lifts himself and mankind, of which he is a part, above that which is given towards that which can and should be done." He continues, "But today the gift of intelligence has developed so one-sidedly that man can use it for total destruction of the delicate bridges between mind and Nature, between knowledge and the deeper self, in other words, between external civilization and the true *cultura animi*."[11]

In the executive suite, it may be appropriate at this stage of our development as a civilization to press aggressively for education in this spirit. The arts and the humanities, to balance the hitherto stronger emphasis on science and technology, need more than comforting words; and the creativity they promise cannot be bought cheaply.

The other quotation is from Sir Herbert Read: "Art is a dialectical activity; it confronts one thesis, say that of reason, with its antithesis, say that of imagination, and evolves a new unity or synthesis in which the contradictions are reconciled." The artist's capacity to create a synthetic and self-consistent world he regarded as a convincing representation "of the totality of experience: a mode, therefore, of envisaging the individual's perception of some aspect of universal truth."[12]

Corporate policy norms concerning education—both within a company and in its relations with other institutions—might follow the leads suggested in the integrating capabilities of the artistic genius. It is more than doubtful that these capabilities have ever been tapped by the world of business except superficially and tangentially. To think of the arts as occasionally useful is hardly to believe in the possibility of an American culture, of which the corporation is an integral part. To seek actively the common goals of art, business, and education, is to come into the mainstream of the American culture of tomorrow.

Man the Maker

Art is a way of knowing. As a unique path to knowledge, art is an indispensable part of education. In education the institutions of the arts and the corporation meet; both are concerned with the development, assimilation, and transmission of knowledge. This, in itself, makes a strong case for the nexus that binds the corporation and the arts. Yet the argument may be vulnerable because of the premise that art is a way of knowing, a premise that has been attacked with some cogency by Etienne Gilson.[13] It is worthwhile to examine this attack and his alternative approach to art. For in his approach to art as "*ars artefaciens*," or the art that makes things, we find an even stronger nexus.

In his view of the artist as a "maker" Gilson emphatically rejects the view of Lucien Febvre (in the *Encyclopédie française*) that "Assuredly, art is a kind of knowledge." He is especially critical of that word "assuredly," for he concedes that the immense majority of men take the position that art expresses and communicates cognitions of some kind, whether as to the sphere of nature or the affairs of men. This view, Gilson complains, has even worked its way into the schools, where children are expected to "express themselves" in clay, oils, and so on. He deplores the confusion of art appreciation and the practice of the arts. *Whistler's Mother* regarded as a likeness or the expression of a mood is one thing; the painter's *Arrangement in Gray and Black*—Whistler's own name for the picture—is an *ars artefacta* that we examine from the more realistic point of view of the artist who makes things.

Gilson sharply distinguishes the "making" of art from talking and writing about it. Making things and talking about the maker and the things he makes are different occupations. And the talk, even among the profoundest of philosophers does not, in Gilson's view, usually get at the art that wrought a work of art. The talk may get at other matters of no little interest: the *ars artefacta* regarded as an example of realism, expressionism, or abstraction; the artist as a social critic or a visionary; the psychology of artistic creation; the biography of the artist; the history of the fine arts. To Gilson these are all legitimate subjects of discourse provided that one does not forget the essence of the matter: art as a relation between the artist and his work.

Art thus belongs "in another order" than that of knowledge, namely in the order of making or factivity. This does not at all exclude the role of intelligence in art. To know and to think, however, is not to produce a work of art; more is required. The idea of a novel is not a novel. Books have to be made. In every doing and making of any kind there is art. In the fine arts, which Gilson designates as the arts of the beautiful, the end or aim of applying knowledge, intelligence, and invention is "the making of beauty." It is not that truth is the handmaid of beauty, nor that art is subservient to philosophy, but only that it is the artist's business to make truth and knowledge subservient to art as matter is subservient to form. "The perfect artist is not he who puts the highest art at the service of the highest truth, but he who puts the highest truth at the service of the most perfect art."[14]

Man the Maker (*homo faber*) thus becomes the center of attention; a "making being" notable for his activity as a craftsman. Industrial production has increased astronomically since *homo faber* invented the machine tool. Science depends on a series of exchanges between knowing and making, and technology emphasizes the importance of the making being. In the unwritten history of factivity in *all* of its manifestations a systematic analysis would show the relation between the arts and the modern industrial corporation in an especially revealing light. Short of such a history we can imagine some of the delineations.

The practical goals and disinterested purposes of Man the Maker might be distinguished logically, but they tend to fuse in practice. The most "useful" things today often derive from things that men at first made simply for the pleasure of making them, and perhaps for the esthetic pleasure pure and simple. No unbridgeable chasm separates the fine arts and the practical arts. That is not only true historically, it is also a good maxim for a corporate policy and for the artist's heraldic motto. The broad spectrum of arts and crafts serves admirably the canons of utility and beauty at the same time, as in a glistening jet liner aloft, a Crystal Palace, a Saarinen womb-chair.

The beauty of these things is the beauty of artifacts, and not necessarily the beauty characteristic of things produced by the fine arts. But all are products of Man the Maker. The radiance, the quality that catches the eye, the ear, the mind, and makes us want again to perceive the thing that was made by the artist, may be there in the thing made for use, as well as in the beautiful work of art per se. It is this perceptive action—the perceiving of beauty in things made either for use or otherwise—that esthetics (from *aisthetikos*: belonging to perception to sight) takes for its province; the *apprehension* of beauty, not the *making* of it in works of art.

The philosophy of art, in Gilson's view, is concerned with this making and not with the apprehending, which is the domain of esthetics. "To apprehend is not to make, it is to know."[15] The philosopher of art, he says, tries to abstract from the always complex activities of man what makes some of these activities artistic with respect to the production of the beautiful. This leaves us with the permissible inference that in the world of industrial production,

238

insofar as the beautiful is involved (and useful things are also made deliberately beautiful), there is room for the philosopher of art. In other words, the philosophy of art is not alien to the philosophy of the corporation. This is especially the case when one subsumes under the rubric *homo faber* all men who are engaged in production. The artist and the industrialist are on common ground there; nor do they depart this ground merely because one aims solely at beauty and the other at beauty combined with utility.

Such inferences would not be entirely acceptable to Gilson or those who follow his precepts. It does seem inescapable, however, that both esthetics and the philosophy of art are common meeting grounds for the artist and the industrialist. Both are concerned primarily with factivity in the role of Man the Maker; but they are also *perceiving* men who cannot avoid the question of esthetic judgment. A layer of colored pigment on canvas, sounds produced by horsehair drawn across catgut, these are the painter's and the musician's products that are hardly more beautiful as physical phenomena than the material products of a plant operating for nonartists. They are perceptible, however, in terms of beauty, and so are many of the articles of trade. The esthetician's line ought not to be drawn dogmatically against the latter. The canons of beauty are not fixed forever, nor are our categories of men who make beautiful things. Is the jetliner designer an artist, or just an engineer? And what of architects and city planners? The couturier? The creative chef?

Gilson bases his reflections on art upon the commonly accepted distinction between knowing, doing, and making and thus concludes that "the fine arts are answerable directly neither to knowledge nor to action, but to production, and that, in this order, the specific distinction of art lies in its proper end, which is to make things of beauty."[16] Whether this is the proper and only end of art is debatable. But art as *making* is hardly debatable. It is evident that factivity and this productivity bring the artist right into the world of the corporate executive. Neither artist nor executive is certain to see the implications at once. On the part of the executive there may be little or no understanding of the kind of productivity the artist is capable of, and even less propensity to regard the things artists make as being in the same class as produced commodities. On the part of the artist, there may be little or no understanding of the rapidly growing need on the executive's side for wider views of productivity that will take in the artist's product. Both might well consider with care the implications of the passing of the age of scarcity and the advent of the age of abundance: implications both for art and for business enterprise.

What are the millions of people who can no longer produce *economic* goods (for an age of scarcity) going to produce in an age of abundance? Caught on the horn of plenty, as Walton Ferry[17] puts it, how are we to shelve gracefully the outworn economic doctrines of full employment and accept instead the possibility of a new style of civilization that is greatly productive, but productive of different kinds of goods than those we already have in abundance? Our preoccupation with the economic machinery may have to give way to preoccupation with the special factivity that Gilson is talking about: the making of beautiful things. We will have more time for philosophy—the business of knowing—and for "doing" in spheres that were closed to us in an age of scarcity.

It would be fanciful to suppose that the age of scarcity has disappeared throughout the globe. But it is fast disappearing in the more advantaged parts of it, especially in the northern hemisphere. As we turn to the task of moving the rest of the world toward the age of abundance (only partly an economic problem, and essentially an ecological one involving ideologies at religious, political, and other levels) we will need to have that higher style of civilization which the arts and the humanities offer. The road to that higher plane is not necessarily one that will be alien to the corporate executive, however. He will have understood the virtues and devices of factivity for economic goods. The making of the artist may require quite different norms and designs of production; but has not the corporate executive already been severely tested and educated by the computer, the simulator, the age of space technology, and the welfare state? He cannot be completely resistant to the arts of the age of abundance.

240

The task of adaptation will be more difficult for the world of art. The surrealist strain in art and culture which defies society and employs a peculiarly violent strategy for exploring the "crisis of consciousness"[18] of our time will have no ground to work on. Inertia may keep a cry of protest in the air. The problem will be to help Man the Maker see the profound change that has come in the world of abundance, in his immediate vicinity, and to expect a shift of production to new fields. The age of the artist may be much nearer than most artists suspect. Alfred North Whitehead remarked that religion had been powerful in the nineteenth century; then came science at the turn of the century; in the thirties came the educationists. He guessed that "in another generation or so, the germinating power in American civilization may be the artists—using that term in its broadest sense—the creators."[19] He had in mind more than Gilson's production of beautiful things, and in broadening the definition of making, of creativity, he would have included, had he lived, the productivity of the Space Age.

The Corporation, the Arts, and High Culture

A high culture, as reflected in the state of the arts, science, philosophy, literature, and scholarship, is one of our national goals. In some respects we have gone far toward this goal; in others we lag. What is the role of the corporation in this effort? To survive as a social institution, the corporation must keep near the mainstream of the civilization that sustains it and that it serves. Is it, then, a corporate function to adopt positions and to act in accord with policies that move the country toward a higher culture than we now enjoy? Or is all this a matter if great indifference to corporate executives?

The answer is that it is not in fact, nor can it properly be, a matter of indifference to the men who direct large business corporations. Business leaders in the leading companies usually have personal and avocational interests in one or more fields essential to a high culture. Despite the rigid exclusion of corporate purpose from cultural fields, on the ground that profitability is the only legitimate corporate objective, business institutions are run by men and not automatons; and man has a wondrously complex set of motivations. It is manifestly impossible to distil out the entrepreneurial and profit-seeking motive as the sole operational element in the nine-to-five executive.

But the case for corporate involvement in the national effort toward a high culture is not based on such human contingencies. The case is grounded rather on the meaning of high culture for the corporation as a major social institution. It is essential not to underestimate or neglect the importance of this involvement. It can already be seen in corporate interest in the advancement of science. This is new. Traditionally our American culture has been characterized by neglect of abstract thinking and the esthetic side of life, with emphasis instead on resourcefulness in mastering the physical environment of a new continent with an abundance of creative energy and courage, backed up by the conviction that nothing in the world was beyond one's power to accomplish. Now we must add: nothing in space or in the microcosm of the atom.

In these new efforts to master the environment, corporate action has been salient, along with government. And because of the nature of the endeavor, demanding as it does sophistication in science and technology, the corporate interest in abstract thinking is now notable. Even a generation ago one did not find page after page of help-wanted company advertisements seeking solid-state physicists and esoteric mathematicians. At least in the scientific realms of the high culture the nation has arrived by force of circumstance.

There is a new respect for pure science in business board rooms as well as in universities. Basic research has proved its worth to "practical" men who once hooted at theoretical scholars in their ivory towers. Now it is generally accepted that scientific abstractions are "practical." The explosion of scientific knowledge, moreover, leaves corporate managers buried in masses of information that have to be sorted out, analyzed, stored systematically, and retrieved instantaneously by methods that make old techniques obsolete. The computerized, automated, and otherwise modernized production processes of today have brought into business corporations a new awareness of the meaning of high culture, at least in its scientific aspects.

But this awareness does not stop at science and technology. Even the philosophers and the poets are beginning to achieve a certain recognition. It is a slow beginning. There is not yet the same drive toward corporate involvement in the nonscientific and nontechnological aspects of culture. Military hardware and space technology are marketable commodities. The arts do not yet seem to offer the same dazzling inducements. Corporate concern for the arts and other nonscientific aspects of the high culture still seems to be peripheral. The corporate-arts nexus thus is often treated, as we have noted, as purely incidental to the donative power of corporations. That this is a truncated and immature view of the matter is a major theme of this book; the donative power is but one—and not even the major—corporate power to be exercised in the interplay of the corporation and high culture. This appears more clearly when we (1) consider the threefold task of intellectuals as the practitioners and custodians of the various genres of high culture, and (2) assay the role of the corporation in this task.

Three Tasks in High Culture

The corporation is necessarily aligned with both practitioners and custodians of high culture: scientists, artists, scholars, and philosophers. This is a fact that is slowly gaining recognition. The threefold task of the custodians and practitioners of high culture as defined by Shils[20] is: (1) discovery and creation, (2) conservation and interpretation, and (3) maintenance and extension. The first part of the task is the discovery or creation of something true, genuine, and important to perceived experience, expressed in ways that add to and enhance the value of the stock of culture of the human race. Then there is the matter of conserving and reinterpreting this inheritance. Finally, the influence of a high culture has to be main-

243

tained and extended to other sectors of society beyond the centers of discovery, creation, conservation, and interpretation.

In every phase of this threefold task, the modern corporation is involved. It has both opportunities and responsibilities. It has responsibilities to the practitioners and the custodians of high culture. The responsibilities are, in some instances, indirect, and require support (not necessarily or exclusively financial) of those who more directly practice and care for the elements of culture. But, in other instances, the corporation can and should take a direct and active part. Those who work for a corporation will of course take an active part as members of their several communities of interest. But the corporation, as a collective entity, has responsibilities that have to be assumed explicitly by board and executive action concerning company policy.

Corporate opportunities are equally significant. Discovery and creation are less immediately the task of the corporation than the other aspects of conservation, interpretation, maintenance, and extension of culture. But even here, issues of corporate policy arise. The centers of discovery and creativity are, it is true, not characteristically in corporate hands. The poets, philosophers, and artists— to take outstanding examples of the creators and discoverers of our high culture—are located elsewhere, and so are most of the scientists.

By preference these creators and discoverers inhabit the sequestered zones of society, preserves for their activity that are shielded from the rush of affairs. They are found in the universities, conservatories, museums, and scientific institutions. Even alienation, misery, and poverty have been historically the conditions of life for some of our greatest creative minds. There persists a school of thought that demands privation as a condition precedent to creativity, but most corporations have abandoned the idea, at least where scientists are concerned.

Where shall one look for the seminal ideas from which tomorrow's science and technology will burgeon into vast new industrial fields? It is not considered good corporate policy to discourage affluence among the potential scientific creators and discoverers. Rather, one

244

searches out these people when they are as young as possible and makes sure that they get every educational advantage and are then offered high rewards. Nor is the search for talent confined to technics and the application by science to engineering problems. Increasingly, it is recognized not only that basic and "pure" science are essential fields to foster, but also that the future leaders of business must be drawn from many disciplinary areas.

The creative mind, the mind of Gilson's maker of things, may be nurtured in many kinds of academic departments or outside the groves of academe altogether. We learn eventually that there are many royal roads, and that we must encourage the paupers as well as the princes. We try, perhaps too fitfully and too uncomprehendingly, to lower the barriers against the budding discoverers and creators. We see that discovery is more than scientific work in the laboratory or exploration on earth and in space.

The undiscovered realms of future knowledge of human motivation and action are too numerous for comfort in an age that prides itself on scientific achievement. The discoverers are people who are willing and able to push out the frontiers of knowledge in every conceivable direction, and not least in the arts. We need discoverers of new ways of penetrating the mysteries of human behavior, of man's vertical reach for the spiritual verities, of the way we learn about nature and about each other. There are barriers to such discovery.

Barriers

We pride ourselves on our open society, with its relative freedom of inquiry. We despise the communist and fascist totalitarian and authoritarian prisons of the mind. Yet the battle against suppression and censorship, in many guises, goes on in our midst, even as the twentieth century draws toward its close. What we can read, and what we can see and experience in the theater, for example, are still bound by conventions and laws that differ only in degree from the authoritarian prohibition that we, as a free people, detest.

The young potential discoverers and creative minds are inhibited by these restrictions. They rebel against them—often in vain. These rebels need corporate allies. Corporate policy cannot be indifferent to the barriers standing athwart our national movement toward a high culture that all will benefit from. Some of the barriers are rooted in custom and the prejudices of a cruder age. As a culture we in the United States have not favored the arts, and especially not the "fine" arts. In the Far West and the Middle West they have often been suspect as effete or worse, though the picture has changed radically in the last generation or two.

Today, with mass media exceeding in power all those of previous generations, the danger is of another kind: all parts of the country respond to the purveyors of entertainment over the air and on the screen and in print that "sells." The purveyor, it is charged, is afraid to raise the readers' and the viewers' standards even one inch above the average level of demand for fear that there might be a mass flight from the medium. But the leveling down also involves a kind of self-censorship by the purveyors. Certain fields are bypassed for fear of unfavorable public reaction. Whole areas of thought and human interest are deliberately excluded from television and theater screens, thus restricting the field of creative writing at the source, and cutting off the stimuli that would otherwise reach potential creators and discoverers in the audience.

New Opportunities

There are more subtle forces at work to inhibit creativity in our mass-production economy. The "devil theory" that the purveyors themselves keep the content of the mass media at a low cultural level does not help much to get at these subtler forces. Nor do neo-Marxist interpretations. We could do with more gadflies such as Marshall McLuhan, whose *Understanding Media*[21] raises some very pointed questions. Is not "the medium the message," he asks, and if so who are the creative people that are going to discover ways of using the mass media toward new levels of high culture? Is our "eye culture" too obsessed with the printed page and the logic of written language? Are media in the process of changing democratic institutions in basic ways? Are not the rebels in the arts opening new vistas for us, against our will perhaps, so that we can have less "hot" or data-laden messages for use in perceiving and communicating meanings that have been hidden from us because we shun the "cool"? Is not art on a par with the scientific method in telling us what is happening to the old, received culture—a kind of DEW-line warning of things to come?

The explosively hostile reactions to such questions indicate a trend that the longheaded business executive will not ignore. There are suggestions from McLuhan and other communications specialists that will interest many outside the business of televising and publishing, for they indicate new directions in creativity. Who knows what the implications will be for any business in large corporate form? On the profit-and-loss side alone, trends in the arts can open up vast new terrain for enterprise and close down some old overworked fields. It is well known that this is true in technics; the truth is not so widely recognized as to the arts. Even this late in the day, of course, there are still many corporate executives who do not face up to the need for basic research in science because they cannot see a quick payoff. Such shortsighted managers will not be receptive to the significance of the corporate-arts nexus. But their competitors will. And creativity in art teamed up with creativity in enterprise will in all probability lead to startling market quotations in the next decade.

On the other hand, one should not overlook the fact that disengagement of the world of business from the world of art has been historically valid in many fields of enterprise. There was simply no reward in the offing, either for the businessman or for the artist. This disengagement has been defended—rather urged—on the artist's side for entirely philosophic reasons, however.

Maritain's view is that a true sense of the common good understands that art and poetry play an indispensable part in the existence of mankind precisely "because they deal with an object independent in itself of the rules and standards of human life and

the human community"; they do so because "men cannot live a genuine human life except by participating to some extent in the supra-
human life of the spirit, or of what is external to him." Man needs
poets and poetry (Maritain uses these terms to cover many arts)
as he keeps "aloof from the sad business and standards of the rational animal's maintenance and guidance" and gives "testimony to
the freedom of the spirit." So it is just to the extent that poetry is
"useless and disengaged" that it is necessary, "because it brings to
men a vision of reality-beyond-reality, an experience of the secret
meaning of things, an obscure insight into the universe of beauty,
without which men could neither live nor live morally." Leave the
artist to his art, Maritain insists, for he serves the community better
than the engineer or the tradesman. Art serves the community in its
very freedom from the interests of the social group. We can be grateful to the poets, "not only as lovers of beauty, but also as men concerned with the mystery of their own destiny."[22]

This notion goes far, and not all artists would agree with it. It
does, however, indicate one reason for the general reluctance of men
of affairs to engage themselves with the state of the arts as a practical
matter. The aloofness of the artist is not good ground for such a disengagement of interest. Men of affairs are expected to take these
attitudes of others in stride, to pursue the rational method (their
forte) in integrating all of the factors of production, not only of
the firm but of the economy. This rationalism now extends to the
political economy and even to the cultural matrix as a whole. One
expects it of men of affairs in political capitals. The private sector,
if it is to sustain its vitality in the social fabric, must likewise broaden
the planning vision.

Among the relevant cultural factors are poetry and poets, for the
very reason that Maritain insists upon: independence of spirit. That
poetic independence is an invaluable resource in a society headed
toward or maintaining high culture. It is probably a prerequisite
of the discoveries and the creations that make high culture what it
is. We cannot live entirely on the inheritance of past discoveries and
creations. Our age must continue to produce them, and as richly as

possible. In art, as well as in science, these continuing contributions must flow freely.

At this point the man of affairs, and especially the corporate director and executive, faces a dilemma. Conceding that he has an interest in the arts, not as a private person alone but particularly as one who acts on behalf of a business firm, in which direction shall he go? Shall the corporation support the general principle of culture for the masses or an elitist position on high culture? "More is less," so goes the dictum against culture for the masses, a supposed dilution and downgrading of culture. This position is vulnerable as undemocratic and unsuited to an economy based on mass production and mass distribution as vital to the life of trade.

A different position might be one of rigorous neutrality. This is not a position that is open to most corporations, which are ineluctably involved. The artist may well, and properly, choose the poet's Maritainian aloofness from the world of affairs; the man of affairs cannot do so. And nowadays the high culture is so vital to the state of the economy that he would not ordinarily choose to do so. Nor can he dodge the "two cultures" issue that C. P. Snow posed for England, but which is an issue in another form for us on this side of the Atlantic. The modern corporation is already deeply involved in science as one of these "cultures," and now the humanities are making their claim, not only in political capitals but in board rooms where issues of donative power arise. The problem, as we have seen, reached far beyond the proper exercise of the donative power.

Laissez-faire in these two cultures is no longer possible—if it ever was. Both policies of governments and the corporate policies of large collectivities in the private sector have moved irreversibly into both fields. Organized society, in short, has now moved in to do something about the promotion of the sciences and the arts on a large scale. National foundations of the sciences, the arts, and the humanities are here to stay. They will work in collaboration with the vast network of semipublic and private associations in these fields. Private and voluntary action are necessary correlatives of public action in all. The corporation will be called upon to fortify this pluralistic principle of public-private collaboration, both to avoid the dangers of statism and to vitalize the whole effort at the grassroots. A deliberate attempt will be made, especially in the arts, to minimize central, federal dictation of cultural policy and to maximize local autonomy, initiative, and diffusion of control over the discoverers and the creators in science and art.

CHAPTER X

New Guidelines for
Support of the Arts

Democracy as Patron of the Arts

The task of putting political and economic democracy to work as a patron of the arts, without at the same time depressing the standards of our culture to dull mediocrity or worse, has now begun. Ingenious leaders, both in private and in public sectors, are seeking their way through the complex maze of conflicting ideas on the subject. And, of course, the way can be found, just as it has been found in education.

Despite some failures in public education, the nation as a whole has no reason to apologize for the attempt initiated more than a century ago to combine mass education with the achievement of high standards. We still have a long way to go, but we are enroute and there is no turning back—nor even any thought of turning back. It will be the same for public support of the arts. We have come thus far in education through a combined attack on the problem in public and private sectors.

Similar results can be expected with regard to the arts. On the other hand, it also seems likely that a long time will elapse before the arts and culture receive the same measure of public support that developed for public education. In the meantime, many gaps will have to be filled with private aid and encouragement. The corporation of tomorrow cannot sidestep its share of this burden.

What is the corporate share? Part of the answer is to be found in prior consideration of the government's share. The question is still an open one. We have done no more, at present, than to concede that the government must share the burden and not leave it all to charity and the artist's self-subsidization. That in itself was quite a step forward, though a belated one. Far-sighted politicians do not seem to have much difficulty in subsidizing scientific and technical research, especially since Sputnik in 1957. The long-range benefits of science and technology are taken for granted now, and even moon shots can be defended on grounds of national policy of clearly pragmatic value. More difficult has been the task of gaining comparable recognition of the work of artists and humanists. Their work is also a form of service to society that cannot be remunerated solely according to the laws of supply and demand. Yet we do not have any quantitative answer to the question of social value in cultural fields.

In other countries there might be found certain guidelines that are relevant at least to their national goals.[1] These guidelines will not necessarily be ours; nevertheless, they may be indicative of eventual policy in our own country. In Denmark, where a Ministry of Cultural Affairs was established less than a decade ago, a Government Art Fund now makes available for literature, music, and visual art some 4.5 million crowns a year—or about $652,000—administered and distributed by three-man committees in each of these fields. The Danish national budget runs to something like 10 billion crowns a year. The Government Art Fund does not, of course, cover other state contributions to culture, such as the support of universities, museums, television and public education at primary levels. But the Art Fund alone, in a country of less than five million people, would amount to some $25 million in United States terms of reference.

In Great Britain, the Arts Council, established in 1946, is the national patron of the arts. Even during the war the British government had decided to match the grant of the Pilgrim Trust to CEMA (the Committee for the Encouragement of Music and the Arts, a privately sponsored group) up to £50,000. In its first year the Council received from the Exchequer a total grant of £235,000 ($658,000), which increased in ten years to £820,000 ($2,296,000). Most of this money goes to carefully selected institutions that are expected to maintain high standards as exemplary proponents of the arts. Orchestras, theaters, ballet and opera companies, the BBC, and other arts institutions also receive other types of grants from the British Council and from local governments, as well as from private sources.

Although experts concede that Britain's program for the arts is of a high quality, they recognize that other countries far exceed the United Kingdom in financial support. Austria, for example, with a population one-seventh that of Great Britain, spends twice as much. Switzerland, Holland, West Germany, France, and Italy all surpass the British in their arts budgets. The Arts Council of Great Britain recently estimated that £12.5 million a year would be adequate to aid the performing arts on a nation-wide basis. In comparable population terms, the United States would require $25 million for the national support of the performing arts alone.

But these are merely comparative budget figures that say little about the larger problem of national commitment to culture. Putting aside the federal question—the question of division of powers and responsibilities among federal and state governments for the support of the arts—can it be said that we are ready, willing, and able as a people to speak up for culture through *governmental* action, and if so, how purposefully? Assuming there should be government action in this area, to what extent should responsibility be shunted off to the private sector?

The Public Sector and the Corporate Role

This issue will be debated increasingly now that we have the National Foundation on the Arts and Humanities Act of 1965, which establishes a National Endowment for the Arts and a National Endowment for the Humanities and authorizes appropriations of about $20 million a year for the first three years. The figure is small, but it may increase with time. The actual appropriations doubtless will call up, every year, debate on the nature of our pluralistic society and the role of governmental support of the arts in such a society. How much support should come from the private sector? To what extent will public support endanger freedom of artistic expression? Is the indicated wilting of traditional congressional prejudice against federal support for culture a laudable step that relieves the corporate sector from much of its obligation toward the arts? Or will this small start toward national backing of the artistic phase of high culture lead (just because it is small and may be kept small) to substantial matching grant programs by states, cities, corporations, and private individuals? Most of all, will the new Act give impetus to private-sector recognition of the arts and the humanities as indispensable elements in high culture, and pave the way for policies in the private-sector groups—especially business corporations —that underline this recognition?

In the Senate Hearings, Dr. Glenn Seaborg, chairman of the Atomic Energy Commission and a Nobel Laureate in Chemistry, said in support of the legislation: "We cannot afford to drift physically, morally, or esthetically in a world in which the current moves so rapidly perhaps toward an abyss. Science and technology are providing us with the means to travel swiftly. But what course do we take? This is the question that no computer can answer for us."

In the momentous step taken by the United States in establishing the National Foundation on the Arts and the Humanities, there is a partial answer to this question. President Johnson, in proposing the bill, declared that no government should seek to restrict the freedom of the artist, for "in proportion as freedom is diminished so is the prospect of artistic achievement." He further observed that the government could recognize achievement in the arts, help "those who seek to enlarge creative understanding," increase "the access of our people to the work of our artists," and establish the arts in the public mind "as part of the pursuit of American greatness."

Senator Claiborne Pell of Rhode Island, a sponsor of the bill, said that for the first time in this country a president has supported a measure that "combines the two areas most significant to our nation's cultural advancement and to the full growth of a truly great society." Frederick H. Burkhardt, president of the American Council of Learned Societies, testified that "the National Foundation for the Humanities and the Arts would be a dynamic institution dedicated to creative cultural work, a visible, living monument to human knowledge and action."

There were outspoken opponents of the bill. Some warned of the danger of entry of the government into the world of ideas. There would be a "despotism of taste" imposed by the Foundation. The "cultural czars" heading the two endowments would have the power to disburse millions of dollars at their own discretion, setting standards that recipients would have to meet. "Regal taste-making not seen since the days of Catherine the Great" would pervade the cultural life of the nation, demanding that public funds, gathered under compulsion of the tax laws, be withheld from novelists, biographers, musicians, painters, sculptors, and choreographers whose work could be brushed aside as having no significant merit.

One critic said that the nation was stumbling into the arts with all the grace of a two-ton Tony Galento trying to do the minuet. The *Wall Street Journal* said that the bill would create "a pattern for surrealistic bureaucratic confusion" with its hydra-headed foundation-council setup for deciding which applicants for grants would meet federal standards of "substantial" artistic and "cultural" significance under the terms of the bill.

The prognoses of doom have not been realized. The powers of the "czars" are quite limited, and they are under scrutiny of the councils as well as the public eye—more so, indeed, than any previous large-scale effort to advance art. The institutions created by the Act—a National Repertory Theater, a National Opera Company, a National Ballet Company, an American Film Institute—have not yet been granted enough money to do much. But a principle has been established: that the Government of the United States commits itself to an official regard for the arts and humanities. Congress has endorsed the concept that the nation has a duty toward the arts as they relate to the lives of Americans. The opposing view that high culture is somehow un-American has been laid to rest.

A rejection of the arts as an integral part of American culture is now meaningless. The debates that will arise over the implementation of the Act, the meaning of its clauses, and the purposes of its paragraphs in the national effort at the high-culture level, can be bitter and prolonged. But for the first time in our history it will be a debate with a new flavor, a serious inquiry into the meaning of art for national purpose.

Nevertheless, there will be room for quite diverse views on the role of private sectors in this purpose. The course of the debate will determine whether we can bring to bear both government and corporate resources, together with other resources in the pivate sectors, without impinging on freedom of expression. This task involves, as we have said, in the previous chapter, the creation of arts, its conservation and interpretation, and its maintenance and extension. No one aspect of this task can be safely neglected—or left in the hands of any "czars," public or private. It remains to be seen whether those who effectuate the purposes of the Act of 1965 and who work at state, local, and corporate levels toward the fulfillment of the threefold tasks referred to earlier, will sustain a proper balance among the elements named.

The question of balance of power between the public and private sectors of American life is a well-worn theme in the political economy. It is a theme less understood with respect to the arts. We are now facing the question for the first time. During the Great Depression there were temporary governmental incursions into the arts; the purpose was subordinated to economic recovery. Today a long-range program will have to be worked out, and the program ought to stand on its own.

The authoritative bodies established under the National Foundation on the Arts and Humanities Act of 1965 will be dealing with this issue for a long time to come. So will Congress, as annual appropriations come up for debate. The President and the Bureau of the Budget will have to face the issue regularly, as will every level of government down to municipal and local units. There is no reason to suppose that the larger corporations will be able to avoid the issue, if only on the question of matching grants for which corporate support will be sought more and more urgently.

But for corporations, it is not merely a question of matching grants for the purpose of aiding art institutions to meet financial conditions set by public bodies. If, as we may suppose is the case, there is to be a strong new impetus to the growth of the arts in this country, corporate enterprise will be affected in many ways, only some of which can now be predicted. The practitioners and custodians of the arts are going to enjoy higher status than they did before. They will demand, and receive, a larger share of the national income. They will be more influential in the determination of public policy on such issues as urban planning, architecture, and the role of the arts in public education, in our international relations, in highway design, the layout of parks and recreational areas, the use of public buildings, patent and copyright law, the uses of leisure time, and so forth.

Pluralistic Aspects

As the practitioners and custodians of art move up to the table of power in the United States, the more traditional power-holders will have to make room, listen to their proposals, and come to terms with them as a social and political force. We must expect to see the rise of new associations and the strengthening of the established ones in the arts for the exercise of this new power. Corporate policy will have to deal with this new power just as it has had to deal with the power of labor. The parallel need not be overdrawn. It is a question of degree. But there is a strong tendency among all professional and trade associations to assume a guildlike character. In raising standards for a profession, a characteristic move is toward exclusivity.

Insiders tend to give the cold shoulder to outsiders. In the name of freedom to raise artistic standards, the freedom of individual artists may be jeopardized. Also, other, nonartist competing power blocs in society will have an interest in any guildlike tendencies among the arts. Insofar as the corporation is a user of the arts, a buyer of talent, and employer of the resources of arts institutions, it is inevitable that clashes of economic interest will arise, requiring comity and conciliation.

The harmonizing of a social complex into which the new power of the arts is introduced raises political questions that only now begin to show on the horizon. A plea for the complete exclusion of public governments from the realm of art may be anticipated. But this could only mean the tacit approval of private power pyramids in the arts, uncontrolled either by government or by competition.

Pluralism in the nation's mosaic of art institutions may turn out to be as important to freedom as the pluralistic economic structure —a basic tenet in our constitutional system, broadly conceived. And just as most business leaders now recognize that they have a real stake in the preservation of a pluralistic economy, with its numerous decision centers as against one authoritarian center alone, so may corporate leaders of tomorrow come to realize the value of a pluralistic culture for the arts.

Quite aside from any issues of corporate giving in support of the arts, there is then the more fundamental question of corporate support of cultural freedom. It is vitally important to business that optimum social conditions for innovation, creativity, and discovery be maintained. This principle applies equally to the arts, the humanities, science, and technology, all of which hold the promise of a healthy culture, as well as a growing economy.

The problems of pluralism in a high culture promoted by government should not be underestimated. During the hearings on the 1965 Arts and Humanities Act, Kingman Brewster, Jr., president of Yale University, warned against the troubles to be faced when potentially controversial areas in the arts come up for subsidies. As to the humanities, he favored government support of libraries and places

258

"where the selection of who you like and who you don't like is not necessary," leaving the support of areas of potential controversy to "the calculated anarchy of charitable private enterprise."[2]

There is a kind of calculated anarchy in our cultural pluralism as a whole; but there is also need for the common view, the comprehensive understanding. In our age of specialization we have lost some of the ability to talk with one another in a community. "The public sector of our lives," President Brewster declared in his testimony, "what we have and hold in common, has suffered, as have the illumination of the arts, the deepening of justice and virtue, the enabling of power and of our common discourse. We are less men for this." The new movement of government into the field of the arts indicates a sensing of this danger. Government can be expected to act for "Society, Inc." when common action is required and voluntary action is wanting.

Yet this common action does not rule out the vital role of private-sector groups. In the arts, both in conservative and innovating categories, private-sector groups are necessary. The venerable private institutions are trustees of certain standards and are a main line of defense against the debasement of values. Even so, they must be held in check by new and innovating artists and groups that provide yeast, ferment, and vitality to the arts, give them a growing edge.

Bold experimentation is as necessary as the maintenance of standards and traditions. As in science, the "chance to fail" is a necessary condition for success in new ventures. If an Art Establishment gets the upper hand, due to the inactivity of government and business in supporting and encouraging the common interest in innovation, the chance to fail disappears. Authoritarian strangleholds on art are deadly.

In the corporate-government-arts complex the question always arises: how much pluralism can we stand? How much pluralism, generally speaking, is necessary to implement national goal-values?[3] How much can we have without disrupting the social order as descending into a "farrago of fanaticisms"?[4] The problem may be less acute in the arts than in the political economy, but it is not irrelevant. The most important thing about pluralism, as a social philosophy, is that it regards centralization of authority with suspicion, puts centralists on notice that they justify transfers of power from local and individual instances to central organs of any kind. At best, pluralism is highly individualistic and not merely a case for a parochial groupism that may, in the end, turn out to be quite as hostile to human freedom as centralized authorities.

A considerable degree of centralization of authority, both in public governments and in private associations, is indispensable in order to achieve a good life; but to the extent compatible with this requisite, power should be left or devolved to all kinds of bodies—political, economic, cultural, religious, educational—according to their functions. The greatest possible autonomy of these bodies is not only necessary for freedom but for the proper exercise of their functions. Their powers need to be strong enough to attract energetic and talented people, and so far as possible, their financial status has to be independent of central authorities.

Because of the increasing interest in recent years in this pluralistic argument for corporate support of the private sectors, an argument now extended to the support of the arts by business, one needs to take a penetrating look at the reasoning. In many respects it is an unassailable argument and one that has convinced many businessmen that they have a duty to make charitable contributions for the strengthening of the private sectors of our society. A free society, they believe, is not merely one that writes into its fundamental laws certain rights of persons and their property, but one that also nourishes as a matter of principle those organizations that extend to the person, so to speak, and offer him the means of self-help against encroachments on his rights. A free society is a pluralistic society in that it encourages *many* such organizations and self-help associations, which tend not only to balance off the power of governments but also the power of each other. In the interstices of the mosaic there is individual liberty in addition to those protections of liberty written into constitutions and laws and provided by the individual's extended self through his chosen organizational instruments.

Wise business leaders know that there are many private sectors, as well as their own corporate sector that must be preserved if this pluralistic social structure is to be maintained. The support of private-sector groups with corporate funds is regarded as not so much a civic duty as a matter of enlightened self-interest; an investment in a protective corporate environment. The argument is not the crude one that all private sectors must help each other to stand up against the government. It is rather that in a free society the public government does not attempt to be omnipotent and omnipresent, and the job of governing men and getting the world's work done has to be shared by public and private sectors, and that when the private sectors fall down on the job the public governments perforce move in with their coercive machinery, to the great disadvantage of everyone. This is as true of the arts as it is of other activities.

Pluralism, as a social theory, is not uniformly praised. On the contrary, there are political philosophers who attack pluralistic theory and practice on the ground that it dissipates authority to pressure groups at a time in history when we desperately need adequately integrated authority to represent the general will and advance the public interest. To such critics, the corporate espousal of pluralistic doctrine seems to be nothing better than the old "rugged individualism" dressed up to look like good contemporary philosophy. This notion is charged with being nothing more than warmed-over laissez-faire.

A good case can be made for corporate financial support of the arts on the ground that freedom is thereby advanced in creative private sectors of substantial interest to the corporate business world. But the intellectual problem is acute. One must be able to show substantial corporate interest in a donation, at least on a prudential theory, proving that corporate support of the arts is a good investment of corporate funds. Using the pluralistic argument in this connection one must go on to show that a *pluralistic and not a monistic* structure of the world of the arts is promoted and preserved by the donation. When these norms are applied to corporate-support programming in specific companies there will have to be considerable soul-searching about some of the grants that are now being made.

Some corporate donors, for example, prefer to give to local arts and cultural councils, rather than to individual art groups or persons. One thereby avoids deciding who gets what. But in avoiding this Scylla, what about the Charybdis danger that the united-funds method threatens the very pluralism of artistic effort that has been so much praised? United funds are not so likely to encourage the unorthodox, which in the arts are sometimes the most creative. The pluralistic argument is surely sound, but corporations that use it should be prepared to "put their money where their mouth is." It is a hard rule to follow, for the donor who follows it must set up defensible criteria in artistic fields where fierce battles rage over questions of taste.

Imagine some conservative corporate donor extending support to a contemporary composer comparable with Brahms, who at age 43 wrote his first symphony. As late as 1893, a celebrated music critic declared that Brahm's *First* was "the apotheosis of ignorance." Critics here and in Europe suggested signs in concert halls reading "Exit in case of Brahms." Will the corporate supporter of the arts today steer clear of the controversial writers, composers, choreographers, and performers, electing instead to aid an Arts Establishment? If it does so choose, disregarding the new, the venturesome, the creative, the corporation will move against a pluralistic structure of the arts, and move instead toward uniformity and a controlling Establishment.

This is looking on the negative side of the question. Assuming a positive program of corporate support of the arts—positive, that is, from the standpoint of pluralistic doctrine—one may very well imagine a vigorous growth of architectural, musical, dramatic, and balletic activity if business companies set out deliberately to encourage the unorthodox, the new, the untried. In that case, programming of corporate support will have to be geared to norms not now widely accepted in the world of corporate donors, norms that would defend the search for new talent as a kind of artistic risk comparable with business risk-taking. The corporation that takes the lead in this kind of programming will make a name for itself, and yet it will be in the best tradition of liberty.

Non-Donative Support

We have just been considering the pluralistic aspects of the case mainly as to corporate donative action. Actually, the possibilities of corporate action in constructive support of cultural pluralism are greater in other areas of corporate policy than corporate giving. Because of its influence in the community, a corporation can affect public policy by taking positions on many issues that will either hinder or help the arts. The "good corporate citizen" cannot afford to be neutral on these issues if cultural pluralism is at stake and the vitality of a center of art is threatened. The issues of federal policy in particular, require study, and not dismissal with pat answers. For example, on the question of federal subsidies and matching grants for the arts under the 1965 Act, a standard policy line of retrenchment in public expenditures is not informative. Government encouragement of the arts and the humanities may or may not strengthen cultural pluralism in America, but a company's position on this issue ought to bear some relation to its own policy on art.

To take another example: a company's position on a bond issue for a cultural center for the local community or for an arts council. It is not to be assumed offhand that the proposal is good or bad, from the company's point of view. Some degree of sophistication on these matters is required if a stand is taken, and increasingly it is difficult for a major company in a community to avoid such an issue. Traditionally these issues are referred to certain desks, perhaps that of the company legal counsel or the corporate secretary, or to community services or to some donative component. Generally, it may be supposed that "public relations" could handle the matter.

But what does "public relations" know about the arts and about the case for cultural pluralism in the community? Advertising may be the extent of its competence.

The irreversible trend toward corporate involvement in the arts calls for special competence in dealing with these new relationships. They are not primarily donative relationships, nor relationships with the public in the usual sense. They involve the common goals of art and enterprise, and understanding requires high-level attention in any corporation. It is especially important at this juncture to enter a caveat against the assignment, within a company, of the corporate-arts relationship to staff components dealing primarily with employee relations on the ground that their free time is the heart of the issue.

The Leisure Problem

Today there is a "leisure problem," or one might better say a complex of problems that seem to cluster about the idea of leisure. More likely, they cluster instead about another idea: the notion that we are approaching an unprecedented age of free time for everybody. There is concern that newly-won free time will be badly spent; that those who use their free time badly will undermine the high culture and even civilization; and hope that wise policy could open the way to a high culture on a democratic basis never before known to man.

These and other issues associated with "leisure" become a matter of interest to a student of corporate institutions because the policies of these institutions are widely expected to affect the outcome of the leisure problem. Specifically, as to the corporation-arts interplay, is there a way that business corporations can help to solve this leisure problem, or complex of problems, through constructive relations with the arts?

Although there is no certainty that we will have as much "free time" for the mass of men as we think, there are already gloomy prognoses of the unhealthy state of affairs that free time precipitates. There is, for example, the psychiatric view that Western man is quite unprepared, emotionally and psychologically, for the free time that modern civilization presumably offers. Some persons are said to become alienated from themselves and from their fellows, or to become compulsive participants in "leisure-time" activities that do not really answer their basic need. Instead of enjoying their free time from work, they look for a second job; and this may be the symptom of an inability to adapt to free time and not necessarily a response to economic necessity.

Leisure-time marketeers are beginning to flood the markets with facilities and proffered activities that are supposed to improve our external resources. But it is charged that people everywhere are overestimating and misconceiving these external resources and facilities as the answer to the "leisure problem." Rather, the underlying need is held to be the development of one's own inner resources, to relax, to do things for the sake of doing them, to seek satisfactions that money cannot buy and marketeers cannot sell. This kind of adaptation to "free time" is blocked by a number of things in our culture. The "shapers of choice" do not in fact make leisure widely possible today in the United States. Sebastian de Grazia, in *Of Time, Work, and Leisure*, corrects many errors in the facile talk about "free time" and the true nature of a life of leisure, which is too often simply equated with time off the job.[5]

At the twenty-fifth anniversary of the Association for the Advancement of Psychoanalysis in New York City in November, 1965, a two-day symposium—sponsored by the Association, the American Institute for Psychoanalysis and the Karen Horney Clinic —was held on the subject of "The Changing Image of Man: A Challenge to Psychoanalysis." At this meeting one speaker rejected the notion that academic education and exposure to the arts, sciences, and humanities would guarantee creative adaptation to new expanses of free time. Public health problems, in fact, seem to have arisen from the new situation. Seriously maladjusted people resort to psychiatry to free themselves from dangers related to so-called leisure time. The issue needs clarification, and it is by no means an issue solely for the guardians of health. The problem of leisure has large dimensions and a long history.

The whole struggle of the human race was divided into two chapters by President Garfield in 1880 at Lake Chautauqua: "first, the fight to get leisure; and then the second fight of civilization—what shall we do with our leisure time when we get it?"[6] The second chapter cannot yet be written, for we are still struggling. We have some free time, but our so-called leisure becomes a mere parenthesis in the lives of men and women who conform to the method of work and time. How vacuous will these parentheses be? How richly filled, and to what extent by the arts, might they be?

Garfield probably had his sequences wrong. There has always been a life of leisure for the few. According to Aristotle, the only fit life for a Greek citizen, a free man, was a life of leisure. He did not mean "spared from work." A free man did none of the work of a slave, who was essentially an instrument and not a free man at all. Thus, the Aristotelian dictum: "We call a man free when he exists for his own sake and not for another."[7] Philosophizing was time-consuming; but it was the free man's way to escape from ignorance; work could have its affirmative aspects in the search for truth, goodness, and beauty.

Art for art's sake is work of a noninstrumental nature. The maker of things, in Gilson's sense of "making," is an artist and a free man. This kind of leisurely life has always been a boon and a goal of humane civilization. Our cybernetic age of limited hours of work and automation is not the first to see a leisure class. Many men have always labored without any hope of leisure, whereas others have never allowed circumstance to deprive them of it. This was true in ancient Athens. Garfield's chapters are, therefore, not historically sequential.

A good state, a great society, must offer all men leisure. That is the real difference. Here we have to distinguish between leisure and time off the job, and between being "out of work" and having noninstrumental work to do for its own sake. Time off the job or time on one's hands because one is out of a job and needs it, is no door to leisure. The identification of leisure with free time can lead to erratic conclusions about our vaunted progress toward more leisure for more people.

De Grazia argues that free time, realistically calculated, has not increased appreciably since 1850, although it is greater when compared with the old sweatshops of New York.[8] Alongside modern rural Greece or ancient Greece, medieval or ancient Rome—counting out all the holidays, festivals, games, and days off that people enjoyed then, free time today suffers by comparison; and leisure suffers even more. There is a modern fear of free time, related perhaps to the work ethic or the Sunday neurosis, the panic of a day without guided hours of work, which is embedded somehow in our Calvinistic roots.

This complicates the matter in any careful consideration of the meaning of leisure in contemporary society. De Grazia declares that although lip service is paid to the idea that leisure is a wonderful thing, there has never before been such a high proportion of the population at work. And people do not seem to long for more time free from work. The "overtime hog" wants to work more hours per day. The executive's work day is hard to calculate. It is interspersed with activities that others might call leisure-time activities that may be a part of his job although not in his office.

Consider the day of a shoemaker before the middle of the nineteenth century, before the Ten Hour Movement. He had shoes to make or repair, but not all of the time. "When he was playing cards at the alehouse he wasn't making shoes, but neither was he spending free time. Time in the modern sense had no part of the scheme. He had shoes to make, ale to drink, and cards to play, all of which he did without need of the words work and leisure."[9] With the arrival of the 10-hour day he did have free time, but all in "a lump of concentrated nothingness he never had before," observes de Grazia. The split between work and free time had thus arrived with the arrival of specified hours on the job in factories. And so, work time and free time have remained split to this day. This, at least, is de Grazia's somewhat pessimistic view of the matter.

The Ten Hour Act gave workmen who had been drawn to cities this "lump of time," but the urban mess took much of it away. For they lost space, and with it both time and money. In England the towns provided no places for recreation and games. Sunday was a bore, if it existed at all as a holiday, and free time meant idleness and drinking, especially on Saturday night. When the Puritanical frown began to vanish later in the nineteenth century and enterprises discovered a vast new market in workers' free time for spending, "idleness" won a new name: leisure. Diversion in many forms became a marketable commodity: commercial sports, outings with travel, pets, gardening, music halls, and taverns. Now the free time tends to be gobbled up by work that we put in to make enough money to buy the things we want for use in free time. It is a cycle that can destroy leisure.

Free time, spare time, pastime, and leisure are all distinguishable. Free time is, for all practical purposes, time away from work. It is time for nonwork. Leisure and pastime have affirmative rather than negative connotations. But there is still a strong tendency to regard leisure-time with suspicion as wasted time or worse. It can be seen in a "work ethic" as badly spent time that had better be spent on work. Leisure has as a positive ingredient the pursuit of happiness.

But can this ideal leisure be democratized? According to de Grazia, an ideal of leisure no longer exists in the United States, though it once was articulated by aristocratic eighteenth-century gentlemen such as Jefferson, George Mason, John Adams, and Franklin. Their ideal has been replaced, he says, by a "commercial spirit," both in government and in business in this country, which insists on attaching spending to the idea of leisure; it is an ideal of free time, of the good life, the good life consisting of "people's enjoyment of whatever industry produces, advertisers sell, and government orders."[10]

268

We have reached a new level of life; but is it not a life without leisure? We must be free of the clock if we hope to "transform the lead of free time into the gold of leisure."[11] The clock sets it off from leisure, fragmentizes it, "mesmerizes it." Automation does not help. Relatively few will do the mainly intellectual work required; the rest may live on Easy Street, with a great deal of free time. But that free time may never be spent on more than bread and circuses. Critics fear gross misuse of the free time workers already have, and especially of the vastly greater amount of it they believe automation will yield. They argue that if moonlighting does not absorb a man's free time, he will most likely seek out low entertainment, with a net loss for high culture.

Surely this is a parade of imaginary horribles. Quite aside from the bigotry of such a judgment, there seems to be little chance that we shall have either much free time or much leisure. This, at least is de Grazia's rather pessimistic view of it. He sees in our commodity-oriented culture, bent on higher and higher productivity and mass distribution of products, a "free-time/work-time duality" that severely limits any real free time.[12] Free time has limited payoff from the strictly economic point of view. The life of leisure, on the contrary, can promise nothing, even though it could accomplish much for the society that undertakes to foster it. Freedom, truth, beauty —these are the religion of the life of leisure, letting "who will go whoring after commodities, and money, fame, wars, and power, too."[13] Our ideas about work, time, and equality (a potent idea in both economic and political spheres of democracy) bar the way to an improvement in taste, as well as in the development of a life of leisure for those who elect to pursue it. The work ethic condemns off-work time as idleness unless it is spent in rest for the next work period or for other purposes good for the economy. Play is no longer sinful, yet men work as much as they did before. Rest for work's sake, repose earned by work, work for the sake of subsistence, are all excluded from the life of leisure. It is life of *"otium, scholē, theoria,* and *sophia"* for their own sake.[14]

The leisure kind play hard, but they are not bound to work-time/free-time intervals imposed by other necessities than the pursuit of these goals. The ideal of leisure can, therefore, be attacked as dangerous and subversive, and not least by the very people who are bound to the work-time/free-time oscillation of essentially unfree men. According to contemporary notions of work and equality, "the life of leisure is antidemocratic, antisocial, against organization, opposed to work and to most of the things men work for, and indifferent to home, mother, and perhaps even country."[15]

So there is not much danger of too much free time of the affirmative sort that the life of leisure requires. "A leisure class, in order to develop, must . . . live where existing political and religious beliefs set store by the cultivation of ideas. If contemplating, study, meditating, and speculation are held to be the pastimes of incompetents, the community will be hostile in ways flagrant and subtle . . . to those who live for these things."[16] To nurture in a rudimentary leisure class the idea that everybody must work for a living has to be banished in favor of a climate that deliberately encourages such a class.

On the dangers of too much free time (time off the job and away from the world's required work), de Grazia also has something to say. The real danger is not a life of bad taste; it is rather an unfree life in the guise of free time. A man can be unfree without knowing it, like a life-sentence prisoner suddenly pardoned and too-long subject to necessity to leave prison once the gate is opened. He is incapable of freedom and certainly of a life of leisure. Only a proper upbringing and conditioning of those who work, and then have more and more time off the job, can prepare them for the "better" things of life.

Here de Grazia leaves an open question: how conditioned and how nurtured, if one is to be of the nonleisure kind and cannot in fact escape the work-time/free-time syndrome? Evidently the standards for such nurturing and conditioning are to be set by the leisure kind who are creative, and these standards are not to be contaminated by either the democracy of politics or the democracy of the market.

Leisurists and the Arts

Having looked at the leisure problem through de Grazian eyes, let us now turn to another view of it. Recently a comprehensive plan for the wise use of leisure was drawn up by James C. Charlesworth, who introduced the useful terms "leisurists" and "leisurites."[17] The leisurists are the new specialists on the uses of leisure; the leisurites are people who are in a position to make good use of free time. The latter are categorized as old people, children and teenagers, wives with time on their hands after housework, vacationers, weekenders, sinecurists. Other people have time on their hands, but they are not free to use it as they please: patients in mental and general hospitals under prescribed therapy; members of the armed forces whose leisure is presided over by their officers; prisoners; and the unemployed, who have no true leisure but much free time. Excluded from the categories of people with time on their hands are working wives; farmers; some heavily dedicated professional persons; and moonlighters, whom Charlesworth calculated at some 7 per cent of the employed in 1963.

This approach to the leisure problem is somewhat different from de Grazia's. Although qualitative, Charlesworth's conception of leisure is more nearly "free time," and is not so heavily influenced by the aristocratic Greek view of high culture. He declares that leisure is growing much faster than our capacity to use it wisely; also that the more monotonous a worker's job the more monotonous the recreation he seeks in his free time. Both, he concedes, are value judgments, but then he faces the question of what to do about the leisure problem. As a result of automation and semiautomation there is a problem of "barren boredom," quite aside from the problem of unemployment. What can be done to overcome the boredom and to raise the standards of recreation?

Long hours of relatively interesting work and no leisure may or may not be better than short hours of relatively interesting work followed by vacuous free time. The question is academic inasmuch as we cannot go back to long hours. Nor, declares Charlesworth, can we expect much help from the leaders of our industrial civilization in answering the real question that recreationists and educators must face: how, in view of urbanism, stultifying jobs, long leisure hours (de Grazia would say "time off the job"), gadgets, and a residual heritage of the pro-work ethos, can we "strengthen the philosophy of recreation and extend existing programs both in scope and depth"? Like de Grazia, Charlesworth deplores the national ethos that holds that recreation for adults is a sign of a weak and improvident character, a belief, deeply ingrained by the Protestant ethic, "that work is good for its own sake and that the Lord favors the industrious." This basic ethos, together with the confrontation between East and West, with overwork due to our having too few in some occupations and too many in others, with the inundation of the consumer public by advertising to promote the keeping-up-with-the-Joneses complex, affects our leisure potential and operates to reduce it.

So we must start from such a factual situation, and not from some wished-for state of things in American society. In Charlesworth's philosophy of leisure there are several clear points:[18]

1. The wise use of leisure is more wholesome, creative, and elevating than work.

2. Programs for the wise use of leisure are a public and governmental responsibility.

3. The present preoccupation with the gross national product and growth for growth's sake should be repudiated.

4. In place of the copybook maxims that work is its own reward we must substitute the doctrine that we work in order to enjoy leisure.

5. Our leisure pattern must not be imitative but based rather on indigenous philosophy of leisure that is compatible with our economic income, our cultural pluralism, our fetish of quality, and our social intelligence.

The Charlesworthian formula is challenging to corporate executives concerned with the corporate-arts nexus. It demands, first of all, that the government should take the prime responsibility for the wise use of leisure; and by implication this means heavy government responsibility for the arts as a part of the American philosophy of leisure. The government has primary responsibility for a number of reasons. A major one is that the "leaders who preside over our industrial civilization are individualists who make no pretense of being architects of societies"; they are "neither trained nor motivated in the general public interest." Accordingly, "civic-minded people, like educators and recreationists, must follow after the industrialists, assess the social and cultural effects of what they are doing, and periodically enunciate social programs to supplement or correct those effects."[19]

Why is this primarily a governmental responsibility? For Charlesworth the answer is clear. It is a gradual evolution away from extreme laissez-faire. Traditionally, there was shock even at governmental assumption of the task of education. Then came public health, public welfare, and so on. These tasks are now all acceptable; so will be the task of dealing with the wise use of leisure. Charlesworth would avoid federal centralization. He insists that we need in every state a department of leisure with financial and legal status coordinate with that of other departments for education, health, and highways. There will also be regional and district organizations, perhaps coterminous with counties and the larger municipalities. State programs, devolved administratively so far as possible to the lower administrative echelons, would include a number of kinds of activities to be developed by the professional "leisurists." The objectives in leisure programs would include:[20]

1. Intellectual development (not training of any kind).
2. Esthetic appreciation.
3. Grace and ease in socializing.
4. Skill in nonathletic games.
5. Skill in athletic games.
6. Sightseeing, covering man-made works as well as natural scenery.

7. Nature study and outdoor life.

8. Skill in noncompetitive hobbies and sports.

9. Loafing and resting (because the fruitful use of leisure can itself become an obsession).

The programs thus designed would be for the young and the old particularly, but with an eye to the middle years when people will have been properly prepared for the wise use of leisure. Not the use of leisure for other public programs, such as the abatement of juvenile delinquency, mental and physical therapy of the ill, and prevention of disorder in correctional institutions. The leisure program must not be adjectival, but an end in itself, the one exception being the aid it offers to the integration of cultures and races for the enrichment of the mind and a broader and deeper understanding of other ways of life.

Whereas Charlesworth would make all of this primarily a governmental responsibility, he would expect private sector organizations to devote the time and effort of their staffs to coordinate programs. He specifies universities, churches and synagogues, clubs and organizations created for particular leisure activities, neighborhood circles, housing developers, housing authorities and settlement houses. Corporations are not on the list. Nor does one find any major emphasis on the arts. One of the general objectives is "esthetic appreciation," a debatable term for practitioners and custodians of the arts. Is the modern corporation, then, to be excluded from the leisurists—specialists in the wise use of leisure? And are the arts to be regarded as a minor element in the leisurist's program?

In the symposium (on "Leisure in America: Blessing or Curse?") to which Charlesworth contributed, the arts had no special place on the agenda. Perhaps this was because the role of the arts (like that of the humanities and of science) in American life was not regarded as essentially a *recreational* role, a major concern of the symposium. The conference concluded with a tentative proposal for a "Council on Social Values" to "provide informational statistics about how free time is utilized, supply economic data on income and consumer sectors, develop time budgets for use in recreational programming, prepare cooperative informational programs for the maximum utilization of the mass media, and establish normative yardsticks to see how certain agreed-upon values in the use of free time are being realized for the well-being of man."[21] Such a council, it was suggested, might spur leadership in implementing a comprehensive plan for the wise use of leisure, allied with the critics in the arts, the drama, literature, telecasting, and music.

Leisure was defined early in this symposium as "all time beyond the existence and subsistence time."[22] Another definition made it "that portion of the day not used for meeting the exigencies of existence,"[23] or free time subject to two restrictions. These were that "free time" should not preclude the performance of necessary work, and that it must not be used for the sake of work. Among the ends properly sought, under the latter definition of leisure, are those "final goods of the arts, to be enjoyed for what they are"; and it is suggested that without losing this value the arts can be engaged in actively, to make possible a greater range of sensitivity. "No one knows what capacities one has in these directions until one has experimented with multiple media, techniques, instruments. A leisure time is well used if men will not only enjoy the arts but pursue them."[24] Implementation of this principle was not developed in the symposium.

In the discussions following the presentation of papers at this conference it appeared that there was disagreement about the alleged antimony of the "work ethic" and the "leisure ethic." The distinction was dismissed by some as spurious. The values relating to work and to leisure might be different, but they were not necessarily regarded as incompatible. Nor was there agreement about the scope and objectives of recreational policies and programs. There was no general plea for the "good life" of an Athenian free man of the Golden Age of Greece, as described by Plato and Aristotle; it seems to have been assumed that their ideal does not necessarily connote the leisure goals of modern man in a democratic society.

Nor was the "mass man" of Ortega y Gasset, an opprobrious caricature, accepted as the proper tastemaker of modern democracy of a capitalistic era. The proper content of leisure was regarded as a relative matter depending on time and place. It was even suggested at one point that the professional "recreators" should only provide a "showcase of recreational opportunities" for people, who then take their choice. In a democratic society, popular taste has to be satisfied, as well as the taste of others who seek greater rewards in self-fulfillment. The pursuit of happiness cannot be dictated by an elite in our brand of political and economic democracy.

There was, however, a reference to the role of employers in encouraging the wise use of leisure. No anachronistic paternalism was intended; but it was suggested that employers should instill attitudes during work time which would lead to a more fruitful use of all time, both work and leisure.[25] Direct reference to corporate responsibilities does not otherwise appear in the report. Yet much that was said had important implications. There was general agreement that government must take the primary responsibility for comprehensiveness and balance in planning and implementing the wise use of leisure.

Voices were raised in this symposium in favor of considerable voluntary and private-sector action that would presumably include business corporations to some undefined extent. The idea, so heavily underlined in de Grazia's analysis, that a reconstruction of our ethos is required if the highest goals in leisure are to be reached, was not much developed. Some institutional change was implied, however. Participants could not agree on the interpretation of current social and economic trends as related to the better use of leisure. A conservative view left it to the established institutions to make the needed adjustments; the more revolutionary approach called for outright repudiation of some tenacious doctrines that can make or break golden plans for the leisure life envisaged, say, by de Grazia. Some of the doctrines requiring repudiation, in this view, would strike close to the executive suite.

The Corporate-Arts Nexus in a New Light

These ruminations extend far beyond the specific question of the corporate-arts relationship. Yet it is difficult to see how one can deal

276

adequately with that subject except on a broader societal canvas. The arts cannot be regarded *in vacuo* any more than the corporation can be abstracted from its social context. The arts are part of a social complex—seen at the symposium we have just reviewed, for example, as a part of the entire problem of recreation and leisure— that has far reaches into education, religion, ethics, and human ecology.

When the corporation makes an attempt to move closer to "the arts" or to almost undefinable Art, for the purpose of establishing some meaningful relationship, the corporate executive must become aware of these long reaches. For the artist, it is equally necessary to be aware of the institutional complex called "the modern corporation," which too many artists seem now to define as simplistically as the lawyers and the economists once did. On both sides, in short, the corporate-arts nexus ought to be seen in a new light. It should not be cut to fit old procrustean beds of outworn doctrine.

The corporate-arts nexus, thus seen in new perspectives, is one that suggests policies both for institutions among the arts and for business corporations. We cannot here enlarge on the former kinds of policy. What the artist must do in order to relate to the business community is not the subject of this book. It is a problem for the several specialists in the arts, more particularly for the practitioners and custodians of the arts rather than for estheticians and critics. No doubt it is true that there are still too few practitioners and custodians of the arts who have been willing to make any penetrating study of the nature of the modern corporation as a social institution. But there must be some, and the numbers hopefully will grow.

Instead of the polemics and apologetics that too often characterize artists' commentary on the corporate-arts nexus, we urgently need analysis and careful prescription of policy from that vital nonbusiness quarter. Instead of a generalized theory of art in a capitalistic and democratic society, we need from dramatists, poets, novelists, painters, sculptors, architects, dancers, musicians, urban planners, designers in every field, ceramists, the producers of art for the mass media, and, yes, even the practitioners in those so-called lowly categories of the arts "beneath" the fine arts, serious thinking about their working relationships *as artists* with the world of corporate business.

The relationship to the corporate world of the artist as artist—and not as a political or economic critic—has to be emphasized. The economists, the political scientists, and the sociologists can take on that job, and do it more or less professionally. But not the same kind of a job that one wants from artist *qua* artist. Yet when the artist attempts it, he often leaves unsaid precisely the things that we want most to hear and may utter platitudes that we have heard too often. The voice of Art, directed specifically at the executive suite, carrying the artist's own message is almost never heard—and is perhaps seldom raised. The fault is not entirely the artist's. At the executive suite there are seldom any antennae directed toward the arts. Things are changing.

The wide discretionary authority of corporate governments—that is to say, of directors and executive managers, not to speak of many managers down the line whose decisions on countless matters of company policy are, for all practical purposes, final—has large implications for the corporation as a social institution. The governments of corporations make decisions on a very broad spectrum of issues that reach far beyond the simple problem of profitability. The spectrum of issues that in fact confronts directors and managers every day in the thousands of companies in the private economic sector would astonish those who still cling tenaciously to ivory-tower corporation theory.

The point here is that some of these issues directly or indirectly involve goal values that the practitioners and custodians of the arts might regard as exclusively theirs. The fact is, however, that the modern corporation as a social institution of major proportions, actually operates with goal values that concern the pursuit of Truth through science and education, the promotion of the Good beyond economic goods, and the creation of the Beautiful through the arts. Social institutions cannot realistically be contained in watertight, logical goal-value categories.

The corporation cannot neatly categorize social institutions as seekers respectively after the Good, the True, and the Beautiful. Nor is one to conclude that the sole interest of the modern corporation in the arts is the creation of beauty. The arts have other aims, and corporate interest in these other aims is often parallel with the interests of the practitioners and custodians of the arts. There are differences of opinion among estheticians and philosophers of art concerning the aims of art, the norms of artistic criticism, and relationships between the Good, the True, and the Beautiful.

For some, art is one of the indispensable paths to truth, to the understanding of the nature of man and the universe. For others, this is anathema, since art is said to be its own reward, an autonomous discipline. For still others, there is an indissoluble tie between the Good and the Beautiful, thus making the artist a kind of moralist. These and other philosophic issues do not deter the modern corporation from becoming deeply involved in the arts—and the primary reason is that the governors of the corporation cannot escape the involvement, given both the nature of the modern corporation and the fact that its governors are multivalue goal seekers.

To take the latter point first, it seems undeniable that corporate governors will of necessity be men of rather broad-gauged value systems. The popular caricature runs to the contrary proposition that they are all money-grubbing men on the model of the "economic man" in classical economics. In this view, they are drawn as having no other motives than profitability for the firm. The difficulties with the caricature are many. As "economic men," these governors could not logically be interested only in the firm to the exclusion of their own personal economic interests; profitability for the corporate entity must be a completely subordinate goal. Critics of the modern corporation, looking at executive salaries, bonuses, and stock options will retort that this may be true; yet these high incomes are miniscule portions of the corporate usufruct, they are subject to public scrutiny, and they are seldom repudiated by the stockholders, who are said to be interested in company profitability, also a disputable point.

The main difficulty with the caricature of the single-track mind of the corporate executive, however, is of a different order. It goes to the psychology of men, an understanding of their motivations, and a more penetrating look at what it takes to govern a great enterprise. This is not the place to penetrate these questions very deeply, but even superficial observation of the corporate governors at work, as distinguished from the caricatures often presented in literature, reveals the multiple-goaled man of everyday life, and not the single-tracked mind of an "economic" or corporate man of imagination.

The complexity of personal value systems in a single individual, and the "conflict of moralities" in organizations (Chester Barnard's term) are not separable issues. They merge in the minds of any corporate executive. One striking bit of evidence of this is the contemporary debate about "corporate social responsibilities." Brought down to individual psychology, to the analysis of the thinking of corporate governors themselves, this debate is about the Barnardian conflict of moralities going on inside the heads of corporate governors. They ask themselves: as we sit here in the seats of power as corporate decision-makers, what norms must we follow, what standards of conduct must we adhere to? Are they so different from our personal norms, *sui generis*, and disparate in kind?

The answers are not easily arrived at. One may question whether, as corporate governors, these men are to think mainly of their *responsibilities* instead of their powers, of their obligations instead of their opportunities, of their limitations rather than their potentialities in directing the affairs of great enterprises essential to the political economy. Of course, they must think of both. But as men of action, and not primarily of the contemplative life, they are makers and doers and they have to move organizations toward getting things done on a large scale that affects hundreds of thousands of people.

Executives in the public and private sectors are expected to be creative, always prepared to act when action is called for, and to provide leadership. The dynamism of the task precludes protracted contemplative concern about responsibility. And although it is elementary that corporate governors are responsible to stockholders, they are also responsible to many other groups of people: employees, customers, vendors, the public in all its complexity, and so on.

The so-called social responsibilities of the corporation sometimes are read to embrace all of these, sometimes only a part of them, conservatively only the stockholders. When now we enter into the picture the community of Artists, with its many practitioners and custodians, there is no clear and simple answer to the question: what is the responsibility of the modern corporation to the arts?

There is not only no clear answer; perhaps there is *no responsibility* at all. The key to the corporate-arts nexus lies there. If it is difficult to decide the nature and extent of corporate responsibilities in general, how can one proceed at once to answer the question of responsibility to Art? At the most there are *mutual* responsibilities for Art and Corporation. Another tack is more promising. Looking away from the negative aspects of corporate external relations (those aspects, that is, which speak of what corporations ought to do and not to do in order to help someone else), it is more rewarding to seek the corporate-arts nexus in the common goals of the two institutions.

This is not to say that mutual responsibilities are irrelevant. But if there are such mutual responsibilities between the corporation and the arts, then it seems more likely that they are both discoverable and statable in acceptable terms after one has stated what they both are after. Our inquiry has shown that they both seek goals that are closely related, if not entirely congruent; and that the relationship among common goal-values is striking. It is so striking, in fact, that one must dismiss the case of those who deny any nexus between the corporation and the arts. Instead, one must entertain a strong case for developing the presently tenuous nexus into something of value to both.

New Paths of Corporate Policy

In view of the new perspectives open to those who look at the corporate-arts nexus in a new light, what courses of action can be recommended? There are two sides to this question; both the corporation and arts must act. For the arts, the requirements of wise action are beyond our province, as we have said. The most we can do here is to indicate the nature of the modern corporation so that the practitioners and custodians of the arts may frame their own policies more realistically.

These policies on the side of the arts include far more than enlightened approaches to corporations as potential donors. Corporate giving, as we have seen, is but one aspect of the whole. It is not an unimportant one. For art institutions to concentrate on this approach to the exclusion of others is to miss many opportunities for mutual benefit for both arts and the corporation. Moreover, to regard the corporate business community as a Big Rock Candy Mountain from which the major financial resources will flow into the arts is an illusion.

The needs of the arts in the decades ahead cannot be met primarily, or even to any great extent, by corporate giving, although it is certain that companies will make increasingly large expenditures for business reasons for the work of the artists. It seems inescapable that very large subventions by government will be required, together with more aggressive entrepreneurial activity on the part of the artistic community. These are matters of concern for the practitioners and custodians of the arts in our society as it moves upward toward a higher culture.

Procedural Aspects

So far as the corporation is concerned, however, it is possible to be more explicit. Corporate policy, as it relates to the arts, subdivides into substantive and procedural aspects. The procedural aspects— how to go about establishing the necessary relationships with the world of art, its institutions, leaders, critics, estheticians, practitioners, and custodians of the arts—present an unexplored field for corporate management. What the administrative requirements are cannot as yet be stated with any exactitude. It is possible that specialized components within the very large corporations may be needed. Or, it may be preferable to rely heavily upon outside consultants.

One thing seems certain: there are too few managers today who have any knowledge of the currents of thought in the world of art. A great noise is sometimes made by people who will have no lasting influence on art and esthetic standards, but who nevertheless take the spotlight and may thereby deflect corporate policy unduly. The question is relevant not only to industrial design and architecture but also to urban planning, corporate support of the arts as part of education, and the positioning of companies on salient issues of public policy relating to the arts.

Corporate management must possess at least some degree of sophistication in these matters in order to meet the artists, estheticians, planners, and public policy-makers on their own ground. On many issues presented a company management ought to take a firmly negative stand and refuse to be put in a defensive position on some proposals, for example, on corporate support of the arts. The wiser course may be for a company to initiate its own programs of support for the arts, or for working out mutual relationships with the world of art that may not necessarily meet the criteria set by outsiders.

The procedural question in the corporate-arts relationship is perhaps most interesting in connection with the field of criticism. Critics have the capability of intimidating, as well as instructing. When critics have access to mass media, such as the press, they can make or break artists, new trends in the arts, and perhaps even new trends in the corporate-arts nexus. One of the most important tasks of management is to establish independent, but optimum, use of critics. Critics are not necessarily the best consultants for a company about to set up systematic relationships with certain art institutions or to branch out into new areas of art support.

There are notable exceptions. A Robert Brustein, for example, can aid immeasurably in distinguishing the genuine from the fake, the inspired from the commonplace, the flashy upstart from the durable genius, in the theater arts. With critics of this caliber at his elbow a manager may hope to avoid elementary errors of judgment in relationships with the esoteric world of art. Critics who have a strong sense of art as a part of the life we live are to be preferred to those whose interests are remote from the world of affairs and whose judgments derive from a highly abstract system of esthetics. The art critic is a much-needed man. His liaison function in interpreting art to the layman with humility, devotion, and integrity is an indispensable one. He is creative in his subservience to those very creative forces that make art what it is. These qualities are hard to find in much of today's criticism. Corporations may face the task of deliberately educating a new generation of critics on whom managers can rely.

A major reason for this proposal—the deliberate corporate development of good and reliable art criticism—is that the mass market that makes big enterprise possible is also a market that threatens to undermine the defender of high standards against the popularized pseudoart which mass marketing encourages. Responsible and discriminating inquiry into the nature of popular culture is not new. Matthew Arnold's *Culture and Anarchy* (1869) is still profitable reading for the corporate specialist in art relationships. Richard Hoggart's recent *On the Uses of Literacy* and *The Popular Arts* by Stuart Hall and Paddy Whannel (1965) are additional and recent titles.

It has become intellectually fashionable to elevate the popular arts to high status, as though Pop Art somehow distils out from contaminated surroundings an unparalleled esthetic purity. At the other extreme is the morality of indignation, the doleful verdict that everything is going to the dogs. Somehow corporate managers must find the *via media* here and insist upon the development of critical abilities in consultants that steer a sober line in the midst of mass culture.

Brian O'Doherty has put the matter succinctly: the popular arts have to be studied and criticized in relation to contemporary institutions; they are "the arts of free enterprise, the iconography of capitalism, and this context of production, distribution and consumption, inseparable from popular art, is the proper framework for criticism." He rejects the notion that the mass media are corrupt; it is simply that "their functional use precedes their artistic use" and that "their conventions are formed by business, not art." He speaks of a positive development in the liaison of exclusive and popular art:

"the development of a sensibility that can scan a barrage of stimuli and select the input—a computer-like response enabling survival and action in situations of instability and change."[26] These remarks suggest the need for critics who can make *timely* distinctions, who are not overwhelmed by the current Camp, but are not overburdened by classic dogma either.

Criticism is a misleading term. As applied to the arts, one thinks at once of writing for the press about theatrical productions, concerts, and exhibitions. The appraisive or judicial function of the critic, as required by editors, is generally too pressing to permit critics to carry out their other functions—orientation and recreation. As defined by Theodore M. Greene, these latter functions demand of the critic time for study and practice of the arts; a critical writer for the press rarely if ever has a chance to pursue these objectives very far. The public suffers as much as he does. In the years ahead, as the corporation gets deeper into the arts, the larger companies will have to develop their own critics and free them from press deadlines. These critics, moreover, will have to be provided with an opportunity to orient themselves in the thinking of both the corporate and arts worlds, and to develop that Gilsonian facility of "making" that distinguishes the artist from the mere talker about art.

These are some of the *procedural* aspects of corporate policy as it relates to the arts, and there are many others that cannot be elaborated here. But they need to be distinguished from the substantive aspects, which deal with those matters that corporate executives and people in the world of art have to consider in common.

Substantive Aspects

Substantively, corporate policy on the arts touches practically all the major functions of a company: in manufacturing, sales, employee relations, relations with vendors, engineering, research, community relations. In these and other functions managers run into problems that require relationships with both practitioners and custodians of the arts. During the course of this book we have considered many of them at length. Here we review them summarily and add others that require more exploration than can be made at this point in time in the evolution of the corporate-arts nexus.

The first and most important substantive matter concerns the basic issue of corporate ecology—the relationship between the modern corporation and its environment—with special reference to those resources in the environment which depend on a high culture, of which the arts are an integral part. The arts are among the essentials in the human and man-made environment that sustains corporate enterprise. It is notorious that there has been short-sightedness in the business community generally concerning both the natural and the man-made ecosystems that sustain the economy.

Heedless depletion of water resources and pollution of streams is beginning to exact its toll. Nature has been bountiful, but we have drawn on the bank dangerously. So it is with the sources of creativity and beauty which once seemed to "practical" men so remote from business interests and now loom large in respectable R&D prognoses.

The subproblems of this general ecological issue are many. One has to do with the future of our cities. A good life is impossible in the world's ugliest cities, too many of which we have right here in the United States. Urban renewal and design demand esthetic as well as legal, economic, and political approaches. Most of the population lives in cities. That is where the industrial complex is focused. That is where the seats of corporate control are situated. The corporation, as a social institution, is inextricably tied to the ecological urban problem; and it is therefore tied to the esthetic aspects of it.

Corporate executives must either set up specialized internal components to deal with architects, urban planners, cultural-center designers, and others related to the world of arts, or be prepared to retain outside consultants who can establish and maintain these relationships as they affect corporate policy. Obviously, the range of corporate policies involved can be extensive. There are legal issues, questions of taxation, the location of company plants, the company's position on accessibility of an attractive urban life for employees and indeed their very health as dependent on the reduction of effi- ciency-reducing and even death-dealing atmosphere so prevalent in many badly planned sites.

The air we breathe in many cities threatens health and deposits tons of soot on clothing, buildings, and vegetation. This airborne sewage costs cities, and the companies in them, millions of dollars every year. Air pollution control also is expensive. Is it worth the money, from the corporate point of view, not only in direct health dividends but also in what it does for the observing eye? And outside the cities, in the rural parts of the country, there are similar issues on which corporate policy may have to take a stand.

A "wilderness bill of rights," together with a united front against the despoilers of nature, will be costly to some enterprisers and bit- terly opposed by others. Yet predatory man has made disastrous inroads on our forests, our seashores, our wild rivers, and the habitats of endangered species of wildlife. Lovers of the beauties of nature are rising up against the "effluent" society that spews its destructive products about. When the president of the United States sends to Congress a Message on Natural Beauty, which happened for the first time in 1965, corporate policy will not lag where business lead- ers are steering the ship into the cultural midstream.

We live in the latter half of a century that has finally awakened to the *total* ecological problem and the menacing calamities of the nuclear arms race and widespread starvation. These two salient issues for the human race are so urgent that the search for beauty in our own affluent society, in this privileged part of the earth, may soon be engulfed in frantic efforts to avert the two major disasters we all face as earthlings unless we find the way out. In corporate board rooms the immediate and overriding company economic issues, together with these global ones that impinge on every man today, will tend to edge out the ecological issues related to the arts. Therein lies a serious danger to corporate survival. The downgrading of the arts as an integral part of the environment is a danger that few per- ceive or will even consider seriously.

The failure to make the causal link between proper development of the esthetic sense through education and the survival of the race is not due, however, mainly to businessmen and politicians. It is due, primarily, if Alfred North Whitehead is correct, to the stoneblind policies of the educators themselves—backed, to be sure, by the more puritanical elements of the community who control educational policies through lay boards. The arts have simply been shunted aside as irrelevant or evil. Only recently has there been a revival of learning in this indispensable area of *paideia*. The educational process, whole and balanced, must continue into adulthood and permeate the society that cherishes the arts and sciences.

The educators who deserve the blame are not only at primary, secondary, and advanced levels, but include as well all those who are practitioners and custodians of high culture. Our tardy inclusion of education in the arts only now has begun to influence the upcoming generation of men and women who will eventually lay down the necessary and broader principles for education in this wide sense. It is the business leaders of tomorrow to whom one must look for this better conception of the role of the arts in society, in the hope that they will implement this understanding in appropriate corporate policy.

Among those who must assume responsibility for this change in basic principles governing the role of the arts in education are the artists themselves, in all branches of art. The elitists among the practitioners and custodians of the arts will find this difficult to do if they persist in holding art as a kind of private preserve too precious for a democratic populace. Equally hostile to the inclusion of the arts in a broadly conceived educational process are those who, at the other end of the scale, condemn all taste-makers as a useless aristocracy with absurd esthetic standards. There is an internecine warfare of standards in the community of the arts, with both sides being aided and abetted by economic and political forces having ulterior motives. The preservation of our great social heritage of art, and the effort to establish and maintain the necessary conditions of creativity in the arts, are both threatened by this grab for gain and the push for power.

Corporate policy-makers, then, are likely to be caught between the upper and nether millstones of a struggle that they would like to avoid. Yet bystanders in this contest enjoy immunities that business leaders, especially in big corporations with institutional status, cannot claim. Whatever the aim and purpose of art in society—whether the pursuit of the Beautiful or some other goal—the corporate world will be drawn increasingly into the contest of forces.

There will be problems of the allocation of economic resources at national and local levels that demand position-taking on public issues, as in zoning regulations, land use, building codes, the formation of quasipublic and quasiprivate action groups for planning Megalopolis and the urban-rural oscillatory rhythm of life for men of the twenty-first century, national-local relationships of educational planning and administration, and so on. In some of these battles, the practitioners and the custodians of the arts will be near the center of controversy; in others they will be nearer the periphery. They will seldom be entirely absent.

The ecological aspects of the future nexus of the arts and the corporation are many. Several of these aspects deserve restatement here. One is the simple issue of profitable art. Corporate survival depends on continued profitability in company operations. It has dawned on not a few business leaders that art pays. In its crudest form, this acceptance of art into the house of business is the corporate art collection: paintings and sculpture, whether they are "good" or not, may become capital gainers. The development of fine corporate collections by certain large companies[27] is not to be underestimated as a constructive force. Yet "Tycoonart"[28] has properly come in for much derision. It may neither be good for the arts nor for companies. Contemporary objets d'art in the Executive Suite do not necessarily improve the firm's image and may hold it up to richly deserved ridicule.

Some of the great company collections, on the other hand, do, by example, make a strong case for corporate patronage of the arts. And on purely financial grounds the great international art market of today seems to justify measured esthetic corporate investment. A Vermeer—*The Portrait of a Young Girl*—that sold in Rotterdam in 1816 for 3 florins (in current dollars about $1.80) was bought by an American collector a few years ago for $350,000. In 1955 its value was estimated at $1,252 per square inch; the picture measures 17 1/4 by 15 3/4 inches. In Wall Street the House of Morgan stood at the time on land that was valued at only $2.10 per square inch.[29] *Aristotle Viewing the Bust of Homer* would strike an even greater contrast. A company with artistic investments of this kind would not do badly in profitability. But there are hazards, and it is doubtful that art consultants are available to advise a business firm on reserves of this kind.

The more prevalent use of art in business is that described by Russell Lynes in his account of John Rogers, popular American sculptor of the nineteenth century.[30] Rogers' art was mass-produced for the home. He was in business. His art sold. After he went to Rome to study sculpture he soon declared that he had not the slightest intention of following the classical style of Greenough and Powers. "High art" was beyond his depth, he said. He would stick to "small figures in bronze and very nice plaster." In this way, if he could get his "name up for that style and represent *human nature*" he could "make a living by it as well as enjoying it exceedingly."

James Jackson Jarvis aroused some opposition by his favorable criticism of these small figures—later to be sought zealously by connoisseurs of indigenous American art. Said Jarvis: this was "a genuine production of our own soil, enlivening the fancy, enkindling patriotism, and warming the affections." It was "not high art," but it was genuine art nonetheless. It was "art of a highly naturalistic order, based on true feeling and a right appreciation of humanity." Similarly, Lynes calls our attention to the work of Currier & Ives. They married the practical with the esthetic and built their reputations on the principle that there need be nothing toplofty about art. It was "a commodity that people could use and enjoy without pretensions or large bank accounts."

Today the vast market in the plastic arts, in music, in the theater arts by film, and so on, for *reproductions* of the best, as well as the mediocre, raises new questions. It is not enough to denounce the corporate-arts nexus on the ground that profit is sought in the mass distribution of Toscanini's reading of Beethoven's Ninth. The art business is here to stay. Replication of great performances certainly does something to art that was never done before. Repeated hearings of *Air for the G String* under all possible circumstances of daily life, some far from poetic, as the music floats out from ubiquitous speaker systems can dull the sensitivities. But what do we do about that? Organize an Association for the Stamping Out of Canned Music? No, the way out is to use the canning processes to enhance the practice and custodianship of the arts, and these activities in themselves demand innovation and creativity. We must go on from where we are, not back to some irretrievable and not altogether attractive past state of affairs in the world of art. This relationship between artistic replication and corporate business will be an important field for both the executives and the artists of the future.

There are other implications of profitability in the corporate-arts nexus that will not escape the discerning. It is now established practice among leading companies to expose their promising junior executives to the arts and the social sciences as a normal part of in-company education and training. Engineering firms have found that it does not pay to overload their pools of potential managers with technicians innocent of the humanities.

Companies often send their more promising men and women to the leading universities for balance, for communication with people in other disciplines and the outside world. They are exposed to the history of Greek civilization and comparative literature, for example. They become aware of the cultures of Asia and Africa, whereas in college they might have done well to glimpse some bits of the history of Western culture.

The theme could be extended indefinitely. Consider, for example, the big waves in advertising waters caused by Marshall McLuhan, director of the Center for Culture and Technology at the University of Toronto. He has atypical theories of viewing culture, and these theories are related to new views of art, the theory of communication, and technology. His view that the "medium is the message" gives pause to even the most astute advertisers. "Pop art is a better indicator of what is happening in advertising than the advertisers know. . . . Advertising creates environments and these are very effective as long as they are invisible. Some think that an ad is good if it is noticed. That is quite mistaken. The work of an ad is totally subconscious. As soon as you realize it is an ad, it is not serving its function."[31] The art of advertising may be beyond the pale to the world of estheticians. It has never been so to the world of business. Now the Executive Suite had better give ear to the avant garde in communication theory of the future corporate-arts nexus.

By orthodox standards of esthetics, these are heretical ideas. But orthodoxy will rule neither the Executive Suite nor the Artist's Modernized Garret (possibly a penthouse) in the decade ahead. The glum view of interplanetary space travel as the culmination of posthistoric man's starvation of life and reduction to the physiological functions of breathing, eating, and excretion, as pictured by Lewis Mumford, has to be contrasted with the astronauts' discovery for us of new beauty. The Space Age lends new meaning for life in humanistic as well as scientific terms. If we can ever learn to live together without mutual extermination, mankind could be on the threshold of a far more amply dimensioned Good Life than had ever been imagined in the century of the dismal science. Then, economics could not have been more remote from art. But today, arts, science, humanistics, and business are sitting around the same table—and they are actually enjoying the experience.

When all is said and done perhaps the most important function of art is its revolutionary function, its capabilities of helping us to overcome absurd limitations of mind which, for centuries, have prevented mankind from facing his own problems squarely so that solutions can be found. Perhaps the artist can help us to discard the blinders, to see realities where words, logic, and science have failed in getting at the kernel.

In an interesting passage in his autobiography, Judge Thurman Arnold observes that man is slave to his vocabulary.[32] Writing more specifically of the problems facing the American economy, and especially the problem of unused productive capacity, which he thinks is lamentably far greater than that of any nation in history, Judge Arnold says that "adjustment to the industrial revolution will be accomplished only when we invent new words to describe the problem that faces us." Will new words be enough? And can we find them with verbal devices alone? In another passage the distinguished jurist sees life as "a gorgeous ballet with a whole variety of dancers moving back and forth across the stage to create a scene of beauty and rhythm." Perhaps this is the key to what we really hope for: some kind of esthetic model that will give us a more truthful view of our society as it now is and as it can become.

NOTES

1. Thomas Munro, *The Arts and Their Interrelations* (Indianapolis: Bobbs-Merrill, 1949), esp. p. 543.

2. "The distinction between 'fine' and 'useful' arts was not widely made until the eighteenth century. Before then, 'art' covered all useful skills, including those which aimed at beauty (along with other ends) and those of a more purely utilitarian nature, such as iron mining." See Thomas Munro, *Toward Science in Aesthetics* (New York: Liberal Arts Press, 1956), p. 136.

3. Edward S. Corwin, *Constitution of the United States, Edited and Annotated* (Washington, D. C.: U. S. Government Printing Office, 1953), p. 271 f.

4. 88th Congress, 1st Session, Senate Document No. 28, May 28, 1963.

5. See *United States Supreme Court Reports, Annotated,* October Term, 1953, 98 L ed 644, an annotation on statutory copyright protection of "works of art." Federal cases indicate that copyright protection of works of art extends only to their nonmechanical and nonutilitarian aspects, and that one of the most difficult legal issues has been whether the fact that a particular design is copyrightable (or patentable) bars it from being patented (or copyrighted); protection afforded by a copyright is not coextensive with that afforded by a patent.

6. I have borrowed the term "isolationist" as applied to estheticians from Melvin Rader (ed.), *A Modern Book of Esthetics: An Anthology,* 3d ed. (New York: Holt, Rinehart, and Winston, 1960), "The Question of Definition," xv-xviii. He finds the isolationist point of view in the writings of Benedetto Croce, Roger Fry, Ortega y Gasset, Hugo Münsterberg, and others. Rader contrasts the isolationists with the "contextualists."

7. John Dewey, *Art as Experience* (New York: Minton, Balch & Co., 1934), pp. 337–338.

8. Dewey, p. 341.

9. Dewey, p. 344. Dewey insisted on the need for a worker's esthetic satisfaction in the products of his work, a satisfaction that could come only after radical changes in "industrial oligarchy." "The psychological conditions resulting from private control of the labor of other men for the sake of private gain, rather than any fixed psychological or economic law, are the forces that suppress and limit esthetic quality in the experience that accompanies processes of production." (pp. 343–344) The end could not be attained by any revolution that stopped short of "affecting the imagination and emotions of man." The values leading to production and intelligent enjoyment of art would have to be incorporated into the system of social relationships. Art itself was not secure under modern conditions "until the mass of men and women who do the useful work of the world have the opportunity to be free in conducting the processes of production and are richly endowed in capacity for enjoying the fruits of collective work."

10. Harold Taylor, in a review of the Rockefeller Panel Report on the Performing Arts in *Book Week*, March 28, 1965. He criticized the report for its emphasis on organizations and edifices that virtually excluded new directions in art-oriented education.

11. Dewey, p. 344.

12. Anthony West, "A Painting of Pattern," *The Washington Post*, March 28, 1965.

13. Quoted by Van Wyck Brooks, *John Sloan: a Painter's Life* (New York: E. P. Dutton, 1955).

14. Susanne K. Langer, *Feeling and Form* (New York: Chas. Scribners Sons, 1953), p. 60.

15. Kenneth Clark, *The Nude* (New York: Doubleday Book Co., 1959), p. 49.

16. This seems to be the position of William Snaith in *The Irresponsible Arts* (New York: Atheneum, 1964). He attacks *l'art pour l'art* repeatedly as a heretical doctrine that has led to the "irresponsibility" of contemporary artists.

17. Rader's anthology indicates the scope.

18. Morris Weitz, *Philosophy of the Arts* (Cambridge, Mass.: Harvard University Press, 1950), cited and quoted in Rader.

19. Rader, xvi, citing E. F. Carritt, *An Introduction to Aesthetics* (London, 1950). Professor Carritt is one of the contributors to the article on "Aesthetics" in the latest edition of the *Encyclopaedia Britannica*. He is the author of *Philosophies of Beauty from Socrates to Robert Bridges* (an anthology) (New York, 1931), and *The Theory of Beauty*, 3d ed. (London, 1928).

20. Rader, xxii.

21. Susanne K. Langer, *Philosophical Sketches: A Study of the Human Mind in Relation to Feeling, Explored Through Art, Language and Symbol* (New York: Mentor Books, 1964), p. 76. This book was first published by the Johns Hopkins University Press in 1962. The passage quoted is from the chapter on "The Cultural Importance of Art," a lecture delivered at Syracuse University and reprinted in *Philosophical Sketches* from M. F. Andrews, ed., *Aesthetic Form and Education* (Syracuse, 1958).

22. Langer, p. 80.

23. Langer, p. 87.

24. Herbert Read, *Art and Society* (New York: The Macmillan Co., 1937), pp. 134–135.

25. Frances Herring, "Touch—the Neglected Sense," *Journal of Aesthetics*, VII (1949), pp. 199–215.

26. Curt Sachs, *World History of the Dance*, trans. Bessie Schönberg (New York: The Seven Arts Press, 1952), p. 3. Published originally in Germany under the title *Eine Weltgeschichte des Tanzes*. Sachs (1881–1959), a distinguished ethnomusicologist, held important academic and museum posts in Europe and the United States and was at the time of his death adjunct professor at Columbia University.

27. Sachs, p. 6.

28. Dewey, p. 4.

29. Dewey, p. 326.

30. Read, p. 127.

31. Read, p. 127.

32. Read, p. 135.

33. Huntington Hartford, *Art or Anarchy? How the Extremists and Exploiters Have Reduced the Fine Arts to Chaos and Commercialism* (New York: Doubleday Book Co., 1964).

34. Snaith, passim.

35. Walter Gropius, *The New Architecture and the Bauhaus*, trans. Morton Shand (London, 1935); quoted by Read, p. 127.

36. Read, pp. 126–127.

37. Ernst Kris, *Psychoanalytic Explorations in Art* (New York: International Universities Press, 1952), p. 39.

38. Munro, *Toward Science in Aesthetics*, p. 257 f.

39. Harold D. Lasswell, *The Future of Political Science* (New York: Atherton Press, 1963), p. 185.

40. Among the *Heritage* TV tapes by WQED, Pittsburgh, Penn., there is a delightful series in which T. V. Smith is interviewed. In one of these programs he states that art "helps us to be whole men, to absolve ourselves from tension, to take the High Road." But his approach is not through the definition of Beauty, but rather through talk about the price we have to pay, the discipline we have to undertake, in pursuing the ideals of Truth, Goodness, and Beauty. Civilization may pursue only one of these goals at the cost of the others but only at the peril of sterility. Instead of adhering to this monolithic view, democratic societies are pluralistic and tolerant; they love variety. But if no one of the triad is a sufficient ideal in itself, it means that we must produce more scientists, artists, and statesmen. And for each category a special kind of discipline is required. For the scientist, the discipline of doubt; for the statesman, the discipline of sympathy for others' points of view; for the artist, the opening of all the windows of the soul—"a sensitization that is costly." In Platonic fashion, "T. V." (as he was affectionately known by his colleagues) urged the balanced development of all three disciplines in each generation. He rejected the monistic theory in favor of the "pluralistic enterprise of democracy" where one starts with many ideals and refuses to subsume everything under any single Ideal. On art, "the discipline of Beauty," he said that imagination plus techniques are the heavy requirements of the artist, who pays an enormous price in mastery of his medium but also in creating through imagination. There is, too, a discipline in the audience, the discipline of the people, a trained receptivity (which is not common) in following the artist in his creative search, in "trusting the surmise" (after Wordsworth), in learning to understand the artist's symbols. Beauty "doesn't come free," either to the artists or to a disciplined people ready to receive it; it has to be developed through skills of hand, mind, and heart. The weakest spot in our democracy, according to "T. V.," is the lack of pride and joy in skill, something valuable for its own sake. To "stretch the human soul" to open "all its windows to sight and sound," not only as to fine arts but the menial arts as well, is to send one on the road to Beauty. Art is one of the "disciplines of democracy," for Beauty is as indispensable there as are Truth and Goodness. Politics is "the discipline of Goodness," and the citizen's discipline in politics is "to accept compromise and to avoid coercion."

41. "A perspective is a pattern of identifications, demands, and expectations" observable in the way persons identify themselves symbolically as members of certain groups; for example, the way they express their values in terms of preferred outcomes and goal events, and symbolize past, present, and future occurrences or general state of affairs. "The persons active in politics make demands for values (on themselves and others) on the basis of various expectations. Patterns of attention, sentiment, interest, loyalty, and faith are among the perspectives of political action." Harold D. Lasswell and Abraham Kaplan, *Power and Society: A Framework for Political Inquiry* (New Haven: Yale University Press, 1950), Ch. 2.

42. Lasswell, p. 185. The eight values which Lasswell usually lists are the four "deference" values of power, respect, rectitude, and affection, together with the "welfare" values of well-being, wealth, skill, and enlight-

enment. To what extent can the esthetic quest be associated, in Lasswell's analysis, with such goal values as rectitude, affection, skill, well-being, and enlightenment? The problem is discussed later in this book, when corporate and art goals are compared.

43. *The Arts in Society,* ed. Robert N. Wilson (Englewood Cliffs, N. J.: Prentice-Hall, 1964).

44. James H. Barnett, "The Sociology of Art," in *Sociology Today: Problems and Prospects,* ed. Robert K. Merton, Leonard Broom, and Leonard S. Cottrell, Jr. (New York: Basic Books, 1959), pp. 197–214.

45. Wilson, p. vi.

46. Barnett, pp. 198–199.

47. See note 42 above.

48. Arnold J. Toynbee, *A Study of History,* Abridgment of Vols. I–VI by D. C. Somervell (New York & London: Oxford University Press, 1947), p. 241.

49. Meyer Schapiro, "Style," in A. L. Kroeber et al., *Anthropology Today: An Encyclopedic Inventory* (Chicago: University of Chicago Press, 1953), p. 287 f.

50. Here, I am following to some extent the account of Barnett together with the section on "The Scientific Approach to Aesthetics" by Helmut Hungerland in the article on "Aesthetics" in *Encyclopaedia Britannica,* I, pp. 272–273.

51. Vernon Louis Parrington, *Main Currents in American Thought* (New York: Harcourt Brace & Co., 1927, 1930), I, p. 357.

52. Hippolyte Taine, *History of English Literature* (New York, 1886), I, p. 30.

53. P. R. Farnsworth, *Musical Taste: Its Measurement and Cultural Nature* (Stanford: Stanford University Press, 1950). See also R. W. Lundin, *An Objective Psychology of Music* (New York, 1953).

54. Barnett, p. 210.

55. Barnett, p. 210.

56. Barnett, p. 211.

57. Barnett, p. 211.

58. Barnett, p. 211.

59. Barnett, p. 212.

60. Barnett, p. 212. Barnett cites the thesis of Leo Lowenthal, in *Literature and the Image of Man* (1957), that creative writers, through their selection, often unconscious, of plots, characterizations, depictions of milieus, and emphasis on values, convincingly portray man's relation to his society and his times. Creative literature, and perhaps by extension the other arts, thus provide a species of documentation for the study of social structure and cultural change. But even more than this, Lowenthal takes the position that "creative writers are sensitive to incipient changes in man's relation to his society and often reflect this awareness in their work." Barnett, p. 209.

61. As in the Ajax and Omega commercials and the potato chips commercials starring Beatrice Lillie and Bert Lahr. See Paul Gardner, "TV Commercials Gain Art Status," *The New York Times*, February 15, 1965, reporting the views of Marshall Lewis in preparing a festival of TV commercials and documentaries for the Bleecker Street Cinema.

62. "New Groups, New Manifestoes, Maybe New Ideas," *The New York Times*, December 27, 1964.

63. *The New York Times*, May 10, 1965. Similar breadth of view has been demonstrated in awards made in 1965 by the New York Board of Trade to companies selected for projects through which they have furthered the arts. The fifteen awards—the first ever made in the fields of the arts by the Board—included the following:

> The winners in the fine arts were: S. C. Johnson and Sons, Inc., for their touring exhibition of modern paintings, principally by artists of the United States.
>
> Hallmark Cards, for a sponsorship of the arts since 1949, when it established the international Hallmark Art Awards with the Wildenstein Gallery here.
>
> The International Business Machines Corporation, for a program that includes a collection of art from 79 countries exhibited here and lent to museums, as well as for sponsoring 10 major exhibitions a year at its gallery here.
>
> Lever Brothers, for a continuing display of art in its Park Avenue exhibition hall, which showed the way for similar use of other lobbies.
>
> The Pepsi-Cola Company, for continuous presentation in its Park Avenue gallery of noncommercial educational and cultural shows.
>
> The Pantene Company (American Roche), for a grant to the American Ballet Theater to restage "Les Sylphides," paying for new scenery and costumes.
>
> The Union Dime Savings Bank, for its sponsorship, with the New York Public Library, of summer noon-time recorded concerts in Bryant Park since 1949.
>
> The Dell Publishing Company, for supporting the New York Shakespeare Festival and contributing to construction of Central Park's Delacorte Theater.

Texaco, Inc., for 25-years' sponsorship of Metropolitan Opera broadcasts without sales messages.

American Export-Isbrandtsen Lines, for underwriting a complete restaging of "Aida" by the Metropolitan Opera.

Standard Oil (New Jersey), for presenting "The Play of the Week" on Channel 13 as a public service.

A general award went to Lord & Taylor for participating in such projects as benefits for the Museum of Modern Art, in campaigns to save Carnegie Hall and to restore Central Park's Bethesda Fountain and for underwriting of the cost of a box at the new Metropolitan Opera house.

The Seagram Building, for its "elegant form and utilization of materials" and for the benefits to the community its plaza provides.

The Columbia Broadcasting System Building, not yet completed, for its "simplicity of concepts, the form and materials of its continuous piers and the sunken plaza which surrounds the entire building."

The Hotel Corporation of America, for maintaining and refurbishing the Plaza Hotel while retaining its "distinctive charm and appeal."

The New York Times, May 17, 1965.

NOTES FOR CHAPTER III: *Freedom of Creativity and Innovation*

1. The freedom of "free societies" is so variously described that one wishes for a neutral definition. Freedom, as Felix E. Oppenheim has pointed out in an essay attempting a definition that is valuationally neutral and empirically grounded, is a watchword for liberals and antiliberals alike. He prefers to interpret the notion of freedom as referring to relationships of interaction among persons or groups, and begins with attention to "interpersonal unfreedom." See his *Dimensions of Freedom* (New York: St. Martin's Press, 1961). John Stuart Mill, in his famous essay, *On Liberty*, limits his discussion to the "power which can be legitimately exercised by society over the individual"—a sentence that certainly "cries for analysis," as Frank H. Knight has said in "Some Notes on Political Freedom and a Famous Essay," in *Nomos IV: Liberty*, ed. C. J. Friedrich

(New York: Atherton Press, 1962), pp. 110–118. The analysis is still going on. In *Nomos IV*, Arnold Brecht (in his essay on "Liberty and Truth: The Responsibility of Science") makes the appropriate observation that it is the function of social scientists, in dealing with ends and means, "not to proclaim dogmas or to criticize one dogma from the platform of another but to show the risks and consequences involved in taking one road or the other." In my use of the term, "the free society," I would like to heed this warning; yet it seems to me that "risks" and "consequences" cannot easily be set forth with complete and empirical neutrality. "Risk" implies negative norms. On the other hand, Karl W. Deutsch, in an essay in the same volume ("Strategies of Freedom: The Widening of Choices and the Change of Goals") does offer a most useful hint in defining freedom as "the range of effective choices open to an actor, such as an individual or a group of persons," and adding that "the choices of action or policy open to a group can eventually be translated by virtue of their consequences into indirect choices for individuals." He specifies at least four major aspects or preconditions of freedom in this view of it as effective range of choice: the absence of restraint; the presence of opportunity; the capacity to act; and the awareness of the realities in terms of external "unrestrainedness" and opportunity and the actor's own capacity. In the present chapter I accept this view of the nature of freedom.

2. I use the term *constitutionalism* in the sense in which it has been defined in Richard Eells and Clarence Walton, *Conceptual Foundations of Business; An Outline of the Major Ideas Sustaining Business Enterprise in the Western World* (Homewood, Ill.: Richard D. Irwin, 1961), Ch. 17. There, the two essential aspects of constitutionalism are discussed in some detail—the energizing and canalizing of public power, and the protection of private interest against unauthorized use of that power. Constitutionalism is, as Charles H. McIlwain has said, a legal limitation on government, the antithesis of arbitrary rule; its opposite is despotic government. McIlwain stressed the ancient doctrines of the rule of law. Others, such as Carl J. Friedrich, have emphasized the system of effective restraints upon governmental action. The two approaches are complementary. It seems wise today to insist that constitutionalism be made applicable in fact and theory to the domains of private, as well as public power, especially in plural societies such as ours where the deliberate dispersion of the power to govern is an integral part of the system of effective restraints on power. The private sectors, in other words, are not only the well-springs of initiative, innovation, and creativity; they are also reserved areas where public power is admitted sparingly, and where, for that reason, many kinds of private government necessarily prevail. Where freedom is cherished, it

is quite as necessary to have effective restraints on these private powers as it is to constitutionalize the public governments themselves.

3. Pluralism, as the term is used here, is discussed in Eells and Walton, Ch. 16.

4. On the general characteristics of totalitarian dictatorships, the types of totalitarian ideology, the directed economy, and the cultural implications, see Carl J. Friedrich and Zbigniew K. Brzezinski, *Totalitarian Dictatorship and Autocracy,* 2d ed. (Cambridge, Mass.: Harvard University Press, 1965).

5. Adolf Hitler, *Mein Kampf,* trans., ed., and annotated by John Chamberlain and others (New York: Reynal and Hitchcock, 1939), p. 354.

6. Stephen H. Roberts, *The House That Hitler Built* (New York: Harper and Row, 1938), p. 242. *Cf.* George L. Mosse, *Nazi Culture: Intellectual, Cultural and Social Life in the Third Reich,* trans. from the German by Salvator Attanasio and others (New York: Grosset & Dunlap, 1966).

7. This passage, from Meissner and Kaiserberg, *Staat und Verwaltung im dritten Reich,* is quoted by Wm. M. McGovern, *From Luther to Hitler: The History of Fascist-Nazi Political Philosophy* (Boston: Houghton Mifflin, 1941), p. 655.

8. George H. Sabine, *A History of Political Theory,* 3d. ed. (New York: Holt, Rinehart and Winston, 1961), p. 921.

9. Sabine, p. 921.

10. Priscilla Johnson and Leopold Labedz, *Khrushchev and the Arts: The Politics of Soviet Culture, 1962–1964* (M. I. T. Press, 1965). See also Ralph Blum, "Freeze and Thaw: The Artist in Russia," *The New Yorker,* August 28, September 4, and September 11, 1965.

11. As quoted by George Feifer, "Art for Marx' Sake," *The New York Times Magazine,* December 20, 1964.

12. Georg Lukács, Hungarian philosopher, is the author of a monumental work, *Esthetics,* which was published by the Hungarian Academy of Science in connection with his 80th birthday in 1965. See note 31, Chapter V, below.

13. See S. L. Schneiderman, "A Visit With Georg Lukács," *The New York Times Book Review,* May 9, 1965. Lukács conceded that "Kafka was wonderful in his vision of the oncoming dark times which we have lived through."

14. Henry Tanner, "Moscow Affirms Curbs on Artists," *The New York Times,* January 10, 1965.

15. The Theaters Act provides that "one copy of every new stage play, and of every act, scene or epilogue and of every new part added to an old prologue or epilogue, intended to be produced and acted for hire at any theater in Great Britain shall be sent to the Lord Chamberlain of Her Majesty's Household." The Act was invoked as recently as 1965 to prevent the public presentation of John Osborne's *A Patriot for Me.*

16. The Arts and the National Government, Report to the President Submitted by August Heckscher, Special Consultant on the Arts, May 28, 1963, Senate Doc. No. 28, 88th Congress, 1st Sess., p. 28.

17. The Kennedy Administration gave historic impetus to concern for the arts in Washington. But the roots of the movement lie much deeper. What is now the John Fitzgerald Kennedy Memorial Center for the Performing Arts originated during the Eisenhower Administration as a national center for these arts. Efforts on Capitol Hill to advance legislation in support of the arts date from the beginning of the republic. But in the nature of our federal system, where the arts are mentioned in the U. S. Constitution only with reference to the "useful arts" as related to the copyright and patent powers of Congress, it was long assumed that any governmental efforts on behalf of the arts aside from the exercise of these powers would originate at state and local levels. And even at the state and local levels it was long the rule that the "police powers"—that is, the reserved powers of the states—were very limited in the regulation of property rights so as to promote civic beauty. The constitutionality of zoning and other laws for the latter purpose has now been put on a firmer basis; and as the Rockefeller Panel Report has stated, one of the most encouraging signs on the American cultural scene is the increasing concern of state governments with the arts; social legislation of carefully designed nonesthetic content is no longer the rule. But even at the national level there has long been a concern by leading legislators and administrators for the cultural side of national policies. George Washington declared that "the arts and sciences are essential to the prosperity of the state and to the ornament and happiness of human life." The gradual development of the capital city as one of the world's most elegant had its beginnings in the esthetic sense of the earliest planners. The enactment of the law establishing the National Council on the arts in 1964 was the culmination of legislative efforts dating back to the nineteenth century. See note 42, Chapter V, below.

18. The number was later increased to 40 and then reduced by law.

19. President Johnson's advisory group consisted of Lucius D. Battle, an Assistant Secretary of State; Isaac Stern, violinist; Abe Fortas, lawyer; and Pierre Salinger, former White House Press Secretary.

20. Howard Taubman, "A Sign of Grace; U. S. Takes a Modest First Step in the Arts," *The New York Times,* Sunday, September 20, 1964, Section 2. Two years later Taubman wrote that the National Arts Endowment, under the chairmanship of Roger L. Stevens and his advisers, was "confounding the Cassandras who glumly prophesied that public funds would be spent on cautious principles and unadventurous programs." The reverse had been true. "The endowment has taken chances, brought quick help to worthwhile institutions in mortal danger, been hospitable to new ideas and to fresh approaches, and has been alert to the needs of the creators as well as to the performing artists." Seldom had a new government program, "especially one so beset with possible booby traps, been implemented with so much imagination and dispatch." He noted the wide range of interests in grants by the Arts Council and the richness of opportunities remaining: "Early fears were expressed that the government, seemingly in competition with the foundations, would run out of worthy programs and activities to support. These fears turn out to be illusory. There are vast areas in this country and huge publics with only the most rudimentary experience in the arts. As they learn to know the enchantment and the power of the arts they will ask for more and better things, and there will be unlimited room for the government, the foundations, and private enterprise to make salient contributions." (Taubman, "Adventuresome Course," *The New York Times,* September 1, 1966.) Writing on *The Foundations and the Arts* (New York: The Twentieth Century Fund, 1966), August Heckscher struck a similar note on the open field of opportunity: "Today a new factor is tending to inhibit the foundations in their approach to the arts. This is the growing role of government. From thinking that government would never act at all in this area, we have gone to the opposite conclusion of thinking that perhaps government is going to do everything. Now it is absolutely incumbent upon the foundations to move along with government, to match and to supplement its efforts, lest the cultural life of the country grow dependent upon funds from one source." The Fund has taken steps to improve the situation, notably in the study by William J. Baumol and William G. Bowen, *Performing Arts—The Economic Dilemma* (New York: The Twentieth Century Fund, 1966).

21. James J. Kilpatrick, "Johnson Arts Bill Lacks Limits," *The Washington Star,* March 18, 1965.

22. *The Performing Arts: Problems and Prospects,* p. 148.

23. The panel reports that the Federal Theater Project was "plagued in the halls of Congress," almost 10 per cent of the major titles produced by the Project having been criticized by congressmen or witnesses before congressional committees. "In June, 1939, in passing an appropriation of $1.75 billion for the Works Project Administration, the House of Representatives made a specific proviso that none of the money could be spent

on the Federal Theater Project—a provision to which the Senate yielded, although it was actually willing to have the program continue." (*The Performing Arts,* p. 130.)

24. *The Performing Arts,* p. 113.

25. The direct and indirect forms of governmental support of the arts are discussed in the Rockefeller Panel Report on pages 132 f.

26. Current public attention to the uses of the Fourteenth Amendment in defense of civil liberties, and especially the rights of accused and of racial minorities, tends to obscure the fact—clear to all corporation lawyers and students of American constitutional history—that the drafters of the amendment and leaders of bench and bar in the years just after the Civil War were deeply cognizant of the value of this addition to the basic charter. The due-process and equal-protection clauses, in particular, were invoked, together with the commerce power, to throw a cloak of protection about the corporate structure in business as against hostile state legislation. The story begins in the early part of the nineteenth century and builds up to a climax at the time of the New Deal. It has been told entertainingly and authoritatively by Edward S. Corwin: "The Doctrine of Due Process of Law Before the Civil War," *Harvard Law Review,* XXIV (1911), pp. 366–385 and 460–479; "The Basic Doctrine of American Constitutional Law," *Michigan Law Review,* XII (1914), pp. 247–276; *Twilight of the Supreme Court, A History of Our Constitutional Theory* (New Haven: Yale University Press, 1934); and *The Commerce Power and State Rights* (Princeton: Princeton University Press, 1936). See also C. Herman Pritchett, *The American Constitution* (New York: McGraw-Hill Book Co., 1959), Chapters 14, 15, 16, and p. 571: "It is rather anomalous that the Fourteenth Amendment for a half century after its adoption should have been of very little value to the Negroes in whose behalf it was primarily adopted, while it should so quickly have been accepted by the Court as a protector of corporate rights"; but in common with most authorities on constitutional history he rejects the "conspiracy theory" that the Amendment was a deliberate Trojan horse smuggled into the Constitution under the pretext of protecting the Negroes while in fact introducing a new and powerful instrument of judicial review over state legislation affecting corporate property interests. Attempts to get the Court to reverse a half century of holdings on this basis and to declare that the original intention was not to protect corporations have all failed. The due-process clause is on very solid ground today as a protection of both procedural and substantive rights of natural and artificial persons.

27. See note 1, above.

NOTES FOR CHAPTER IV: *The Knowing Artist*

1. See *The Creative Process: A Symposium,* ed. Brewster Ghiselin (Berkeley: University of California Press, 1952), also published as a Mentor Book (1955). Arthur Koestler's *The Act of Creation* (New York: Macmillan Co., 1965), examines at length the problem of artistic and scientific creation. His book develops Plato's suggestion that genius is the capacity to bring apparent disparates into significant relation. Koestler notes, with Bergson and Freud, this genius of "bisociation" in wit and the creativity of laughter, a "sudden glory" of intelligence, a vibrant intersection of habitually incompatible frames of reference, a collision that yields in a brief flash a glimpse of a world newly ordered. Major discoveries in science, according to Koestler, are products of creative acts that bear a close family resemblance to the creative acts of artists. In both there is a seeming irrelevance, a lapse of consequent argument, that can lead to the creative leap of the mind, while the built-in routines of order and official logic may blindfold the free-creative act of comprehension. In both art and science Koestler sees the work of a purposeful logic of the unconscious, even though artist and scientist translate their visions into an objective medium with different devices: the poet and painter using the codes of perspective, rhythm, contrast, key-relations, prosody; the scientist using mathematical and technical inference. These summary statements about the book, together with a critique, will be found in a review by George Steiner in *Book Week,* October 25, 1964. Steiner points out that there is nothing new or startling in Koestler's treatise and that the view of creative insight as "the relocation of reality concepts through collision, reversal or juxtaposition is thoroughly standard"; that Kekulé's "dream-discovery" of molecular structure, which Koestler invokes many times, is "a hoary chestnut and very possibly a literary myth after the fact"; that Koestler fails to touch new developments in linguistics, in the analysis of modern logic, in the theory of mathematical inference, in the problem of musical invention, and in relational metaphors in language and mathematical propositions (Wittgenstein); and that the book is to be regarded as *haute vulgarisation*—"A popularization and summation of certain aspects of esthetics, psychology and the history of science." Steiner makes a brief but provocative reference to "the obscure but vital puzzle of musical invention—an area which

may contain decisive clues to the way in which the perception of energy levels and psychic unbalance can be shaped into conscious expression."

2. Alfred North Whitehead, *Science and the Modern World* (New York: The Macmillan Co., 1925), p. 298. Whitehead foresaw the dangers —and the inevitability—of wandering, even though he saw no orbiting astronauts: "Modern science has imposed on humanity the necessity for wandering. Its progressive thought and its progressive technology make the transition through time, from generation to generation, a true migration into uncharted seas of adventure. The very benefit of wandering is that it is dangerous and needs skill to avert evils. We must expect, therefore, that the future will disclose dangers. It is the business of the future to be dangerous; and it is among the merits of science that it equips the future for its duties." On the whole he regarded the great ages as unstable ages; and clearly he thought the adventures of "passionate feeling" and thought, and the adventures of esthetic experience, quite as significant as the physical wandering. "Art flourishes when there is a sense of adventure, a sense of nothing having been done before, of complete freedom to experiment; but when caution comes in you get repetition, and repetition is the death of art." *The Dialogues of Alfred North Whitehead as Recorded by Lucien Price* (New York: Mentor Books, 1956), p. 142. My quotations from Whitehead are drawn from these two sources together with his *Adventures of Ideas*.

3. Kenneth Clark, *The Nude*, p. 33: ". . . in our Diogenes search for physical beauty our instinctive desire is not to imitate but to perfect."

4. D'Arcy Wentworth Thompson, *On Growth and Form* (Cambridge: Cambridge University Press, 1942).

5. The empirical-inductive and theoretical-inductive methods and the requirement of both in education are discussed by James Bryant Conant in *Two Modes of Thought: My Encounter With Science and Education* (New York: Trident Press, 1964).

6. For Maritain the words "intellect" and "reason" convey more than they do in most current discourse. For "intellect, as well as the imagination, is at the core of poetry," and "reason, or the intellect, is not merely logical reason; it involves an exceedingly more profound—and more obscure —life, which is revealed to us in proportion as we endeavor to penetrate the hidden recesses of poetic activity. In other words, poetry obliges us to consider the intellect both in its secret wellsprings inside the human soul and as functioning in a nonrational (I do not say antirational) way." The universe of the intellect is one with which the artist must be free to communicate. The normal climate of art is intelligence and knowledge, "its normal soil, the civilized heritage of a consistent and integrated sys-

tem of beliefs and values; its normal horizon, the infinity of human experience enlightened by the passionate insights of anguish or the intellectual
virtues of the contemplative mind." Jacques Maritain, *Creative Intuition
in Art and Poetry* (New York: Meridian Books, 1955), pp. 3–4 and p. 49.

7. See Bertrand Russell's observation, in his *Mysticism and Logic*
(1918), pp. 11–12, that the "mystical way of feeling"—essentially emotional and therefore related especially to religion and art—teaches an element of wisdom not to be learned in any other way; for while "mysticism
is to be commended as an attitude towards life" and "not as a creed about
the world" or a basis for metaphysics, the mystical emotion "as coloring
and informing all other thoughts and feelings, is the inspirer of whatever
is best in man." And he added that "even the cautious and patient investigator of truth by science, which seems the very antithesis of the mystic's
swift certainty, may be fostered and nourished by that very spirit of reverence in which mysticism lives and moves." *In Human Knowledge: Its
Scope and Limits* (1948), xv–xvi, Russell said that "knowledge" was far
less a precise concept than was generally thought, and that it "has deeper
roots in unverbalized animal behavior than most philosophers have been
willing to admit." "The logically based assumptions to which our analysis
leads," he added, "are psychologically the end of a long series of refinements which starts from habits of expectations in animals, such as that
what has a certain kind of smell will be good to eat."

8. César Graña, "John Dewey's Social Art and the Sociology of Art,"
in *The Arts in Society*, ed. Robert N. Wilson (Englewood Cliffs, N. J.:
Prentice-Hall, Inc., 1964), p. 189.

9. C. E. M. Joad, *Guide to Philosophy* (New York: Dover Publications, 1936), p. 348 f., on "Clive Bell's Theory of Significant Form."

10. "The most distinctive feature of Professor Whitehead's philosophy
is the postulation of eternal objects which, entering into the flux of events,
confer upon the physical world the characteristics which it is seen to
possess," and these eternal objects "bear a strong resemblance to Plato's
Forms, both in respect of their intrinsic nature and of their relation to
what Plato called the world of becoming." Joad, p. 357. In Joad's view,
there is a necessary connection betweeen a picture that we call "beautiful"
and the Form of Beauty in this Platonic sense; he declines to find any criterion of the value of a work of art in the work itself but rather in the
Form of Beauty. The relevant question is whether the artist "possesses the
capacity for vision, in virtue of which he is able to disentangle the manifestation of the Form of Beauty from the physical setting in which it
appears"; and this capacity is not, he declares, a matter of training, of
mastery over technique, of discipline such as that which produces a scien-

tific piece of work. "The coming of Form knows no law. It is the incalculable element in all art; it can neither be compelled nor cajoled" (pp. 354–355).

11. Sir Herbert Read, *Art and Society*, 3d ed. (London: Faber and Faber, 1956), p. 95.

12. Read, p. 29. He refers here to Lucien Lévy-Brühl, *How Natives Think*, trans. Lilian A. Clare (London, 1926), pp. 35–36; Lévy-Brühl discusses collective representations as the natives' mode of picturing reality.

13. Ernst Kris, *Psychoanalytic Explorations in Art* (New York: International Universities Press, 1952), p. 25.

14. "What Makes a Company Creative," *Nation's Business*, June 1965, p. 76 f. The experts participating in the special seminar on creativity included Franz Alexander, Chief of Staff, Psychiatric Department and Director of the Psychiatric and Psychosomatic Research Institute at Mt. Sinai Hospital, Los Angeles; Frank Barron, Research Psychologist, Institute of Personality Assessment and Research, University of California; B. E. Bensinger, Chief Executive Officer, Brunswick Corporation; Bernard Berelson, Director, Communication Research Program of the Population Council, New York; Marvin Bower, Managing Director, McKiney & Company, Inc.; Jerome S. Bruner, Professor of Psychology and Co-Director of the Center for Cognitive Studies at Harvard University; Harold Guetzkow, Professor of Psychology, Sociology, and Political Science, Northwestern University; Paul E. Meehl, Professor, Department of Psychology and Neurology, University of Minnesota; Robert K. Merton, Professor, Department of Sociology, Columbia University; David M. Ogilvy, Chairman, Ogilvy, Benson & Mather, Inc.; Peter G. Peterson, President, Bell & Howell Company; Milton Rokeach, Professor, Department of Psychology, Michigan State University; William Shockley, President, Shockley Transistor Corporation; Morris I. Stein, Professor of Psychology and Director of the Center for Human Relations, New York University; Ralph W. Tyler, Director, Center for Advanced Study in the Behavioral Sciences; W. Allen Wallis, President of Rochester University, Rochester, N. Y.; and Gary A. Steiner, Seminar Director, Professor of Psychology, Graduate School of Business, University of Chicago. The article was adapted from the introduction to *The Creative Organization*, ed. Gary A. Steiner (Chicago: University of Chicago Press, 1965).

15. "Aesthetic Probings of Contemporary Man," in *The Journal of Social Issues* (January 1965), a publication of The Society for the Psychological Study of Social Issues (a division of the American Psychological Association), contains further references to current studies, not all psychoanalytic.

16. Susanne K. Langer, "The Social Influence of Design," *University,* Summer 1965, pp. 7–12. (*University* is a Princeton University quarterly.) In this chapter, subsequent quotes from Mrs. Langer are from this article.

17. See also Mrs. Langer's earlier accounts of "feeling" referred to in Chapter 2 of the present book.

18. Mrs. Langer refers specifically to the "vulgar feeling" expressed in many dolls and toys being marketed today. Cf. "Design in America," *Saturday Review,* May 23, 1964, with articles by Katherine Kuh, Walter Dorwin Teague, Vincent Sculby, Wolf von Eckhardt, and Arthur Drexler.

19. Ada Louise Huxtable, "Victory By Default," *The New York Times,* May 23, 1965, a review of "Modern Architecture: U. S. A.," an exposition at the New York Museum of Modern Art of building achievement from 1900 to 1965, arranged by Arthur Drexler and cosponsored by the Graham Foundation for Advanced Studies in the Fine Arts. Miss Huxtable says that Europe, not America, points the way by concentrating on frontiers of design on a community and environmental scale. See also her "Planning for the Nation's Cities," *The New York Times,* March 22, 1965, in which she said that President Johnson's "landmark" message on housing—which dealt more broadly with the needs of 135 million Americans, or over 70 per cent of the population, who live in the country's urban areas—represented "the first broad, progressive, professional approach to environmental and urban problems at the highest executive, policy-making level." But, she added, "the obvious weakness of the President's proposals was the crucial matter of implementation. He had outlined an advanced and experimental planning program that consists of specific suggestions with broad remedial powers, designed to meet problems unknown to any previous generation. . . . Much of it was out of the range of existing government machinery . . . and financing. It could be either the start of one of the century's most significant programs, or . . . go right back to the planners' textbooks."

20. For example: Leo F. Schnore, *The Urban Scene: Human Ecology and Demography* (New York: The Free Press, 1965); Ian Nairn, *The American Landscape: A Critical View* (New York: Random House, 1965) ("America has made the biggest hash of its environment in the history of the world"); Victor Gruen, *The Heart of Our Cities: The Urban Crisis, Diagnosis and Cure* (New York: Simon & Schuster, 1965); John W. Reps, *The Making of Urban America: A History of City Planning in the United States* (Princeton: Princeton University Press, 1965); James A. Wilson, "Urban Renewal Does Not Always Renew," *Harvard Today,* January 1965; Laurence B. Holland (ed.), *Who Designs America?* The American Civilization Conference at Princeton (New York: Doubleday Anchor Books,

1966); Arthur Cort Holden, *Sonnets for My City: An Essay on The Kinship of Art and Finance* (New York: Schulte Publishing Co., 1966), and H. H. Goldstone's review of this book in *Progressive Architecture*, May 1966.

21. Lewis Herber, *Crisis in Our Cities* (Englewood Cliffs, N.J.: Prentice-Hall, 1965), argues that pollution and congestion are approaching epidemic proportions and that drastic quarantine measures are an immediate necessity. The thesis has been supported and attacked by experts in public hearings on the problem of air and water pollution. See *The New York Times*, June 23 and 24, 1965, on The City Council's Special Committee to Investigate Air Pollution, and the editorial, "On Air and Death." *Cf.* Clive Entwistle, "Roads to Ruin," *The New York Times Book Review*, September 4, 1966, p. 3.

22. The fifteen panels of the Conference fell into four general categories: the city, the countryside, highways, and ways and means of accomplishing goals. The last category included citizen action, local, state, and federal government action, and education. Mr. Rockefeller said that the "purpose will not be to pass resolutions that beauty is good; rather it will be to recommend specific actions to the President and to the people of this country of what should be done and how it should be done."

23. Wolf von Eckhardt, in *The Washington Post*, May 30, 1965, said that there was no practicing architect on any of the panels and that "the conference skirted the fundamental issues of economics and the cockeyed values of 'economy,' both public and private, which the prevailing economic wisdom fosters. . . . Only Barbara Ward, the sparkling economist from England, hinted at this issue when she said that 'beauty is more than lace on a corset.' By the corset she must surely have meant our self-imposed conventional wisdom which omits beauty and livability from the economic equation." On the positive side he noted that "with all its rebellious talk against urban freeways, the conference also made clear, for instance, that pleasure driving is America's foremost mode of recreation. The point is not to stop roads but to integrate and design them better, to make them a constructive rather than destructive force in the cityscape."

The financial problem of implementing the goals of the Conference was often raised. For example, "if some talented designer comes up with a plan to integrate a new freeway into a cityscape, he runs up against the Highway Department's well-meant but evil-brewing 'cost-benefit' concept. Or a court rules that the Seagram Building in New York must pay heavier taxes than other buildings because it is more beautiful and thus cost more. But more importantly, it thus comes to pass that our tax system favors the slum lord and makes it almost impossible for free enterprise to build homes low-income people can afford. It favors land speculation and urban sprawl and penalizes improvements, orderly concentration and sound building." As Jane Jacobs, author of "The Death and Life of Great American Cities," pointed out to the conference, there is little sense in talking about the creation of new city parks if the cities don't have the budget to properly maintain the parks they already have. Paul F. Brandwein, education director for the Conservation Foundation, said there was "little sense in talking about instilling school children with a greater awareness of natural beauty when many of their school buildings are monuments to man-made ugliness because of municipal stinginess and mediocrity."

24. Sir Herbert Read, for example, complains that anthropologists rarely regard art as an independent phenomenon. They tend to see it as only one of the subordinate cultural features of a civilization. But he finds that some, like Ruth Benedict, show how art and religion have been separated in certain cultures (Zuñi). Read observes that "the great Iconoclastic Controversy that nearly wrecked Christianity in the seventh and eighth centuries" throws surprising light on the question, and that in Spain with its two cultures (Mohammedan and Christian) side by side for centuries, the one produced great secular art completely divorced from religion, the other a wholly religious art, in the same country with similar economic and climatic conditions. Thus Read speaks of "the dialectical nature of art" which is "not a by-product of social development, but one of the original elements which go to form a society." (pp. 4–5)

25. Robert Redfield, "Relations of Anthropology to the Social Sciences and to the Humanities," in A. L. Kroeber et al., *Anthropology Today: An Encyclopedic Inventory* (Chicago: University of Chicago Press, 1953), pp. 728–738.

26. Redfield mentions among the alternative models the models drawn from history (Evans-Pritchard), the "logical model" in the manner of Sorokin.

27. Redfield, p. 734.

28. John Dewey, *Art as Experience*, pp. 345–346.

29. P. 260 (italics added).

30. Meyer Schapiro, "Style," in Kroeber, *Anthropology Today*, pp. 287–312. Schapiro appends a good bibliography.

31. Paul Frankl, *Das System der Kunstwissenschaft* (1938).

32. Shapiro, p. 287. Cf. Herbert J. Spiro, *Government by Constitution* (New York: Random House, 1959), p. 452 f., "The Style of Politics."

33. Toynbee, p. 429 f.

34. Pp. 255–260.

35. Pp. 465–467.

36. Pitirim A. Sorokin, *The Crisis of Our Age: The Social and Cultural Outlook* (New York: E. P. Dutton & Co., 1957), p. 30. The original edition was published in 1941.

37. Pp. 33–34. In a special category, Sorokin places "eclectic" art as a pseudoart, unintegrated, and a mere mechanical mixture on anything and everything; the "art of a bazaar," with no unifying values and no consistent style.

38. P. 44.

39. P. 78.

40. Here Sorokin makes the connection with the parallel developments in society:

> [Modern art, as hypersensate] is somewhat similar to communism or fascism in the political world. Communism and fascism are materialistic in the highest degree. They elevate the economic factors or those of "race and blood" to the level of a god. In this sense they are the legacy of the bankers and money-lenders, the captains of finance and industry, only still more economically minded than these. On the other hand, they are in revolt against the sensate capitalist system, not because it is materialistic or economically minded, but because it is not sufficiently materialistic, confining luxury and comfort to the few instead of bestowing it on the many. (p. 78)

Like the communists and the fascists, the rebel modernists in art were regarded by Sorokin as essentially "sensate," materialistic, and destructive. They were not constructive builders of a new art system or a new politico-economic system of the future, nor bearers of a permanent new culture. They indicate a period of transition and are a system of revolt against the prevailing forms, and are therefore significant. But they have nothing of the coming ideational culture—if such a culture is permitted to appear—in them, and they only serve to prove that the old sensate art and the old sensate politics have performed their respective missions. They have almost spent their creative force. "After the travail and chaos of the transition period, a new art—probably ideational—will perpetuate in a new guise the perennial creative *élan* of human culture." (p. 79) (Sorokin refers here to his fuller treatment of the whole subject in his *Social and Cultural Dynamics*, I, Chs. 8–13.)

41. Whitehead, *Adventures of Ideas*, p. 271.

42. Dewey, p. 349.

NOTES FOR CHAPTER V: *Art, Business,*

and the Moralities

1. The term "moral creativeness" was used by Chester I. Barnard in *Functions of the Executive* (Cambridge, Mass.: Harvard University Press, 1938, Ch. 7) in discussing the nature of executive responsibility. In a paper on the nature of leadership, in his *Organization and Management: Selected Papers* (Cambridge, Mass.: Harvard University Press, 1948), Barnard defined responsibility as "an emotional condition that gives an individual a sense of acute dissatisfaction because of failure to do what he feels morally bound to do or because of doing what he is morally bound not to do, in particular situations." (p. 95) A responsible person would avoid such dissatisfaction and could be "approximately relied upon" if one knew his beliefs or his sense of what was right.

2. Barnard, *Functions of the Executive,* p. 272.

3. Among the organization codes mentioned by Barnard as requiring conformity by an executive head of an important department of a company are obedience to the general purpose and general methods, including the established systems of objective authority; the general purpose of his department; the general moral (ethical) standards of his subordinates; the technical situation as a whole; the code of the informal executive organization, that is, that official conduct shall be that of a gentleman *as its members* understand it, and that personal conduct shall be so likewise; the code that is suggested in the phrase "the good of the organization as a whole"; the code of the informal organization of the department; the technical requirements of the department as a whole. He adds that there will often be others.

4. The technical demands of a new corporate esthetic code should not be underrated. On the general subject of technical competence, Barnard observes that a condition of complex morality, great activity, and high responsibility cannot continue without commensurate ability. "I do not hesitate to affirm," he adds, "that those whom I believe to be the better and more able executives regard it as a major malefaction to induce or push men of fine character and great sense of responsibility into active positions greatly exceeding their technical capacities. Unless the process can be reversed in time, the result is destructive," by which he means destructive either of ability, or responsibility, or morality, or all three. (Barnard, p. 272.) When new corporate codes are introduced, as in the cases of education and the arts, an elementary requirement is the concomitant introduction of specialized staff to meet the new technical demands on corporate management for these new relationships.

5. Sigmund Freud, *Civilization and Its Discontents,* trans. Joan Riviere (New York: Doubleday Anchor Books, 1958), p. 105. The original German edition was published in 1930, when Freud was 74.

6. "In the special world of the Theatre of the Absurd the word 'absurd' means 'without sense, purposeless,' not 'ridiculous.' In short, it is a rueful description of modern man's Fall from Grace, his present tragicomedy dilemma." Samuel Hirsch, "Theatre of the Absurd (Made in America)," *Journal of Social Issues,* January 1964, p. 49. On some of the antecedents of the Absurd in art Maurice Nadeau, *The History of Surrealism,* trans. Richard Howard (New York: Macmillan Co., 1965), is useful.

7. The quote is from C. E. M. Joad, *Guide to Philosophy,* p. 353. He speaks of emotions aroused by art as being "esthetic emotion . . . felt not for this world but for reality."

8. According to Elizabeth Todd the themes of Indian art have customarily been presented in the guise of religion—love, nature, heroism, conflict, all finding a place in the intricate mythologies that arose "to flank a religion and give it secular intelligibility." "In India the concern of art was not the pursuit of beauty as an esthetic abstraction but the revelation of beauty as a divine condition; not personal sentiment or self-expression but a rigorous adherence to a traditional hieratic canon." She maintains that these have always been the characteristics of Indian art "even when its theme or its purpose were not apparently religious, as in the crafts or secular architecture or occasionally even in painting or sculpture." *Ency. Soc. Sci.,* I, p. 230.

9. Benjamin Rowland, Jr., *Art in East and West: An Introduction Through Comparisons* (Boston: Beacon Press, 1954), p. 1.

10. Rowland, p. 3. Rowland presents many photographs of painting and sculpture to make his point. Technical incompetence, as he indicates, is not necessarily the cause of distortion in nontraditional art: "artists made their representations as 'real' as they wanted."

11. Susanne K. Langer, *Form and Feeling,* p. 253.

12. Langer, *Philosophical Sketches,* pp. 82–83.

13. Ray Lepley, ed., *The Language of Value* (New York: Columbia University Press, 1957), and Ray Lepley, ed., *Value: A Cooperative Inquiry* (New York: Columbia University Press, 1949), are symposia that indicate the difficulties and attempt to clarify the issues.

14. Dewey, *Art as Experience,* p. 189.

15. Dewey, p. 325.

16. Dewey, p. 348.

17. Joseph A. Schumpeter, *Capitalism, Socialism, and Democracy* (New York: Harper and Row, 1942), p. 83.

18. Lillian Smith, author of *Strange Fruit* and *The Journey*, in a message, "The Poet in a World of Demagogues," offered to a national convention of the Women's Division of the American Jewish Congress in Washington, D. C., as reported by *The New York Times*, March 21, 1965. Miss Smith said that much of the suffering and anxiety in the world—school dropouts, drug addiction, poor housing, discrimination and tensions between nations—was, in effect, an aspect of man's insistent hunger "to become more human." "Once we see it; once we begin to realize, by act of imagination and heart, the meaning of what is happening to us, then things will fall into line, chaos will resolve into new forms," she declared, continuing: "And it is the poet's job to show us. For only the poet can look beyond details at the total picture; only the poet can feel the courage beyond fear. It is his job to think in spans of 10,000 years; his job to feel the slow, slow movement of the human spirit evolving; to see that the moment is close for mankind to make another big leap forward."

19. Lewis Mumford, "Constancy and Change," *The New Yorker,* March 6, 1965, p. 162.

20. Sigfried Giedion, *The Eternal Present; A Contribution in Constancy and Change,* 2 vols. (New York: Pantheon, 1962), p. 68; *Space, Time, and Architecture, The Growth of a New Tradition* (Cambridge Mass.: Harvard University Press, 1941), especially Part IV, "The Demand for Morality in Architecture"; *Mechanization Takes Command, A Contribution to Anonymous History* (New York: Oxford University Press, 1948); *The Beginnings of Architecture* (New York: Pantheon, 1964); and *Architecture, You, and Me, The Diary of a Development* (Cambridge, Mass.: Harvard University Press, 1958).

21. Mumford, pp. 165–166.

22. Mumford, p. 166.

23. Mumford, p. 166. The statement is Giedion's.

24. Mumford, p. 170.

25. The debate flares continuously, often with a very moralistic tone, as in Huntington Hartford's *Art or Anarchy?* and William Snaith's *The Irresponsible Arts.* Snaith speaks of a "universal dehumanization of the arts," whereas Giedion and Mumford discern hopeful trends in the modern movement. Much of the criticism of modern art is colored by political premises, as in Hartford's suspicion that today's artist-rebels' thinking has influenced the U. S. Supreme Court in "recent decisions to be tolerant of disloyalty to our government and intolerant of a simple prayer in school." (Hartford, pp. 50–51.) The condemnation of works of art and artists on political grounds is not uncommon in societies less free than ours. Peking's spokesmen for cultural reform in the Communist People's Republic of China now decree that the emperors, gods, and spirits of the old plays and operas must now be replaced by workers, peasants, and soldiers: "heroes imbued with proletarian ideology" to be "praised with enthusiasm, while a critical attitude should be taken toward backward people infected with bourgeois ideology and other influences of the old society in order to help educate them" (from a *New York Times* dispatch from Hong Kong on August 29, 1965, quoting Tao Chu, a deputy premier of the People's Republic). In Moscow, Sergei P. Pavlov, first secretary of Komsomol (the Young Communist League), on the same day denounced the "unhealthy criticism" of Soviet conditions in some works of art and literature. Pavlov said, "It cannot be a matter of indifference to us in which direction the force of literary expression is headed—toward stimulating revolutionary-creative energy or toward promoting in young people a skepticism about all that is pure, advanced, and progressive and constitutes the essence of our society." (*The New York Times*, August 30, 1965.)

26.   In the Rede Lecture in May, 1959, at Cambridge University, C. P. Snow elaborated a thesis he had already presented in an article of "The Two Cultures" in *The New Statesman* (October 6, 1956). The lecture was published as *The Two Cultures and the Scientific Revolution* (Cambridge: Cambridge University Press, 1959), cited hereinafter as *The Two Cultures*. In 1963 he brought out a slightly revised edition to which was added a new section, *The Two Cultures: And a Second Look* (Cambridge: Cambridge University Press, 1963; and New York: Mentor Books, 1964), cited hereinafter as *Second Look* and with reference to the New York edition.

27.   *Second Look*, p. 20.

28.   *Second Look*, pp. 40–41.

29.   Among the English critics was F. R. Leavis, who attacked Snow with acid invective in the Richmond Lecture at Cambridge University; see *The Two Cultures? The Significance of C. P. Snow* (London: Chatto and Windus, 1962).

30.   In the new, added section Snow summed up the argument as follows: "It is dangerous to have two cultures which can't or don't communicate. In a time when science is determining much of our destiny, that is whether we live or die, it is dangerous in the most practical terms. Scientists can give bad advice, and decision-makers can't know whether it is good or bad. On the other hand, scientists in a divided culture provide a knowledge of some potentialities which is theirs alone. All this makes the political process more complex, and in some ways more dangerous, than we should be prepared to tolerate for long, either for the purpose of avoiding

disasters, or for fulfilling—what is waiting as a challenge to our conscience and good will—a definable social hope. . . . The division of our culture is making us more obtuse than we need be: we can repair communications to some extent. . . . With good fortune . . . we can educate a large proportion of our better minds so that they are not ignorant of imaginative experience, both in the arts and in science, nor ignorant either of the endowments of applied science, of the remediable suffering of most of their fellow humans and of the responsibilities which, once they are seen, cannot be denied." (*Second Look*, pp. 90–92.) As to those who "cannot be denied" he wrote in the new section: "Millions of individual lives, in some lucky countries like our own, have, by one gigantic convulsion of applied science over the last hundred and fifty years, been granted some share of the primal things. Billions of individual lives, over the rest of the world, will be granted or will seize the same. This is the indication of time's arrow. It is by far the greatest revolution our kind has known." (p. 79)

31. The "two cultures" debate is of course only one aspect of a more general and world-wide conflict among many schools of thought stirred up by modern scientific and technological revolutions. Marx and his various sectarian followers were among the first to state the conflict in contemporary terms. Of special interest is Georg Lukács who, in *The Meaning of Contemporary Realism* (New York: Merlin Press, 1962), defines modernism in terms of its rejection of narrative objectivity, the dissolution of personality, ahistoricity, and the static view of the human condition. See V. Zitta, *Georg Lukács' Marxism, Alienation, Dialectics, Revolution* (The Hague: Nijhoff, 1964); and Peter Demetz, "The Uses of Lukács," *The Yale Review*, Spring 1965, pp. 435–440. Society is condemned by many writers (who may not even have heard of C. P. Snow) as antihuman and psychopathic. In *Book Week*, June 20, 1965, in a review of Paul Goodman's *People or Personnel: Decentralizing and the Mixed System* (New York: Random House, 1965), Seymour Krim lists James Purdy, William Burroughs, Allen Ginsberg, Edward Albee, Terry Southern, and Hubert Selby as examples of American writers who have done "a slaughterhouse job" on "our glittering synthetic-heap of a culture" in almost monstrous attacks, and notes a "barefaced contradiction between the experience set down by our writers and the cheerful abstractions offered by members of the so-called Establishment." Krim writes that "our writers have too much honest hatred of the indignity and meaninglessness of their environment to kid themselves with lines like "the great society," whereas the White House-scientific architects of our future are too intoxicated envisioning solutions to mass quantitative problems to concern themselves with the desperate condition of the American soul." Goodman's book was concerned, he went on, "with the reformer's task of trying to re-create a dying national morale by advocating methods of decentralization and localization—in order to humanize The Machine and redeem work from cynicism and absurdity." This is a literary view, not necessarily shared by the great body of people who do not write (or read) such books as these and who do manage to live quite well in a country whose folk are alleged to have deteriorated into comas of alienation and powerlessness.

32. Werner Jaeger's great work on *Paideia: The Ideals of Greek Culture* is the basis for my use of the term "paideutics," and not the term's narrower philological derivation, as though paideia referred only to the education of youth. Jaeger saw in Greece of the fourth century B. C. the classic epoch in the history of paideia: the development of a *conscious* ideal of education and culture, with a unique awareness of its problems that distinguished the Greek spirit most clearly from other nations. This awareness, in Plato's works especially, reveals how alive the ancient Greeks were "to every problem, every difficulty confronting them in the general intellectual and moral collapse of the brilliant fifth century" before the Christian era; "they were able to understand the meaning of their own education and culture so clearly as to become the teachers of all succeeding nations. Greece is the school of the Western world." (Jaeger, Vol. II, entitled "In Search of the Divine Center," New York: Oxford University Press, 1943, p. 5.) Athens was for Jaeger the cultural center of Greece, its *paideusis*. The searching minds of Socrates, Plato, and their followers produced a great body of thought in an era of conflict and despair, when men had to rethink their way through numerous disciplines and subjects. A newer and higher ideal of a state and of society was obviously necessary. This realization led to a search for new ideal systems. At the center of the whole intellectual struggle was paideia—a higher unity of philosophy, rhetoric, and science, together with a vast array of practical subjects: politics, economics, law, strategy, hunting, agriculture, travel, and the arts of sculpture, painting, and music. These all were seen as "forces which claim to mould character, to impart culture . . . to explain the principles on which their claim is based. . . . [It was a] bitter but magnificently enthusiastic struggle to determine the nature of true paideia." (Jaeger, pp. 9–10.) The tragic shadow of institutional collapse lay over fourth century Greece; yet with it "the radiance of a providential wisdom." Out of the later Hellenistic paideia and Christian paideia came humanism, according to Jaeger; but it is to this seedbed of Athenian rivalry between philosophical and antiphilosophical forces that he goes back for a fundamental antinomy that runs like a red thread in the history of humanism down to the present day. Paideia, in the words of the poet Menander, is "a haven for all mankind . . . a possession which no one can take away from man."

33. Alfred North Whitehead, *Adventures of Ideas* (New York: Mentor Books, 1955), p. 271 and p. 267.

34. Whitehead, p. 271.

35. Sir Kenneth Clark has observed of a great Dorian sculptor of antiquity—one of "the puritans of art"—that it is not "correct to discuss Polykleitos solely in esthetic terms, for his work was based on an ethical ideal, to which formal questions were subservient. Though his purity of aim may recall the Chinese potter continually refining upon a single shape, the human body is, in fact, inexhaustibly complex and suggestive, and to a Greek of the fifth century it stood for a set of values of which restraint, balance, modesty, proportion, and many others would be applied equally in the ethical and in the esthetic sphere. Polykleitos himself would probably have recognized no real distinction between them, and we need not hesitate to pronounce before his work the word 'moral,' that vague, but not altogether meaningless, word which rumbles in the neighborhood of the nude till the academies of the nineteenth century." (*The Nude*, pp. 68–72.)

36. Le Corbusier, *Toward a New Architecture* (New York: Praeger, 1959; first published in 1923). See also *Le Corbusier Talks with Students* (New York: Orion, 1961); and Françoise Choay, *Le Corbusier* (New York: Braziller, 1960). His works were published in 7 vols. by Geo. Wittenborn, New York, 1946–1952.

37. Wolf von Eckhardt, "Corbusier Anticipated Watts in 1923 Appraisal of Cities," *The Washington Post*, September 5, 1965.

38. Wright, in his philosophy of "organic" architecture, at first sought a relationship in Oriental philosophy, and especially Taoism, but later regarded it as a rejection of architectural borrowings from Europe together with a reach for indigenous American inspiration. "America has always assumed," he wrote in *The Natural House* (New York: Horizon Press, 1954), that culture, to be culture, had to come from European sources—be imported." His idea of organic architecture, therefore, "coming from the tall grass of the Midwestern American prairie, was regarded at home as unacceptable," though when associated with Oriental design it was thought to be worthy of imitation as "imported" from the East; he insisted that although the East had long ago enunciated the idea—that the interior space is the reality of a building, that "the reality of a room was to be found in the space enclosed by the roof and walls, not in the roof and walls themselves"—he had his own way of putting the ancient ideals into practical effect. The idea of organic architecture "that the reality of the building lies in the space within to be lived in, the feeling that we must not enclose ourselves in an envelope which is the building, is not alone Oriental. Democracy, proclaiming the integrity of the individual *per se,* had the feeling if not the words." (pp. 218–221) Laotse may have had the idea, but the organic house now realized the idea. See Peter Blake, *Master Builders* (New York: Alfred A. Knopf, 1960); *Frank Lloyd Wright* (Baltimore, Md.: Pelican, 1964); and Norris K. Smith, *Frank Lloyd Wright: A Study in Architectural Content* (Englewood Cliffs, N.J.: Prentice-Hall Spectrum Book, 1965).

39. Lewis Mumford, *The Highway and the City* (New York: Mentor Books, 1965).

40. Nikolaus Pevsner, *An Outline of European Architecture* (New York: Pelican, 1943); and *Pioneers of Modern Design* (Baltimore, Md.: Penguin, 1965; first published in 1936). For American architecture, see *The People's Architects,* ed. Harry S. Ransom (Chicago: University of Chicago Press, 1964), on seven architects "with a profound feeling of social responsibility"—Reid, Ford, Gruen, Pei, De Mars, Belluschi, and Goodman; and Carl W. Condit, *The Chicago School of Architecture* (Chicago: University of Chicago Press, 1964), on Sullivan, Jenney, Baumann, Adler, Root, and Wright. For a useful survey, see *The Literature of Architecture,* ed. Don Gifford (New York: E. P. Dutton Co., 1966), and Paul Heyer, *Architects on Architecture* (New York: Walker and Company, 1966). Also, Walter Gropius, *Scope of Total Architecture* (New York: Harper and Row, 1943), and Werner Blaser, *Mies Van Der Rohe: the Art of Structure* (New York: Praeger, 1965).

41. Constantine A. Doxiadis, *Architecture in Transition* (New York: Oxford University Press, 1964).

42. The role of the landscape architect in this collaboration is growing. The American Society of Landscape Architects designated 1964–65 as the Centennial Year of Landscape Architecture. The first 40 years of American landscape architecture were practically synonymous with Frederick Law Olmsted, who demonstrated the values accruing from carefully planned outdoor space, and designed major park systems for New York City, Buffalo, Chicago, Philadelphia, Washington, and elsewhere during the 1880's and 1890's. In 1901 Olmsted, at the request of President Eliot of Harvard University, began the first landscape architecture courses ever offered in the United States. A movement started by a few self-taught pioneers is now carried on by technically-trained people who are graduates of seventeen accredited colleges and universities. The society has grown from its original eleven founders to well over one thousand each of members and affiliates. What began with a single park has resulted in professional involvement in park systems that reach from coast to coast, highway, freeway, and parkway programs, innumerable commercial, industrial, institutional, educational, and military projects, both public and private, both here and abroad. The National Park Service is the largest single employer of landscape architects. To save the scenic beauty of the national parks from the hordes of motorized America, the service encouraged the widespread development of state parks for active and intensive recreational use. Civilian Conservation Corps work camps, sponsored by National Park Service, advanced the state parks programs by some 50 years. City and regional planning have engaged the services of landscape architects since Olmsted's day. Agencies involved in town planning, land planning, and housing include these professionally trained personnel on their staffs.

43. At state and local levels public policy can be decisive: "There is much to be done in improved zoning, updated building codes and in the long range planning of our environment. Whereas some farsighted developers are willing to forego some quantity by employing professionally trained men to use the land wisely, far too many belong to the bulldozer school that flattens and denudes land or fills swamps, so that the greatest number of houses may be erected. This is done with little regard for people, who, so in need of housing, buy from necessity rather than choice. . . . What of the future? Modern-day problems challenge the profession (of landscape architecture) as never before. 'America has made the biggest hash of its environment in the history of the world,' " said Ian Nairn, editor of *Architectural Review* of London, after his ten thousand-mile look at the United States. "Our environmental 'hash' is a result of an outmoded attitude that land is a commodity to be exploited. The time is at hand for accepting the ecological concept of land as a community to which man belongs. This community must be guarded and managed so that its growth is amenable and beautiful as well as workable and economic. There is need for more cooperation between the design professions: landscape architects, architects, engineers and planners. The landscape architects must act as the stewards of this larger landscape and the future must produce more and even better designers with even greater vision." Nelson M. Weber, "Milestone for Landscape Architecture," *The New York Times*, April 18, 1965. Cf. Ada Louise Huxtable, "A Code for 20th Century," and news article by Glenn Fowler, "Wide Revisions Outlined for City's Building Code," *The New York Times*, July 9, 1965.

Federal, as well as state and municipal, policies are involved. When the Public Housing Administration in Washington declared recently that it places greater emphasis on the environmental and esthetic aspects of housing than on the promotion of the economy, the General Accounting Office objected, criticizing the PHA for using "outside ornamentation; unusual design for building walls; extra-quality facing brick; hardwood flooring; awning-type aluminum windows; marble interior window sills; high-cost dedication plaques and monuments; ornamental walls and planter curbs, and community facilities," as well as other "elaborate or extravagant" design features. The Public Housing Commissioner had taken a stand against "bare, stark shelter" that resulted from "bowing to pressures for maximum economy." Wolf von Eckhardt, in *The Washington Post*, February 7, 1965, added that GAO's blast at more attractive public housing was in striking contrast to the $125 million or more spent on the new House Office Building, and that it sounded "like the old harassment by misguided real estate interests and speculative builders who consider public subsidies for low-rent housing dangerous socialism and who are imbued with the Victorian notion that poverty is a sin for which its victims must be punished. This is no longer the mood of the country. We have declared war on poverty and we want better and more livable and attractive communities." In New York City the policy of imposing higher assessments upon structures of great architectural merit surrounded by open plazas, such as the Seagram Building, discourages enlightened architects and planners. The proposal of the Committee to Beautify the City of New York that up to one per cent of the total construction costs of all new buildings be allocated for works of art is criticized as a meager measure to combat ugliness by superficial embellishments.

A frontal attack on urban ugliness was long impeded by a narrow judicial construction of the police power of the states, but has now been aided to some extent by the important U. S. Supreme Court decision in *Berman* v. *Parker*, 348 U. S. 26, 99 L ed 27 (1954). In this case Justice Douglas, speaking for the Court, which upheld a federal statute authorizing the use of eminent domain to take a certain piece of land for urban redevelopment, said: "We do not sit to determine whether a particular housing project is or is not desirable. The concept of the public welfare is broad and inclusive. . . . The values it represents are spiritual as well as physical, aesthetic as well as monetary. It is within the power of the legislature to determine that the community should be beautiful as well as healthy, spacious as well as clean, well-balanced as well as carefully patrolled. In the present case, the Congress and its authorized agencies have made determinations that take into account a wide variety of values. It is not for us to reappraise them. If those who govern the District of Columbia decide that the Nation's Capital should be beautiful as well as sanitary, there is nothing in the Fifth Amendment that stands in the way." Congress, acting as legislature for the District of Columbia, had delegated authority to a special development land agency to take title to land in the southwest area of the District. The property involved in this case was land on which a department store stood; the Agency did not claim that the store was slum housing or otherwise objectionable per se; the land was required for the whole development plan. The case establishes, as a matter of constitutional law, that the concept of the public welfare, for the purpose of which Congress acting as the legislature for the District of Columbia may exercise its police power, is broad and inclusive, and that the values it represents are spiritual and esthetic, as well as physical and monetary. A determination that the public welfare requires the community (here, Washington) to be beautiful, spacious, and well-balanced, as well as healthy, clean, and carefully patrolled, is within the power of Congress. The Fifth Amendment was involved in the leading case, but the same principles would apply with respect to the Fourteenth Amendment as a restriction on state legislative action.

Berman v. *Parker* stands in contrast with earlier decisions which sustained zoning ordinances, billboard abatement, and other municipal measures related to urban planning on the ground that the police power thus exercised was confined to matters directly affecting "public health, safety, and morals" but not civic beauty. The prohibition of livery stables, fertilizing plants, and slaughter houses within city limits was upheld, but zoning for esthetic purposes was frowned upon as beyond the police power. As Charles Fairman has put it, "constitutional law in America has been very sensitive to bad smells"; ugliness is something else. Billboard regulation was sustained as a measure against fire hazards, the concealment of criminals and immoral practices, but not because the billboards concealed a beautiful view. Differentiated limitation on the height of buildings was upheld on grounds of public health and fire protection, but it would not have survived as a measure to preserve architectural symmetry and pleasing urban skylines. On the other hand, the Supreme Judicial Court of Massachusetts in 1935 (289 Mass. 149) sustained an amendment to the state constitution authorizing the regulation of advertising billboards "on private property within public view" on the ground that it was "within the reasonable scope of the police power to preserve from destruction the scenic beauties bestowed on the Commonwealth by nature in conjunction with the promotion of safety of travel on the public ways and the protection of travellers from the intrusion of unwelcome advertising."

44. The current trend in university schools of architecture is to integrate architectural design with city planning and engineering principles. There is a great shortage of educators in these fields. At Columbia University in New York the School of Architecture was reorganized in 1965

into three divisions: architecture, urban planning, and architectural technology. The urban planning division will include special studies in urban development in emerging nations. It is also planned to encompass a research Institute of Urban Environment. The division of architectural technology will cooperate with Columbia's School of Engineering and Applied Science in training engineers as consultants in structural, mechanical, electrical, and acoustical fields.

NOTES FOR CHAPTER VI: *The Corporate Reach for New Values*

1. In a famous passage Innocent IV, referring to Justinian's *Digest*, proclaimed that a corporation, as a fictitious person, could commit neither sin nor delict, an offense against law. Maitland, the English legal historian, comments that while Pope Innocent might settle the question of sin and thereby prevent the excommunication of a *universitas*, he could not as a lawyer convince his fellow jurists that a corporation must never be charged with crime or tort. (F. W. Maitland, Introduction to *Political Theories of the Middle Age* by Otto Gierke, which Maitland translated into English; Cambridge: Cambridge University Press, 1900.)

2. The *persona ficta* of the modern law of corporations is often thought to be of Roman-law origin. But, as Maitland reminds us, the texts of Justinian's *Digest* nowhere directly calls the *universitas* a *persona*, and the term *persona ficta* occurs not at all in relation to corporate entities. According to Gierke, the first man to use this famous phrase was Sinibald Fieschi, a great lawyer who became Pope Innocent IV in 1243, and whom Gierke called the father of the "Fiction Theory." Innocent wrote that a corporation is a person, but a person only by fiction; the doctrine was professed alike thereafter by legists and canonists. They were not, of course, speaking of business corporations, nor indeed of any entities that had "liberties and franchises" or rights of self-government claimed by English boroughs and guilds, and later on our modern corporations. They were wheels in the Church's and State's machinery. The fiction theory was closely associated with the concession theory, since the fictitious personality was not inherent in a corporation but only conceded it by grant.

328

The "personification of great industrial enterprise," wrote Thurman Arnold in *The Folklore of Capitalism* (New Haven: Yale University Press, 1937, Ch. VIII), is "one of the essential and central notions which give our industrial feudalism logical symmetry" by endowing great corporations with the rights and prerogatives of free individuals, thereby winning general acceptance of the idea that individual liberty is on a par with the freedom from restraint which large companies enjoy. The corporate personality "is part of our present religion," to which he offered no objection. But he asked for better understanding of the attendant "rituals," particularly in the "ceremonies" surrounding the antitrust laws and the reorganization of insolvent companies. These ceremonies "are designed to perpetuate the illusion that it is men, and not organizations, with whom the Government at Washington is dealing"—individual men buying and selling in a free market, and, in the ritual of corporate reorganization, allegedly men and not companies, "to whom the doctrine of vicarious atonement is applied through which the debts of an industrial organization are forgiven." The corporate personality he was talking about is no *persona ficta* of the legists and canonists. "Institutional personalities," he wrote, "acquire the characters given them by the folklore of the times. Since every character is necessarily a whole bundle of contradictory roles, institutions have to appear in all these contradictory roles."

3. A great gap yawns between the "bloodless apparition" of the corporation in juristic theory and the flesh-and-blood reality of the institutions we see in modern companies, as, for example, in Peter F. Drucker's account of General Motors in *Concept of the Corporation* (New York: John Day, 1946). As Arthur Stone Dewing in *The Financial Policy of Corporations*, 5th ed. (New York: Ronald Press, 1953, I, p. 16 f.) has well said, the modern corporation is one of those *pragmatic* unities produced by social and economic evolution while philosophers were attempting, not very successfully, to define it intellectually in terms of the old problem of the One and the Many. *Legal* corporateness, as we know it in our law, appears far later than the pragmatic unities. To distinguish incorporated from unincorporated bodies historically has been a hard task; in the words of Stewart Kyd (*A Treatise on the Law of Corporations*, London: Butterworth, 1793), "for a considerable period, the shade which separated the one from the other was of a touch so delicate as to require the most minute attention, and the most discerning eye, to distinguish." The first appearance of the corporate group as a right-and-duty-bearing unit is what he, as a lawyer, was after. And it is true that this juristic distinction was very important for the businessman; what he needed, and belatedly got, was a set of legal attributes for the pragmatic unity of a company, which attributes made possible the vast growth of the corporate enterprise system of our day. Legal attributes such as the right to sue and to be sued and to hold property as an artificial person, although not now uniquely corporate rights (legislation may grant these rights to unincorporated associations), were important in the early stages of the evolution of the corporate business system. Limited liability was another significant attribute. But the most important, historically, was the artificial and continuous "personality" grantable by royal charter, and, according to prevailing Austinian doctrine in Anglo-American law, grantable only by the sovereign power (exercisable in the United States by state and federal legislatures). The "Realists" of corporation theory, on the other hand, have always opposed this heady juristic doctrine, together with its corollary concerning the contractual basis of corporateness. Emphasizing the common purpose of those engaged in corporate action, a distinguished Realist of the German school, Otto von Gierke (in *Das Deutsche Genossenschaftsrecht*, Berlin: Weidmann, 1868–1913) insisted that "the essential goal of all corporate organization is the forming of the association into a *living, collective personality*," a tough organic unity rooted in the soil of a community and not at all dependent upon the touch of the sovereign to bring it into being. Gierke's Realism has greatly impressed modern pluralists, such as Maitland, Figgis, and Laski, and, both independently and indirectly, some contemporary writers who defend the autonomy of corporate groups—religious, educational, as well as economic.

4.   Thomas Hobbes, *Leviathan* (1651), Ch. 29.

5.   The royal sanctions employable against towns and other bodies that tried to get away with corporateness without a valid charter were often effective. The king's Attorney-General could descend upon a town (even on London) or an "adulterine guild" with his writ of *quo warranto,* and make "all charters, like the walls of Jericho, fall down before him," returning "laden with surrenders, the spoils of towns." (Cecil T. Carr, *General Principles of the Law of Corporations*, Cambridge: Cambridge University Press, 1905, p. 169, quoting North's *Examen*.) A handsome payment for a new charter would follow successful prosecution before the king's justices in eyre. In a leading case *(King* v. *Passmore)* it was stated that "a *quo warranto* is necessary where there is a body corporate, de facto, who take upon themselves to act as a body corporate, but from some defect in their constitution they cannot legally exercise the powers they affect to use." Edward I applied his statute of *quo warranto* vigorously against boroughs with doubtful charters, or none at all, although some charters of the older boroughs were presumed to be "lost." The practice

obviously served to heighten the royal prerogative. This conception of corporateness by prescription was a fiction that satisfied the king without denying the basic principle that he alone could grant charters. The Italian medieval lawyers, from which this idea may have come, had also used this fiction in connection with their concession theory.

6. "The conception of the juristic person was a legal form exclusively designed for, and applicable to, public property, and the only way in which both societies and foundations could acquire a juristic personality was by being admitted to the circle of public corporations and institutions." (Rudolph Sohm, *The Institutes: A Textbook of the History and System of Roman Private Law*, trans. J. C. Ledlie, 3d ed., Oxford: Clarendon Press, 1926, p. 199.)

7. M. Ivanovich Rostovtzeff, *Social and Economic History of the Roman Empire* (Oxford: Clarendon Press, 1926), p. 160 f. and p. 532, note 22. F. Oertel remarks that one reason for the great insecurity of trade and commerce in the Augustan Empire was that "personal capital only, not joint-stock capital, was sunk in business." ("The Economic Unification of the Mediterranean Region," *Cambridge Ancient History*, X, p. 422.)

8. Julius Goebel, Jr., *Cases and Materials on the Development of Legal Institutions* (1931), p. 586. See further Martin Weinbaum, *The Incorporation of Boroughs* (Manchester University Press, 1937), Intro., pp. 18 and 93–96; Wm. Maitland, *Constitutional History of England* (Cambridge: Cambridge University Press, 1908); C. Stephenson, *Borough and Town: A Study of Urban Origins in England*, Medieval Academic Monographs, No. 7 (1933); H. J. Laski, "The Early History of the Corporation in England," *Harvard Law Review*, XXX, p. 561; Sir Frederick Pollock and F. W. Maitland, *History of English Law*, 2d ed. (1898), I, pp. 486–511 and pp. 634–688; James Tait, *The Medieval English Borough: Studies on Its Origins and Constitutional History* (Manchester University Press, 1936).

9. The most authoritative account of this development is in the writings of Professor Edward S. Corwin, particularly in the chapters on "Dual Federalism versus Nationalism, and the Industrial Process" and on "The Property Right versus Legislative Power in a Democracy," in his *Twilight of the Supreme Court* (New Haven: Yale University Press, 1934), and in more detail in his earlier law review articles cited in these chapters; also in his *Commerce Power versus States Rights* (Princeton: Princeton University Press, 1936). Carl B. Swisher's account, in his *American Constitutional Development*, 2d ed. (Boston: Houghton Mifflin, 1954), Ch. 11, fills in the details of the history. On the ingenious reasoning of Marshall and

Story, laying the basis for corporate *privateness*, see James J. Robbins, "The Private Corporation—Its Constitutional Genesis," *Georgetown Law Journal*, XXVIII (November 1939), pp. 165–183.

10. The charter of a corporation may be regarded simply as a license, a franchise, or a contract. Business corporation charters were originally granted by special statute in the states (under Crown prerogative during British rule) and not under general statutes until about the middle of the 19th century. There were few business corporations chartered until the last decade of the 18th century, when independence and a more promising constitutional system had been established. As the number of charters grew then, and later on in the 19th century, pressures arose to make incorporation little more complicated than granting a license. But the Dartmouth College Case (though the case of a non-profit corporation) set a different tone to the meaning of a corporation charter. There the charter was regarded as more than a franchise constituting a vested or property interest in the hands of the holders, although this vested interest became an important element. In the Dartmouth College Case (1819) the charter (1769) was regarded as the outcome and partial record of a contract between the donors of the college, on the one hand, and the British Crown on the other, which contract still continued in force between the State of New Hampshire, as the successor to the Crown and Government of Great Britain, on the one hand, and on the other the trustees of the college, as successors to the donors. Chief Justice Marshall, in a famous opinion, with his usual ingenuity made this *contractual* point so that there could be no doubt that the contract clause of the federal constitution applied to the case; if the charter had been a mere franchise the United States Supreme Court would not have had jurisdiction. Justice Story went even further in maintaining that Dartmouth College as a corporation *in esse* was a party to the contract, though Berle and Means, in *The Modern Corporation and Private Property* (1932), p. 129, observe that this view does not bear analysis. "It is impossible to have a contract which at once creates the corporation and embodies a bargain between the corporation and the state since a contract presupposes two parties capable of contracting before the negotiations begin." Such logical difficulties have never deterred bench and bar from full acceptance of the Dartmouth College rule, which was soon thereafter applied to business corporations. Chief Justice Waite declared in 1879 (in *Stone* v. *Mississippi*) that "the doctrines announced by this [Supreme] court [in the Dartmouth College Case] have become so embedded in the jurisprudence of the United States as to make them to all intents and purposes a part of the Constitution itself." The same could be said for the network of judicial and legislative interpretations of various clauses of the federal constitution which, when combined, provide a remarkably strong barrier against legislative encroachment on corporate autonomy.

It is true that the powers of Congress over national matters have been more fully recognized than they were before "The Constitutional Revolution, Ltd." (Corwin's term, and the title he gave to a series of lectures at Claremont, Calif.; published under that title by the Claremont Colleges in 1941) occurred and corporate governance thrived in the no-man's-land between the greatly restricted areas of state and federal authority. The older "dual federalism" of constitutional law, which has now disappeared, created this no-man's-land of nongovernment through judicial interpretations of the commerce clause by the Supreme Court from about 1885 to 1935. The commerce clause had been the chief basis of national power in the field of political economy, but the scope of that power had been narrowed down by the judges until the New Deal cases broadened it out again to Marshallian proportions as indicated by the great chief justice in *Gibbons* v. *Ogden* (1819). Other federal powers—especially the taxing, spending, and war powers—have since been used and so broadly interpreted that we have a "mixed" economy in which the business corporation is not, properly speaking, an inhabitant of the so-called private sector entirely. It moves from private to quasi-public sectors, depending on the situation in domestic and world affairs. But even those companies most deeply committed to defense and other public contracts still retain their autonomy if they choose to do so. A narrowing of their range of choice in these matters is not a consequence of constitutional interpretation, but of social forces of a very different order.

11. In my *Government of Corporations* (New York: Free Press, 1962) I have treated the nature of corporate governance at some length, including the question of stockholders as a part of the corporate constituency.

12. The Securities Act of 1933 (the "Truth-in-Securities Law") set up for the first time a federal agency, the Securities and Exchange Commission, to regulate the securities market, but not for the purpose of empowering anyone in Washington to pass on the merits of corporate securities. The aim was to put to work a staff of lawyers, accountants, and security analysts to examine and judge the adequacy of the information corporations provide when they offer securities for sale, and to bar offerings that do not meet the standards of financial accounting set by the Commission. Full-disclosure requirements are backed by criminal penalties provided in the original statute and in succeeding ones: the Securities Exchange Act of 1934, the Public Utility Holding Act of 1935, the Trust Indenture Act of 1939, the Investment Company Act of 1940, and the Investment Advisers Act of 1940, together with various amendments. On the application of these statutes see J. A. Livingston, *The American Stockholder* (Philadelphia: J. B. Lippincott, 1958), Ch. XV. Livingston says that when the Commission was first established, "the regulatees eyed the regulators apprehensively, like youngsters whose stepmother catches them in the jam-pot" since "this was a New Deal Democratic administration, poaching on a Republican preserve—Wall Street and Big Business. . . . Presidents of companies who had been plenipotentiary emperors on their own islands of corporate power had to reckon with a third force in their relations with stockholders. . . . Everyone was tense and uncertain in this brash new world of federal regulation of securities. . . . By the time President Eisenhower took office in 1953, the early distrust and skepticism —the fear and hatred, you could honestly say—had dissipated. Self-searching had become an integral part of Wall Street and corporate practice." But the Commission's standards did not apply to corporations whose stocks were traded in over-the-counter markets, or which were unlisted on any stock exchange. Thus the legislation had neither universal application throughout the corporate sector of the economy nor the effect of introducing "shareholder democracy" as some had hoped and others had feared. It was not "radical" legislation, and repeal would be unthinkable for most businessmen today.

    13. The term "old style capitalism" was used by Calvin B. Hoover in *The Economy, Liberty and the State* (New York: The Twentieth Century Fund, 1959) to refer in general to pre-World War I economies in most Western countries. That war shook the foundations of the old-style capitalism, but it revived somewhat in the United States until the beginning of the Great Depression in the fall of 1929. "Unlike the feudal estate," wrote Hoover, "capitalistic private property gave the absolute right to receive income without the obligation of service rendered," a right "more absolute in the United States than in any other country since it was protected by a written constitution that eventually denied the power of both the federal and state legislatures to impair private property." (p. 15) The New Deal legislation and succeeding judicial interpretations of key constitutional clauses broke down the barriers against democratic *legislative* (as distinguished from private "consumer sovereignty" and corporate) direction of the economy as a whole. Old-style capitalism was overthrown by violence in Russia, Germany, Italy and other countries in Europe; in the United States it was "transformed" peacefully in the thirties. Yet "the first and really decisive step away from an individual-enterprise economy had taken place much earlier when the courts accorded to corporations the status of legal person," thus providing constitutional protections for large organizations as though they were individuals and limiting narrowly the powers of the states to control and regulate the corporate economy until the Supreme Court reversed this policy during the New Deal." (p. 192) But, as Hoover observes, the doctrine of nonintervention by government in the economy had already been substantially breached by the administration of Herbert Hoover at the start of the Great Depression, and the Roosevelt administration's far more extensive intervention, though at first temporarily halted by the judiciary, could not be stopped because the public demanded action, not inaction in Washington. A philosophical justification for the New Deal type of intervention that fell somewhere between extreme laissez-fairism and socialism was not immediately available. Since then, however, we have seen the rise of new doctrine, which does fill the gap here and in Europe. The "concerted economy" in France, developed under the leadership of Jean Monnet, is an example. Keynesian theory played an important role in England and the United States. As Calvin Hoover indicates, the old-style capitalist doctrine based on the outmoded concepts of individual enterprise, has now given way to theories of an organizational economy that is a far cry from socialist collectivism.

14. The new set of corporate responsibilities will be considered in detail in the next chapter, along with a careful look at the concept of responsibility as the term applies to corporate governments. At this point, however, it is well to emphasize that in the traditional concept of the business corporation, the question of responsibility of directors and managers was quite academic and called for no discussion at all: directors and executives worked for the "owners" of the company, i.e., the shareowners. But who really owns a *company*'s assets, if not that fictitious person called the corporation; and what is the power relationship between this person and the real persons who hold the stock? Stockholders, of course, are often corporate persons, too. The path of responsibility from management back to the flesh-and-blood people who are said to be the real owners is often a very tortuous one. The greatest difficulty in applying the older conventional concepts of managerial responsibility to the ultimate owners, whether fictitious or natural persons, is that in the corporation with hundreds of thousands of stockholders, employees, and suppliers, the executive managers are faced with decisions every day that cannot be handled in traditional ways and in accordance with substantive rules of business prudence that govern the actions of small companies and proprietorships. The modern corporation has introduced a new kind of government for business firms, and if the new ways are not entirely satisfactory they are at least a response to new conditions that cannot be expected merely to serve old theory.

15. See "The New Look in Corporation Law," *Law and Contemporary Problems*, XXIII (Spring 1958). "New look," as a fashion-show term, now long outdated, nevertheless still seems to apply to the American Bar Association's Model Business Corporation Act, which was of central interest in the symposium in this issue of the Duke University law review. In the foreword to this symposium, the editor classified the many theories that now abound among legislators and lawyers concerning the role that government should play in corporation law into four main types: (1) the enabling act theory, according to which the privilege of incorporation should be made available quite freely, setting a minimum of special conditions and limitations for the incorporators; (2) a somewhat more restrictive theory that favors legislative safeguards on certain critical matters where experience has indicated that difficulties may rise; (3) the theory that legislation should prescribe limitations that "more systematically impinge on freedom of contract (of incorporators) not only to protect investors and creditors, but to create and preserve the atmosphere of public confidence so necessary for business prosperity"; and (4) the "social responsibility" theory which urges "that corporate power be exercised not primarily for the benefit of investors and creditors, or even to customers and employees, but rather for the benefit of the general public." He adds that "an 'enabling act' philosophy continues to dominate corporation law in this country." Recent attempts, he added, to modernize corporation law, to give it a "new look," may have changed the appearance of the package but not the fundamental contours. In other words, despite the talk about corporate social responsibility, the basic *law* governing corporations fell a decade ago mainly at the other end of the scale and left it essentially to the judgment and contractual terms of the incorporators and their managerial instruments to write their own ticket concerning corporate powers, with little state intervention in the interest of other contributor-claimants than stockholders and creditors, and practically no intervention to force corporations to be "socially responsible." To what extent this is true today is a question examined in the next chapter of this book.

16.   Professor Wilber G. Katz, in the law review symposium cited above, says that as to the contours of the "new look" in the Model Business Corporation Act one commentator (Harris, "The Model Business Corporation Act—Invitation to Irresponsibility?" *Northwestern University Law Review*, L, 1955, p. 1) regards them as a seductive invitation to corporate irresponsibility. Professor Katz, who stated and elaborated the four types of corporation law philosophy referred to above, does not appear to agree with this view. He is critical of "reformers" who want to change the law to make corporations more responsible to society generally: "Perhaps corporation law critics should keep straining to catch Professor Berle's vision" of "The Modern Corporation and the City of God"—referring here

to the title of the last chapter of Berle's *The 20th Century Capitalist Revolution*—but "in the meantime, we need not be defensive about the statutes of North Carolina and Texas—or even those of Illinois and Delaware (all examples of the enabling act theory). None of them, to be sure, is a model ordinance for the City of God. But the corporate organizations they make possible are institutions not inappropriate for economic activity in the Earthly City." (Katz, "The Philosophy of Midcentury Corporation Statutes," *Law and Contemporary Problems,* cited, at p. 192.) The enabling act theory, with its concession of large corporate powers and its absence of *statutory* requirement of socially responsible managerial action does not *command* corporations to be socially responsible, and probably they should not be so commanded by law. But it is quite another thing to argue that the corporate institutions "enabled" so broadly under that theory ought always to restrict themselves to narrowly "economic activity in the Earthly City." The very freedom of action they have as autonomous institutions leaves quite open the question of self-generated social responsibility. A characteristic legalistic view of the matter centers on the statutory and common law requirements of good corporate governance, and leaves practically untouched the equally important issue of the *discretionary uses* of managerial power.

17. Gardiner C. Means, in his 1933 doctoral dissertation at Harvard, which formed the basis of much of the economic analysis in Berle and Means, *Modern Corporation and Private Property,* showed statistically the increasing extent to which economic activity in the United States had been conducted under the corporate form of organization, the increasing role that corporations of great size had come to play, the increasing dispersion of stock ownership, and the increasing separation of ownership and control in "the modern corporation." He sketched the development of corporate activity in this country from the 335 companies of 1800 to the "half million" of the nineteen thirties. In 1927, two years before the onset of the Great Depression, "200 non-financial corporations controlled 45 per cent of non-financial corporate wealth, received over 40 per cent of corporate income, controlled 35 per cent of business wealth, and between 15 and 20 per cent of national wealth." (Gardiner C. Means, *The Corporate Revolution in America,* New York: Collier Books, 1964, pp. 16–17.) He estimated in 1933 that the rate of growth of large corporations between 1909 and 1927 was of such magnitude that, if continued to 1950, it would mean that 80 per cent of corporate wealth would then be in the hands of 200 corporations; but he now notes that concentration actually continued after 1929 at a much slower rate than this.

In a study made under the auspices of the Brookings Institution, A. D.

H. Kaplan showed that, while the corporation was undoubtedly the predominant form of business organization in the economy, the noncorporate area had maintained its relative position with "striking success": 1951 corporation payrolls were 232 per cent, and noncorporate 227 per cent, above 1929 levels, while corporate profits were almost four times their 1929 levels, and entrepreneurial income had increased threefold. Small business in the corporate sector had continued to be substantial: of the 537,000 corporations submitting balance sheets to the Bureau of Internal Revenue in 1948, nearly half had total assets under $50,000 and a net worth of $10,000; and in the category of industrial enterprises, the total financial resources of the small, medium-sized, and giant firms were approximately equal. Of the $230 billion of total assets for all industrial firms (excluding public utilities and financial institutions) he estimated that a third, or $76 billion, was held by the vast majority of proprietorships and corporations having less than $500,000 in assets. The 361 industrials with $50 million or more of assets held $72 billion, slightly less than one-third of the total. The middle group of 34,000 corporations, with assets ranging from $500,000 to $50 million, held the largest segment, its assets totaling $82 billion. The 100 largest industrials in 1948 accounted for about 12 per cent of all income originating in American private business and about 10.6 per cent of the total national payroll, private and governmental. Their assets amounted to nearly $49.2 billion. He pointed out that "these figures fell short by a wide margin of the degree of preponderance of the giant corporations suggested by projecting the findings of Berle and Means," though conceding that "the fact that decisions bearing on the disposition of roughly $50 billion of business resources depend on 100 managements, with some ties of long standing among them, would be cause for concern if this area of centralized managerial control showed a tendency to engulf more and more of the economy." But, "fortunately the 100 largest do not form an integrated whole." He found the structure of the economy as a whole "appropriate to dynamic competition." (Kaplan, *Big Enterprise in a Competitive System*, Washington, D. C.: Brookings Institution, 1954, pp. 238–240.)

The number of business units in the United States (fifty states plus District of Columbia) for all "industries," as defined by the Treasury Department in its *Statistics of Income; U. S. Business Tax Returns*, for the year 1962 was: 9,183,000 sole proprietorships (individually owned businesses and farms), 932,000 active partnerships, and 1,268,000 active corporations. The business receipts and net profits were distributed among these three categories as follows: sole proprietorships—$178.4 billion ($23.89 billion); active partnerships—$72.3 billion ($8.51 billion); active corporations—$895.12 billion ($49.6 billion). (*Statistical Abstract of the United States,* Government Printing Office, Washington, 1965, Table No. 671; these figures include both financial and farm business units as well as public utilities.)

18. I am indebted to Mr. Armand G. Erpf for his ingenious construct of "a spectrum of companies."

19. In oil, wildcatting means sinking a well in unproven acreage and either finding the oil or losing the money, all of this taking place in a brief period of time. The business may be a wildcat, however, even if the period of experiment may be prolonged. There may be large selling for up to $100 million. But there are wildcatters in other fields besides minerals. In all such ventures, the investor takes a calculated risk on the breakthrough either in the markets to which they aspire or in the technological supremacy that they hope to achieve for a many-fold return.

20. In most of the very large, mature companies the growth of sales is not usually expected to exceed that of the overall economy, about 3–4 per cent a year, and this may or may not be translatable into equal earnings growth. Growth at the rate of 8–15 per cent has been seen in the utilities, the process food companies, the mass production and mass distribution companies, education, life insurance, and others. This is exceptional in the category of public corporate capitalism.

21. See "Playing a Civic Role," *Business Week,* April 30, 1966, 100–102: "Of 1,033 U. S. corporations, in the largest sampling ever taken on this subject, 815 have some form of public affairs function. That is a tremendous upsurge from the handful of companies in the 1950s." The NICB report notes, however, that only 172 of the companies have written policies on corporate public affairs. But 309 had public affairs programs that were regarded as "significant" by NICB public affairs research division head Thomas J. Diviney. A "significant" program would contain most of these elements: legislative relations, political and economic education of employees, contributions to and participation in community affairs, and a written policy.

NOTES FOR CHAPTER VII: *The Dialogue and Dilemma*
of Social Responsibility

1.   These estimates of federal impact on the economy are from Merle
Fainsod, B. K. Gordon, and Joseph C. Palamountain, *Government and the
American Economy*, 3d ed. (1959).

2.   The figures on small business are from Eugene P. Foley, *Small
Business Administration: An Agency of the Federal Government, What It
Is, What It Does* (Washington, D. C.: Small Business Administration,
September 1964).

3.   White House Committee on Small Business, *Small Business in the
American Economy* (Washington, D. C.: Small Business Administration,
May 1962).

4.   See especially "The *Fortune* Directory of the 500 Largest U. S.
Industrial Corporations, and the 50 Largest Banks, Merchandising, Trans-
portation, Life-Insurance, and Utility Companies," *Fortune Supplement*,
July 1956, and the comparable directories in *Fortune*, July 1965, and
July 1966.

5.   On corporate endocracy see Eugene V. Rostow, "To Whom and for
What Ends Is Corporate Management Responsible?" in *The Corporation
in Modern Society*, ed. Edward S. Mason (Cambridge, Mass: Harvard
University Press, 1959), pp. 46–71, esp. pp. 51 f. I have discussed the
subject in *The Government of Corporations*, Ch. 12. The internal governing body of the large publicly held corporation of thousands of shareowners
is of necessity a small one: the board. Corporate democracy is hardly possible or desirable under these circumstances.

6.   The term, "mixed economic system," refers here not only to those
European economies described in C. B. Hoover's *The Economy, Liberty
and the State* (New York: The Twentieth Century Fund, 1959), especially
in Chapters 10 and 11, but also to our own changing American economy.
Hoover noted our shift from "the individual-enterprise, laissez-faire,
private-property economy of old-style capitalism" to what he called the
Organizational Economy. He hoped that our system could be preserved
against the trend toward statization that one sees elsewhere: "Whether
the movement towards statization . . . in modern capitalistic economies of
the West can be permanently halted short of the danger zone where liberty
begins to be seriously curtailed remains uncertain, since unfortunately the
limits are nowhere sharply defined." (p. 285) At least the tentative defi-

nition of those limits must be implicit in a systematic approach to the problem of corporate social responsibilities. A major purpose of corporate assumption of social responsibilities is presumably the preservation of liberty in our Organizational Economy.

7. For a more extended discussion of the social responsibility of business corporations see Richard Eells and Clarence Walton, *Conceptual Foundations of Business,* Ch. 20.

NOTES FOR CHAPTER VIII : *New Dimensions of Corporate Donative Power*

1. *Giving U.S.A.,* American Association of Fund-Raising Counsel, Inc., 1966 ed., p. 11.

2. John H. Watson, III (Manager of Company Donations Department, Division of Business Practices, The National Industrial Conference Board), "Report on Company Contributions for 1965," *The Conference Board Record,* October 1966, pp. 45–54. See also his *Industry Aid to Education: Studies in Public Affairs, No. 1,* A Research Report of the Conference Board, 1965.

3. There are important differences among companies in the weight given to "civic and cultural" contributions. The NICB report for 1962 shows that companies with the largest number of employees (10,000 and over) averaged only 4.45 per cent of their contributions budgets for this support area, while all others gave more: 7.48 per cent, for example, in the case of companies with 5,000–9,000 employees, and as much as 12.11 per cent for those with 500–999 employees. Clearly some of the smaller companies were moving more actively into this area than the larger ones. There were differences, too, between companies with and companies without foundations. Companies with foundations gave more (5.7 per cent of their contributions dollar) than those without foundations (4.9 per cent). Industry classifications may also be significant. Highest in the list for "civic and cultural" were textile-mill products (31.04 per cent); stone, clay, and glass products (14.37 per cent); and paper and like products (7.12 per cent). Electrical machinery and equipment (3.42 per cent) and chemical and allied products (3.81 per cent) are examples of classes of industries that fell below the average of more than 5 per cent of the contributions

dollar from corporations for "civic and cultural" activities and organizations.

4. *The Performing Arts: Rockefeller Panel Report on the Future of Theatre, Dance, Music in America; Problems and Prospects* (New York: McGraw-Hill Book Co., 1965), Ch. 5, "Corporate Support for the Performing Arts," based in part on an analysis made by Richard Eells to responses from 100 corporations to a questionnaire on corporate support of the arts.

5. *Hutton v. West Cork Railroad Company,* 23 Ch. Div. 654 (1883).

6. Louis D. Kelso, and Mortimer J. Adler, *The Capitalist Manifesto* (New York: Random House, 1958).

7. *Union Pacific Railroad Co. v. Trustees, Inc., et al.,* 8 Utah (2d) 101, 329 Pac. (2) 398 (1958).

8. *A. P. Smith Manufacturing Co. v. Barlow et al.,* 26 N. J. Super. 106 (1953); affirmed, 98 Atl. (2d) 581; appeal to the U. S. Supreme Court dismissed for want of a substantial federal question, 346 U. S. 861 (1953).

9. A detailed analysis of the *A. P. Smith* case will be found in Richard Eells, *Corporation Giving in Free Society* (New York: Harper and Row, 1956), Ch. 2.

10. B. S. Prunty, Jr., "Love and the Business Corporation," *Virginia Law Review,* April 1960, p. 467. Corporate donative authority is now so widely accepted that we have entered a new phase in corporate support of the arts. At the fiftieth anniversary conference of the NICB David Rockefeller, president of the Chase Manhattan Bank, proposed the establishment of a Council on Business and the Arts to "provide impetus and clearly defined direction" to corporate financial contributions to cultural activities. The council would be composed of businessmen knowledgeable in the arts, cultural leaders, and artists from various fields. It would conduct research on a national basis to provide statistical analyses of the voluntary support being generated on behalf of the arts; provide expert counseling for business firms seeking to initiate programs or expand existing ones; carry on a nationwide program of public information to keep corporations informed of opportunities that exist in the arts and to inform the artistic community on what corporations are doing in their particular fields; and work to increase the effectiveness of cultural organizations in obtaining voluntary support from business and industry and to encourage more businessmen to be trustees of cultural groups. Mr. Rockefeller said that "the corporate community has a long way to go in accepting the arts as an appropriate area for the exercise of its social responsibility," and urged a "massive cooperative effort in which business corporations must assume a much larger role than

they have in the past." On the other hand, he observed that some cultural organizations fail to make the most intelligent and forceful case for themselves when they seek corporate support; "their reasoning is often fuzzy, their documentation fragile" and they often do not come up with a realistic budget and workable plans to attain immediate objectives as well as long-range goals. (*The New York Times*, September 21, 1966.)

NOTES FOR CHAPTER IX: *The Future of the Corporation and the Arts*

1. Etienne Gilson, *The Arts of the Beautiful* (New York: Chas. Scribner's Sons, 1965).

2. Isaiah Berlin, "Political Ideas in the Twentieth Century," *Foreign Affairs*, April 1950. In the view of this Oxford don, a distinguished writer on modern social theory, we face a new situation today. There have been authoritarian regimes before, but the earlier reactionaries did not minimize the importance of the *questions* asked. Today the very questioning is heretical. Earlier attempts to becloud the nature of the issues were associated specifically with the avowed enemies of reason and individual freedom; today there is a persecution not only of science but by science in the name of science—by radicals of all camps. The new attitude rests upon a policy that would diminish strife and misery "by the atrophy of the faculties capable of causing them." This policy is naturally "hostile to, or at least suspicious of, disinterested curiosity (which might end anywhere)." It is a social policy that looks upon the "practice of all arts not obviously useful to society as being at best forms of social frivolity." When they are not a positive menace, such occupations are regarded as "an irritating and wasteful irrelevance, a trivial fiddling, a dissipation or diversion of energy which is difficult enough to accumulate at all and should therefore be directed wholeheartedly and unceasingly to the task of building and maintaining the well-adjusted—sometimes called the 'well-integrated'—social whole." Such terms as "truth" or "honor" or "obligation" or "beauty" thus become "transformed into purely offensive or defense weapons, used by a state or party in the struggle to create a community impervious to influences beyond its own direct control." Technical disciplines that direct natural forces and adjust men to the new order take primacy over humane pursuits—philosophical, historical, artistic. The latter serve, in Berlin's view, at most "only to prop up and embellish the new establishment."

3. The quotation is from Samuel Hirsch, "Theatre of the Absurd (Made in America)," *Journal of Social Issues*, January 1964, p. 58.

4. The quotations are from Max Weber's "Religious Rejections of the World and Their Directions," in H. H. Gerth and C. Wright Mills, *From Max Weber: Essays in Sociology* (New York: Oxford University Press, 1946; Galaxy Book ed., 1958), pp. 144 and 341–343.

5. See *The Arts and the University*, Council on Higher Education in the American Republics, Institute of International Education, New York, 1964. The symposium in this pamphlet is taken from tape recordings of the discussions held in Lima, Peru.

6. *The Arts and the University*, p. 36 f.

7. *The Arts and the University*, p. 23.

8. Lowry speaks from wide experience in making institutional and scholarship grants. On the other hand, Domingo Santa Cruz, dean of the faculty of musical sciences and arts, University of Chile (Santiago), rejected "this duality of conservatory and university" as unjust since "a university can have a so-called conservatory [he rejected the name as absurd] or a school of music." Father Hesburgh, University of Notre Dame (Indiana), pointed to the technically and proficiently trained graduates of Indiana University's distinguished school of music that have been placed in opera companies in Italy and Germany. Chancellor Murphy asked whether it was not too early to pass judgment on art in the university since the development of the arts programs in large state universities is relatively new and many of the artists still young. Lowry did not deny the truth of this; but his first question was still relevant: clarity of an institution's purpose in accepting students in the arts.

9. *The Arts and the Community*, pp. 27–28.

10. See comments by Jerrold Ross, president of the New York College of Music, and Fred Hechinger in *The New York Times*, August 22, 1965; also *Changing Times*, June, 1965, pp. 37–40.

11. Robert Ulich, "On Creativity," in *The University and the New World*, published in association with York University by the University of Toronto Press, Toronto, Canada, 1962, p. 96.

12. Herbert Read, *Art and Society*, p. 2.

13. See note 1. *Cf.* J. Huizinga, *Homo Ludens* (Boston: The Beacon Press, 1955), which stresses Man the Player in art rather than Man the Maker.

14. Gilson, p. 15.

15. Gilson, p. 36.

16. Gilson, p. 133.

17. W. H. Ferry, "Caught on the Horn of Plenty," *Bulletin* of the Center for the Study of Democratic Institutions, January 1962.

18. "The drift of surrealism has always and chiefly been towards a general *crisis in consciousness* and it is only when this is happening, or is shown to be impossible, that the success or historic eclipse of the movement will be decided." André Breton (1930), quoted by Susan Sontag in her review of Maurice Nadeau's *History of Surrealism in Book Week,* November 21, 1965. Miss Sontag observed that the "crisis in consciousness" through which modern man and modern culture are passing has called forth the surrealist strategy as "an acute version of 'crisis thinking,'" and that the real crises cannot be compartmentalized, e.g., into art versus life, thought versus action, and so on, "but require a total and brutal marshalling of one's resources." She rejected the idea that the brutality and the ambitiousness of the surrealist conception could be evaluated as true or false, seemly or unseemly, as phenomena standing alone. Nor would she accept the view that surrealism is a movement in the arts alone; the range in human affairs is wide. On the other hand, she questioned its contemporary relevance and its inevitability as a modern attitude in view of the march of events. Still, she regarded it as "the most viable and continuous tendency of the arts of this century"; and if "it continues to abolish itself," it also generates "new and flexible modes of consciousness that are alive and questioning, not merely resentful and exhibitionistic."

19. *Dialogues of Alfred North Whitehead as Recorded by Lucien Price,* p. 141.

20. Edward Shils, "The High Culture of Our Age," in *The Arts in Society,* ed. Robert N. Wilson (Englewood Cliffs, N.J.: Prentice-Hall, 1964), pp. 317–362.

21. Marshall McLuhan, *Understanding Media: The Extensions of Man* (New York: McGraw-Hill Book Co., 1965). See also Richard Schickel, "Marshall McLuhan: Canada's Intellectual Comet," *Harpers,* November 1965.

22. Jacques Maritain, *The Responsibility of the Artist,* pp. 85–89.

NOTES FOR CHAPTER X: *New Guidelines for Support of the Arts*

1. For the facts and figures in these paragraphs on public support of the arts abroad I am indebted to Frederick Dorian's *Commitment to Culture: Art Patronage in Europe and Its Significance for America* (Pittsburgh: University of Pittsburgh Press, 1964).

2. Quoted by J. Robert Oppenheimer, at the Congress for Cultural Freedom in Berlin in 1960, *The New York Times*, June 17, 1960.

3. On pluralism, as related to business and cultural institutions, see Richard Eells and Clarence Walton, *Conceptual Foundations of Business* (Homewood, Ill.: Richard D. Irwin, 1961), Ch. 16.

4. See Theodore J. Lowi, "American Business, Public Policy, Case Studies, and Political Theories," *World Politics*, July 1964, pp. 677–715.

5. Sebastian de Grazia, *Of Time, Work, and Leisure* (New York: The Twentieth Century Fund, 1962), Ch. 6.

6. J. L. Hurlburt, *The Story of Chautauqua* (New York: G. P. Putnam's Sons, 1921), p. 184, cited in *Leisure in America: Blessing or Curse*, edited by James C. Charlesworth as Monograph 4 in a series sponsored by The American Academy of Political and Social Science, Philadelphia, Pa., April 1964, p. 47.

7. Aristotle, *Metaphysics*, 982b.

8. De Grazia, Ch. 4.

9. De Grazia, p. 201.

10. De Grazia, p. 294.

11. De Grazia, p. 328.

12. De Grazia, p. 432.

13. De Grazia, p. 432.

14. De Grazia, p. 415.

15. De Grazia, p. 431.

16. De Grazia, p. 387.

17. James C. Charlesworth, "A Comprehensive Plan for the Wise Use of Leisure," in *Leisure in America*, pp. 30–46.

18. Charlesworth, pp. 34 f.

19. Charlesworth, p. 33.

20. Charlesworth, pp. 41–42.

21. Paul F. Douglass, and Robert W. Crawford, "Implementation of

a Comprehensive Plan for the Wise Use of Leisure," in *Leisure in America*, pp. 47–69, at pp. 68–69.

22.　Marion Clawson, "How Much Leisure, Now and in the Future?" in *Leisure in America*, p. 1.

23.　Paul Weiss, "A Philosophical Definition of Leisure," in *Leisure in America*, p. 21.

24.　Weiss, pp. 27–28.

25.　Thomas J. Davy, and Lloyd A. Rowe, "Précis of the Conference," in *Leisure in America*, p. 81. Names of 46 participants in the symposium are given at pp. 92–93.

26.　Brian O'Doherty, "Mapping Our Camp Sites," *Book Week*, August 22, 1965.

27.　See *Look Magazine*, March 23, 1965.

28.　Beata Bishop in "Diary of an Art Patron," *Punch*, January 20, 1965, speculates lightly on the report that contemporary objets d'art in the Executive Suite improve the corporate image.

29.　See Eric Hodgins and Parker Lesley, "The Great International Art Market," *Fortune*, December 1955.

30.　Russell Lynes, *The Tastemakers*, pp. 71–79.

31.　*The New York Times*, September 8, 1965.

32.　Thurman Arnold, *Fair Fights and Foul: A Dissenting Lawyer's Autobiography* (New York: Harcourt, Brace & World, 1965).

INDEX

351

Index

high culture and, 241–245
isolationist view of, 11
as a major institution, 1–6
morality and, 139–142
new values, 145–166
principle of perpetuity in, 162
public affairs and, 165–166, 253–257
science and, 118, 123
as a social institution, 155
social responsibility
  boundaries of, 184–187
  content of, 181–183
  corporate ecology and, 177–178
  corporate interests and the public good, 178–181
  large companies, 171–172
  meaning of, 174–177
  relevant social variables, 183–184
  shared aspect of, 168–171
  substantive areas, 187–192
statistics, 169–170
traditional, 146–154, 156
Council on Higher Education in the American Republics (CHEAR), 228–232
Council on Social Values, 274–275
Crafts, Advisory Council on the Arts on, 61
Creativity
freedom of, 46–79
  authoritarian posture, 48–51
  communism and, 54–57

conditions of, 74–79
constitutionalism, 48–51, 57–59
corporate support of, 59–60
the government and, 60–73
processes of, 50–51
structure of, 50–51
totalitarianism and, 47–48, 51–54
moral, 117–119
Cuba, 57
Cubism, 111–112
Culture
definition of, ix
high, 241–245
  tasks in, 243–245
sensate, 110–113
C. P. Snow on, 132–136
Culture and Anarchy (Arnold), 284
Customs barriers, 58

Dadaism, 111–112
Dance
Advisory Council on the Arts on, 61
as a combined art, 41
in historical perspective, 23
as pure art, 40
Dartmouth College Case (1819), 151–152, 154
De Grazia, Sebastian, 265, 267–269, 272, 276
De Staël, Madame, 34
Defense business, 178

About the Author

Richard Eells is Executive Editor, Program for Studies of the Modern Corporation, and Adjunct Professor of Business, Graduate School of Business, Columbia University. Previously, he held the Guggenheim Chair of Aeronautics at the Library of Congress and later was Manager of Public Policy Research for the General Electric Company. He has received various scholarly awards, including research grants from the Alfred P. Sloan Foundation and the Rockefeller Foundation. He serves as an advisor and consultant to various corporations and research organizations and is a trustee of several foundations.

This publication under the Arkville Press imprint was set on the Linotype in Scotch, with display in Monotype Bell and calligraphy by the designer, George Salter. It was composed, printed and bound by The Book Press Incorporated, Brattleboro, Vermont. Paper was supplied by The Oxford Paper Company. The colophon was created by Theodore Roszak.